# The January–May Marriage in Nineteenth-Century British Literature

# The January–May Marriage in Nineteenth-Century British Literature

Esther Godfrey

THE JANUARY–MAY MARRIAGE IN NINETEENTH-CENTURY BRITISH LITERATURE
Copyright © Esther Godfrey, 2009.

All rights reserved.

First published in 2009 by PALGRAVE MACMILLAN® in the United States—a division of St. Martin's Press LLC, 175 Fifth Avenue, New York, NY 10010.

Where this book is distributed in the UK, Europe and the rest of the world, this is by Palgrave Macmillan, a division of Macmillan Publishers Limited, registered in England, company number 785998, of Houndmills, Basingstoke, Hampshire RG21 6XS.

Palgrave Macmillan is the global academic imprint of the above companies and has companies and representatives throughout the world.

Palgrave® and Macmillan® are registered trademarks in the United States, the United Kingdom, Europe and other countries.

ISBN-13: 978-0-230-60673-9
ISBN-10: 0-230-60673-3

Library of Congress Cataloging-in-Publication Data is available from the Library of Congress.

A catalogue record of the book is available from the British Library.

Design by Scribe Inc.

First edition: February 2009

10 9 8 7 6 5 4 3 2 1

Printed in the United States of America.

This book is dedicated to Paul and Waida Godfrey and their January–May marriage.

# Contents

| | | |
|---|---|---|
| List of Illustrations | | ix |
| Acknowledgments | | xi |
| Introduction | | 1 |
| 1 | Intergenerational Marriages in Literature and the Nineteenth-Century Context | 15 |
| 2 | "Old Enough to Be Her Father": Incest Narratives in Dickens | 53 |
| 3 | Visualizing Power: Age, Embodiment, and Aesthetics | 89 |
| 4 | The Horror of Aging: The January–May Marriage as Gothic Nightmare | 113 |
| 5 | Sexual Economies and the January–May Marriage | 147 |
| 6 | January–May Love and the Sacrificial Ideal | 175 |
| Conclusion | | 199 |
| Notes | | 213 |
| Bibliography | | 233 |
| Index | | 249 |

# Illustrations

| | | |
|---|---|---|
| 3.1 | *The First Cloud* by William Quiller Orchardson | 94 |
| 3.2 | *Mariage de Convenance* by William Quiller Orchardson | 95 |
| 3.3 | *Mariage de Convenance—After!* by William Quiller Orchardson | 98 |
| 3.4 | *Till Death Do Us Part* by Edmund Blair Leighton | 99 |
| 4.1 | "Juene" by Anon. | 122 |
| 4.2 | "Tombent" by Anon. | 123 |
| 4.3 | *The Nightmare* by Henry Fuseli | 131 |
| 4.4 | "Cauchemar" by Anon. | 132 |
| 4.5 | *Varney*. Cover Art by Anon. | 136 |
| 4.6 | *Varney*. Art from Chapter 1, by Anon. | 138 |
| 5.1 | *Married for Rank* by John Everett Millais | 152 |

# Acknowledgments

I was able to write this book because of the financial support of numerous organizations. First, I would like to thank the English Department at the University of Tennessee for their support throughout the doctoral work that began this project. I am especially thankful for the Herman Spivey and Bain and Irene Stewart Fellowships, the Norman J. Sanders Dissertation Fellowship, and the John C. Hodges Excellence in Scholarship Award granted by the department. I would also like to thank the P.E.O. Sisterhood for the Scholar Award they gave me in 2005, which allowed me to focus on my initial research and writing. I thank Longwood University and Charles Ross for the Dean's Fund for Scholarship Excellence grant, which enabled me to secure permissions for the numerous illustrations included in the book. I am also indebted to the University of South Carolina Upstate, and the TAPS program for funding the indexing of the book.

A number of individual collectors, private researchers, and archivists at various universities, museums, and galleries also helped me locate and acquire permissions for these illustrations. Longwood University's Tammy Hines was a wonderful resource, acquiring a copy of *Le Livre Sans Titre* from the British Library for me, as well as countless items through interlibrary loan. I am grateful to Humphrey Liu for his kind assistance with images from *Varney the Vampire*. I thank Nicolette Wernick for allowing me to include *Married for Rank*, Michael Holmes for the cover art from *Varney*, and John Schaeffer for *Till Death Do Us Part*, all from their private collections. The generous efforts of Josie Lister at the Bodleian Library and Linda Whiteley and Larissa Haskell at Oxford University enabled me to track down "Cauchemar." I am also thankful to William Lynn for assistance in preparing the images for publication and to Lisa Seamster for administrative support.

I remain indebted to Misty Anderson, who guided the manuscript through the dissertation stage and offered the support and advice that made the project what it was to become. I cannot imagine this book without her inspiration and encouragement, and I am immensely indebted to her as a teacher, scholar, and friend. Several other individuals gave important feedback during early stages of this project. Nancy Moore Goslee, Richard Kelly, David Goslee, Don Cox, and Fred Moffatt all contributed to the growth of my theories. Michael Lund and Derek Taylor each gave me valuable advice as I rewrote the dissertation into book form, and I am particularly indebted to Martha Cook for her encouragement and attention to details in proofreading. Dawn VanNess, Gabrielle Gillis, and Lindsay Lucci were fabulous research assistants, and their efforts prevented several inconsistencies from slipping into the book. I want to give special thanks to my longtime friend Pat Hamilton, who spent many hours editing the final manuscript and advising me during the project's final stages. Because of their collective wisdom, this book is better than anything I could have created alone.

I am truly thankful for the assistance given by the editors and staff at Palgrave Macmillan. Since this was my first book project, they were patient with me through the revising process. I especially want to thank Farideh Koohi-Kamali for believing in the validity of my project, Marilyn Gaull for suggesting stylistic revisions, and Brigitte Shull for listening to and addressing my concerns.

My family and friends deserve more than I could ever express as they lovingly supported me through the long birth of this book, my fourth child. My kids, Ayden, Quinlin, and Roan, have been a source of strength and much needed distraction as I completed the book, and my partner Wayne Robbins has seen me through better and through worse with understanding and humor. My parents, Paul and Waida Godfrey, have been an unwavering source of encouragement and their wonderful, quirky January–May marriage must be credited as a touchstone throughout this project. I also want to thank Gary Duven, Randi Beard, Jenny Rogers, Daniel Godfrey, Janet Coffey, Christy Oehm, Sean Robbins, Matt Robbins, Vickie Burick, Warren and Maida Barnett, William and Lena Liu, Hank and Cathy Robbins, and Helen Liu for their love and friendship.

# Introduction

Zoe, the seventeen-year-old heroine of Geraldine Endsor Jewsbury's novel, *Zoe* (1845), finds that being an unmarried woman limits her will and that, living under the authority of her strict father, she lacks the power to control her daily activities. Zoe's solution to this predicament is marriage. Jewsbury writes, "seriously believing she should die by inches for the want of air and exercise, she speculated on the possibility of persuading one of these ugly old men to marry her, 'For then,' said she, 'I thought that at least I might walk out and be independent like a rational being'" (188). Though nineteenth-century marriage law actually compromised women's legal status, Zoe envisions marriage as a means to social and personal empowerment. Because her father restricts her opportunities for conventional courtship, she must choose from the older men who surround him as friends and advisers, and she realizes that her youth works to her advantage in this marriage market. Marrying Gifford, a wealthy man "about fifty" (182) who was once in love with her mother, Zoe rises in society and influences her provincial circle, while her husband becomes a public laughingstock: "The idea of that little ugly fellow, old enough for her father, being the husband of that lovely creature! *mais tant pis pour lui*" (256).

This book focuses on marriages between older husbands and younger wives in which there are at least fifteen years between the spouses' ages, such as in *Zoe*, and examines the effects of age on gender and power. Adapting Chaucer, I call these relationships January–May marriages.[1] The popularity of this theme in nineteenth-century texts, engaging authors from Jane Austen to Thomas Hardy, conveys that authors and readers found it a useful motif for probing contemporary social issues, and these marriages find their way into poetry, novels, plays, and visual arts created by men and women throughout the nineteenth century. Many of the best-known authors of the period—Byron, Charlotte Brontë, Charles Dickens, Wilkie Collins, Anthony Trollope, George Eliot, Robert Browning, and George Bernard Shaw—take up the theme of intergenerational marriages, and these relationships occupy central positions in canonical texts such as *Sense and Sensibility* (1811) and *Jane Eyre* (1847).

January–May marriages are a literary commonplace in the period because they are a social one. One explanation for this phenomenon is economic: in the rising middle class, men often struggled well into their thirties to accrue sufficient means to support a wife and family. But intergenerational marriages were choices, not necessities. Writing in 1890, an anonymous author in *The Spectator* criticized gender inequalities that stemmed from postponing marriage until men were financially secure: "The men can practically pick and choose, and they prefer, like everybody else, girls younger than themselves, and from whom the bloom has not been rubbed away" ("A Word for Amelia Roper," 83). Though many January–May marriages were second marriages for widowers, men did not marry young women because of a lack of same-aged partners. Pat Thane finds that women enjoyed longer life expectancies than men during the nineteenth century, despite the frequency of women's death in childbirth and that older women outnumbered older men: "Childbirth was never a mass killer of women in western societies. It was not comparable with the ravages of work, war and everyday violence on the lives of men" ("Social Histories of Old Age and Aging," 95). Numerous works like William Hayley's *A Philosophical, Historical, and Moral Essay on Old Maids* (1785) and Francis Power Cobbe's "What Shall We Do with Our Old Maids?" (1862) comment on the abundance of unmarried middle-class women.

January–May marriages were clearly preferences by some, even though inquiries into their motivations reveal complicated discussions about nineteenth-century culture and the relationship between age, gender, and power. In their book *Family Fortunes*, Leonore Davidoff and Catherine Hall conclude that "the cultural norm of child-like innocence as the attractive mode for adult women was confirmed by the practice of men marrying younger women. The higher the status and resources and, presumably, the possibility of choice by the man, the greater the disparity in age" (346). Nineteenth-century law supported this aesthetic predilection for young wives. For much of the century, the age of consent for girls was thirteen—the age of Browning's Pompilia when she marries Guido, who is almost fifty, in *The Ring and the Book* (1869)—and while Parliament raised the age of consent to sixteen in 1885, both laws indulged predilections for infantilized brides. The establishment in 1837 of a national civil registration system required the wife to affirm her age to be at least twenty-one to marry without parental consent, but nineteenth-century records of spouses' ages are incomplete, often citing "of full age" instead of a number. Precise statistics of January–May marriages in the nineteenth century are therefore elusive, but reports in periodicals, court proceedings, contemporary fiction, and private correspondences reveal the widespread practice of January–May marriages. Ginger S. Frost concludes the following from her study of breach-of-promise suits: "In my sample defendants were older than plaintiffs 84 percent of the time.... However, few people involved in the trials disapproved of these age ranges. In several cases a woman in her twenties was considered well suited to a man in his forties or fifties" (94). In *What Jane Austen Ate and Charles Dickens Knew*, Daniel Pool reasons that the January–May marriage "was surely more likely among the English in the 1800s than it is today" (188). Speaking to the housekeeper Mrs. Fairfax, Jane Eyre judges the fifteen-year difference in age between Rochester and Blanche Ingram perfectly acceptable: "More unequal matches are made every day" (163). In Dickens's *Hard Times* (1854), Thomas Gradgrind notes that marriages with "very unequal ages" (77) occur frequently in England and Wales and that statistics prove older husbands far outnumber older wives. Regarding marriages with twenty years between spouses, the narrator of Hardy's *Jude the Obscure* (1895) relates, "many a happy marriage had been made in such conditions of age" (89). Some sources find the marriages common, but problematic. From Italy, Byron writes to his friends back in England of his young lover's aging husband: "He has eighty thousand ducats of rent—and had two wives before—but he is Sixty—he is the first of Ravenna Nobles—but he is sixty" (*Byron's Letters and Journals*, 6:114). And in Trollope's *Orley Farm* (1861), Peregrine Orme protests against social embarrassment: "What does the world always say when an old man like my grandfather marries a young woman?" (376).

January–May marriages may have been more frequent in the nineteenth century, but they resonate with modern readers because they continue to pervade life and art. A number of celebrity January–May marriages and popular images keep these relationships in the public eye. Much of the attraction to Anna Nicole Smith's infamous life, lawsuits, and death stems from her marriage to J. Howard Marshall II, when she was twenty-six and he was eighty-nine. Less sensational unions flood the current media: consider the marriage between Larry King and Shawn Southwick, with a twenty-six-year age difference; between Tony Randall and Heather Harlan, with a fifty-year age difference; between Woody Allen and Soon-Yi Previn, with a thirty-five-year age difference; between Billy Joel and Kate Lee, with a thirty-two-year age difference; and the marriage and divorce of Paul McCartney and Heather Mills, with a twenty-six-year age difference. While women in Great Britain and America today enjoy greater economic independence and legal protection than did nineteenth-century women, cultural preoccupation with these marriages draws from foregone conclusions about how and why such marriages work. Acknowledging the differences between these marriages in the twenty-first and nineteenth centuries, I investigate these shared assumptions and offer new ways to think about intergenerational marriages.

Because of historically unequal economic conditions, criticism about January–May marriages in nineteenth-century literature has often followed the lead of second-wave feminist critics in marshalling these marriages as evidence of the oppression of women, with the beautiful and saintlike heroine existing under the domination of a patriarchal husband. Of Esther Summerson, the young fiancée in Dickens's *Bleak House* (1853), Dianne Sadoff writes, "Once ensconced in John Jarndyce's Bleak House as Little Woman, Dame Durden, and Dame Trot, she happily sees her own name vanish among her nicknames, reposes her entire confidence in her 'fatherly' guardian, and declines to ask him about her past. Esther appears the perfect Dickensian daughter" (*Monsters of Affection*, 52). This critical perspective emphasizes the powerlessness and complacency of the young wife and laments her experiences within the confines of society and marriage. Speaking of the marriage between Dorothea Brooke and Edward Casaubon in Eliot's *Middlemarch* (1872), Barbara Hardy similarly observes that such fictional heroines "are all brought up in a culture where marriage is what is expected of them and is all that is expected of them. The horror and misery of such a system is demonstrated in marriages with men who are old enough to be their fathers, who have little in common with them, and who in various ways fail in sexuality and love. Casaubon is over forty-five, Dorothea nineteen" (70).

I do not claim that Sadoff and Hardy are wrong in their assessments of these types of marriages. Certainly Esther, Dorothea, Zoe, and other young brides sometimes feel "horror and misery" directly related to the generational gaps dividing the spouses that they never expected in their engagements. Yet the distribution of power in these marriages is not unidirectional, and nineteenth-century authors do not use January–May marriages as a blanket method of oppression or liberation in their critiques of gender. While I am indebted to the work of theorists like Sadoff and Hardy, I do not restrict the girl bride to the position of victim. These marriages often reveal complex systems of control, and age marks one way that authors redistribute authority between husbands and wives.

Through the associations they bring with sexual practices that deviate from social norms, January–May marriages offer provocative scenarios for theorizing gender and power. The relative innocence and childish manners of the younger wife associate the January–May marriage with pedophilia, which, as critics James Kincaid and Catherine Robson have demonstrated, transforms gender in texts throughout the century from William Wordsworth to Lewis Carroll. Additionally, through versions of the phrase "he's old enough to be your father," the daddy-daughter aspect of these marriages makes them uncomfortably incestuous. Incest worked as a Romantic weapon for attacking patriarchal authority in works like Percy Shelley's *The Cenci* (1819) and Mary Shelley's *Mathilda* (1819), where explicitly incestuous relations lead to increased female agency and the destruction of male power. The social commentary inspired by pedophilia and incest is more blatant when viewed apart from January–May marriages. Although these marriages raised eyebrows, they also allowed for the subversive dismantling of gender identities within a socially sanctioned, heterosexual rubric that fascinated and repelled the sensibilities of the time. Like pedophilia and incest, the January–May marriage hints at sexual deviancy and hinges on desire. But unlike the more taboo plots, the theme challenges sexual and gendered constructions from a position that is culturally, religiously, and ethically "legitimate" and thereby privileged. Because of its peculiar relation to both standard and non-standard sexualities, the theme is at once dangerous and safe. In this book, I explain some of the various ways writers and artists explored this theme.

While its chapters are not chronological in approach, *The January–May Marriage in Nineteenth-Century British Literature* examines the nineteenth century from Austen's *Sense and Sensibility* (1811) and *Emma* (1816) to *fin-de-siècle* texts like Hardy's *Jude the Obscure*

(1895) and Bram Stoker's *Dracula* (1897). Surveying over twenty works of literature that include epic poems (Byron's 1819–24 *Don Juan*), canonical novels (Dickens's 1850 *David Copperfield*), plays (Shaw's 1898 *Mrs Warren's Profession*), sensation fiction (Mary Elizabeth Braddon's 1862 *Lady Audley's Secret*), and visual arts (Edmund Blair Leighton's 1879 *Till Death Do Us Part*), I trace patterns that emerge in the January–May marriage theme and chart various implications regarding the construction of gender and the distribution of power through age. Not all of these texts present conventional marriages. For example, I read *Dracula* and *The Vampyre* (1819) as Gothic versions of the theme, where partners consummate unions through blood rather than English law. In other examples, one party desires the marriage, but the couple breaks the engagement, often as a direct result of the age difference, as in *Bleak House* and *An Old Man's Love* (1884), yet I maintain that these depictions of abortive January–May marriages should also instruct our readings of age, gender, and power. Furthermore, though some readers may object to my comparison of *Sense and Sensibility*'s thirty-five-year-old Colonel Brandon with *Nicholas Nickleby*'s seventy-year-old Arthur Gride, I insist that common elements exist among these characters when associated with January–May marriages. Marianne's reactions to Brandon's affections underscore, and even exaggerate, the nineteen years between them, making him appear older than his years: "he is old enough to be *my* father; and if he were ever animated enough to be in love, must have long outlived every sensation of the kind. It is too ridiculous! When is a man to be safe from such wit, if age and infirmity will not protect him?" (37). The age difference between Marianne and Colonel Brandon does affect the distribution of power and gender roles in their relationship, and it suggests the diversity of situations in which age-based gender anxieties are manifest.

In stressing both the socially constructed and performative natures of gender identities, I ground my study of the January–May theme in the conditions that fostered such portrayals of gender. Thus, while I move away from an attention to the victimization of women, *The January–May Marriage in Nineteenth-Century Literature* remains connected to materialist feminist concerns with social and economic realities of the period. I reject binary classifications of gender into a masculine and feminine dichotomy; employing gendered terms with caution, I treat them as linguistic signs for codifying power within a specific culture that associates certain characteristics such as passivity or authority with women or men. To a nineteenth-century reader, when a young woman acts with energy or aggressiveness, she becomes more masculine, and when a man shows weakness or becomes enfeebled by age, he becomes more feminine. While I recognize that these assumptions are problematic, I find them useful if taken for what they are: a first step in a larger reconsideration of gender stereotypes and of essentialized sex differences. Consequently, though marriage gives the impression of a fundamentally heterosexual frame, my inquiry into the January–May theme probes a connection between age and gender that overturns such conventional restrictions on identity. At times, the January–May theme so thoroughly undermines stereotypical notions of men and women that such identifications are impossible, and because of this queering of the literary subjects, the theories of Eve Sedgwick and Judith Halberstam inform my critique of the tradition.

I trace several specific patterns within the larger January–May theme, but two broad characteristics extend throughout most of the January–May relationships in the literature that I cover and merit explanation here. Foremost, the January–May theme typically centers on a romantic triangle consisting of the husband, wife, and young male rival for the young wife's affection. Though occasionally more than one suitor vies for the wife's affections, the triangular structure proves dominant, and when multiple suitors exist, they often blend, forming a composite ideal of what the husband is not. Secondly, these January–May marriages operate through a parodic display of excess—excesses of age and youth, impotency and desire, masculinity and femininity, power and powerlessness, ugliness and beauty. These two components—that of the love triangle and that of parodic excess—emerge in almost all of the texts that I examine, and they work independently and synchronously to alter representations of gender within the literature.

Sedgwick's work on male homosocial relationships and the triangulation of desire influences my readings of these January–May relationships. As Sedgwick explores in her chapter "*The Country Wife*: Anatomies of Male Homosocial Desire" in *Between Men*, triangular romances illustrate methods of male bonding. This theory is evident in Dickens's *Bleak House*, which discloses an intricate system of exchange among men, in which a wife can be bought, sold, and passed down as a commodity. Sedgwick is correct in reading these erotic triangles as systems of gender instability and flux, yet I distinguish my position from hers in regard to the activity and passivity of the male and female agents. My reasoning here stems from the January–May marriage theme's emphasis on the importance of female sexual desire. While Sedgwick and other feminist theorists like Gayle Rubin have presented the female in the erotic triangle as the object of the desires of her two active male suitors, I challenge this emphasis on women's passivity. Sedgwick claims, "'To Cuckold' is by definition a sexual act, performed on a man, by another man" (50); however, the word can refer to an act performed by a woman on a man. The verb literally means "to dishonor (a husband) by adultery: said a) of a paramour; b) of a wife."[2] Especially within January–May marriages, where age differences initiate and encourage the erotic triangles, the young wives emerge as vital, active beings who consciously, sometimes forcefully, pursue or resist the affections of men.

    I further argue that the recognition of female desire and agency increases rather than decreases the power asymmetry within the marriage. Subjectivity is not fixed; at times, the texts objectify the younger wives, but they may also objectify the younger male suitors (the objects of female desire for their theoretical ability to please sexually) and the older husbands (objectified as sources of economic stability as well as embodiments of male insufficiency). While I do not hold that the active position of the female within the triangle can result only from her youth, I find that the ages of the wife, the husband, and the lover all affect the triangulation of power and desire, and their ages complicate their relative positions as "men" and "women" within the triangle.

    The January–May structure also encourages excessive displays of conventional traits of masculinity and femininity. Simon Dentith explains parody's *modus operandi*: "One of the typical ways in which parody works is to seize on particular aspects of a manner or a style and exaggerate it to ludicrous effect" (32). The expected gender divisions in a same-age marriage assume a heightened mimetic quality when emphasized by the age differences of a January–May marriage. Both the January and the May figures form gross, often grotesque, caricatures of normative notions of men and women, and when texts graft these caricatures onto a traditional romance narrative, they offer parodies of marriage itself. Moreover, the January–May marriage allows for the exaggeration of specific gender characteristics. If, for example, there were a tendency to oversimplify female morality into a virgin/whore dichotomy, readers could further relegate women to a sexually naïve position when they appeared as child brides, yet at the same time, could heighten the sexual attributes of these young women because of associations of desire and fecundity with youth. Nineteenth-century men, who already enjoyed the privileges of a patriarchal social order, often found their power hyperbolized through their age: A husband, intended to fulfill the protective role of a woman's father upon marriage, grows exponentially more paternal when he is twice her age. But an older husband's age also exaggerates qualities thought to be typical masculine weaknesses, especially those weaknesses of the body, which erupt in numerous tales of impotence and inadequacy within the January–May theme. Through age-based exaggeration, the husband and wife serve individually as parodies of men and women and together as "one flesh" as a parody of a larger social system.[3]

Linda Hutcheon defines parody as "repetition with a critical difference" (20) and explains how it can work in contradictory directions. The repetitive dimension of parody functions as a conservative mechanism, creating what already exists, but the "critical difference" provides for change. In the January–May theme, the reproduction of traditional marriage rituals normalizes gender and power in the text, but the age gap between spouses is the critical difference that undermines marriage as a fixed structure. Although not all authors who draw on intergenerational marriages intend them to be subversive, unavoidable parodic elements nonetheless provide means for subversion. Parody is powerful, sometimes overwhelming authorial control. I read several texts, like some of Dickens's novels, as subversive, not because Dickens necessarily intended them to be so, but because, even when he attempts to reaffirm gender identities through the January–May structure, he instead highlights gender anxieties. Working from within social conventions, the January–May marriage can be effectively seditious. To borrow from Henry Louis Gates's work in race theory, "*only* the master's tools will ever dismantle the master's house" (38).[4] In the January–May marriage, what might appear as stereotypical male fantasy of a subservient, tractable wife proves problematic, uncovering instability within the frame for stability itself.

My first chapter offers an overview of the literary background and historical context for nineteenth-century January–May marriages. Finding it unwieldy to discuss all the literary marriages that contributed to the nineteenth-century examples, I give a general description of the theme's evolution over time, focusing on noteworthy or particularly intriguing examples in the tradition from authors like Chaucer, William Shakespeare, Aphra Behn, Richard Brinsley Sheridan, and Elizabeth Inchbald. Because I believe that the number of these marriages in nineteenth-century literature responds to more than the prevalence of age-disparate relationships in real life, I outline some social and legal changes that threatened traditional gender identities and fostered gender anxieties among men and women of all ages. I demonstrate at the end of this chapter how the January–May tradition contributes to play with gender in a Romantic text: Canto I of Byron's *Don Juan*. Byron's poem depicts the triangular romance and parodic dimension of the January–May marriage with amazing dexterity, and while his rollicking sexual exposé is, in some ways, atypical of most nineteenth-century texts, it attests to contemporary fascination with the ways that intergenerational unions could comment on gender. Subsequent chapters isolate particular ideas or common associations that January–May texts address. My second chapter examines the daddy-daughter aspects of the January–May marriage through Dickens's fiction, including *Nicholas Nickleby* (1839), *The Cricket on the Hearth* (1843), *Hard Times*, and *Little Dorrit* (1857). My attention to familial longing builds on the work of critics like Robert M. Polhemus, who observes, "Ever since people learned that *David Copperfield* was a favorite of Freud's . . . readers have found illuminating signs of the Oedipus complex in the book" ("The Favorite Child," 10). Since I read marriage as essential to Dickens's understanding of family and patriarchy, I claim that the introduction of the incestuous element into marriage (however legitimized by the lack of familial blood) threatens larger social constructions. The daddy-daughter aspect of these relationships undermines patriarchal authority by highlighting the sexually deviant within sanctified marriage unions and by contradicting readings of incest as inherent victimization.

An examination of January–May aesthetics sharpens a critical understanding of the theme's mechanics, and my third chapter explores the visualization of power in January–May marriages and the nineteenth-century fascination with the effects of aging on the body. This chapter is aligned with recent efforts by theorists like Elizabeth Grosz to reassess the corporeality of the physical body without linking gender difference to genitalia. After an initial introduction, the chapter develops in two sections how nineteenth-century aesthetics responded to aging and how those perceptions correspond to power. The first section examines four Victorian paintings that engage the theme of the January–May marriage: William Quiller Orchardson's scries, *The First Cloud* (1887), *Mariage de Convenance* (1883), and *Mariage de Convenance—After!* (1886), as well as Leighton's *Till Death Do Us Part* (1879). All four paintings use the bodies of older men and younger women to conceptualize power, revoking and returning agency along gendered divides. In the second section, I theorize about male embodiment in Eliot's *Middlemarch*, focusing on the attention given to Casaubon's physical appearance. The vivid descriptions of Casaubon, however unkind, heighten the text's dalliances with sexual deviancy and its depiction of marital power, creating aesthetic images of "Old and Young" that both titillate and repulse readers' sentimental and sexual expectations.

The fourth chapter addresses the Gothic element within the January–May marriage theme. Reworking the ideas of critics like Robert Mighall that connect Gothicism to chronological disruptions between the past and the present, I argue that the January–May marriage presents a historical anachronism, merging past (the older husband) and present (the young wife) through the marital union in a manner just as horrifying as a venture into a medieval castle. The horror of the January–May marriage caters to nineteenth-century fears of aging as a rampant disease and is all the more terrible and exciting because of its sexual connotations. "Deviant" sex acts became directly associated with aging and, in turn, aging with deviant sex acts; for example, early nineteenth-century tracts against onanism claimed that the act caused premature aging. In texts like Hardy's *Jude the Obscure*, intergenerational marriages become a form of Gothic nightmare, indicating a correlation between the popularity of the January–May theme in the nineteenth century and the rise of the vampire legend in literature. In addition to *Jude*, I read three vampire texts—*The Vampyre*, *Varney the Vampyre* (1845), and *Dracula*—as contributors to and participants in the January–May marriage theme.

Many texts of the era work from the assumption that young women marry older men for their money, and my fifth chapter considers how authors use the January–May theme to comment on gendered sexual economies. Unfortunately, assumptions about this market are so familiar that readers take them for granted, and they are hence misunderstood. Because the traffic in young women has been so prevalent in Western society and its literature, readers must defamiliarize the texts from overly simplistic suppositions of a male-dominated sexual economy to appreciate the complexities that such exchanges afford. Rubin describes the traditional exchange of women as a system in which "if women are the gifts, then it is men who are the exchange partners" (542), and while she illuminates how economic, psychological, and kinship systems support this market of male privilege, I demonstrate how the emphasis on age in January–May texts reveals that these interrelated systems also contribute to a traffic in men. In John Everett Millais's pen-and-ink drawing *Married for Rank* (1853), the figure of the young wife marginalizes both older husband and younger suitors through the contract of marriage. Similarly, in Austen's *Sense and Sensibility*, Brontë's *Jane Eyre*, and Braddon's *Lady Audley's Secret*, women actively negotiate the marriage market before they marry older husbands. In each instance, capitalist realities override gender customs, and financial resources trump physical masculinity, insinuating that power is not tied to gender or the phallus, but to wealth. Furthermore, mercenary marriages motivated by age expose the economic considerations for all marriages, fostering comparisons between marriage and prostitution that call into question marriage as a legitimate social structure.

The final chapter explains how intergenerational love complicates readings of gender in nineteenth-century texts. *Middlemarch* explores the irrationality of love, and even though no one understands why, "from the wealth of her own love," Dorothea would have liked "to have kissed Mr. Casaubon's coat-sleeve, or to have caressed his shoe-latchet" (127). Several of the marriages that are proposed but not fulfilled offer other examples of love's triumph over pecuniary, aesthetic, or sexual motivations. In Trollope's *An Old Man's Love* (1884), a man initially concerned with gaining the affections of his ward, who "did receive from his hands all that she had—her bread and meat, her bed, her very clothes" (16), surrenders his desire for her, dissolves their engagement, and even provides a dowry so that she can marry a lover who is much closer to her age. For love, John Jarndyce in *Bleak House* also elects to withdraw his offer to Esther, instead establishing her and young Woodcourt in their own "Bleak House." Rather than suggesting that a submissive nature is vital to true love, I claim that such texts support a communitarian ideal that is far removed from the self-centered practices of the older husbands in George du Maurier's *Trilby* (1894) or Collins's *The Woman in White* (1860). These examples of male sacrifice also counter conventional associations of individuality with masculinity and sacrifice with femininity, challenging nineteenth-century concepts of gender and power yet again.

The conclusion contextualizes the January–May texts that I have covered in the book by giving an overview of different age and gender frames in the nineteenth century and in contemporary culture. I briefly examine older woman–younger man reversals of the January–May romance (Don Juan's exploits in later cantos), the tradition in nineteenth-century American literature (Nathaniel Hawthorne's 1850 *The Scarlet Letter* and Henry James's 1871 *Watch and Ward*), and the portrayal of January–May marriages in film and media (*Elegy*, *Northern Exposure*). I also incorporate non-Western traditions that have influenced my theories on the January–May marriage. I find that late nineteenth-century outcry against the practice of child marriage in colonial India redirects British attention from embarrassing pedophiliac tendencies like the W. T. Stead "Maiden Tribute to Modern Babylon" scandal within British culture, and that non-western January–May marriages offer other contexts in which to consider how age affects gender and power. The acclaimed Indian film *Water* (2006) about an eight-year-old widow in the early twentieth century depicts an intricate social conspiracy that promotes the interests of wealthy, older men. Anthropological studies like John Wood's *When Men Are Women* also shed light on the British works that I cover. Wood describes the culture of the Gabra nomads of East Africa, a people who merge age and gender through their culture's concept of *d'abella*, men who become "women" by assuming feminized roles within Gabra society when they reach a certain age. These other contexts attest to the peculiarity of the January–May marriage in nineteenth-century literature, but they also define further issues for discussion.

The aim of this book is to theorize about what these January–May marriages reveal about age, gender, and power. I chose the nineteenth century as the scope of this book because it offers a unique period of gender disruption and anxiety, but the patterns of exchange that its texts reveal can inform our larger understanding of age as a fundamental marker of gender. The danger inherent to such an endeavor, it appears to me, resides in unnecessarily limiting the implications of this line of argument. Certainly, I do not intend to imply that women must be young to wield power, or that such power must be sexual or romantic. One of the most important attributes of age is that age is not a static characteristic of an individual. Any identity that originates from age and its influence on gender is a slippery one. Old men and women were once young, and most young men and women hope to grow old. The temporality of one's age makes it an intrinsically unstable factor within a complex social economy of power. Much work remains to be done to elucidate how age affects gender throughout various ethnic, economic, and historical conditions. This book endeavors to encourage and contribute to that larger conversation.

# Chapter 1

# Intergenerational Marriages in Literature and the Nineteenth-Century Context

Intimate relationships between older men and younger women have a long history of challenging gender relations in literature. Ancient Roman comedy by playwrights like Plautus frequently incorporates the *senex amator* or *senex amans* (aged lover) as a stock character to elicit laughter and contempt from the audience. The older men's lust for younger women leads them into an array of embarrassing situations, and otherwise respectable patriarchs grovel before servants, children, and the women they desire.[1] In the Old Testament, the first book of Kings links loss of male power with age-disparate sexual relationships. Opening with the story of the young and beautiful Abishag being brought to the bed of the aging King David because "he could not get warm," the book employs David's inability to perform sexually to foreground the necessity of his securing a successor (1 Kings 1:1–4). Medieval literature from the continent furthers the theme. The sixth-century Latin poet Maximianus writes cynical elegies about love from the perspective of an aging male. Medieval pageants like those presented at York for Corpus Christi include the theme's assumptions about age and gender to comment on religious narratives. The Pewterers' and Founders' contribution to the cycle, "Joseph's Troubles," presents Joseph as an older husband who wonders if Mary's inexplicable pregnancy is evidence of her unfaithfulness: "My yoonge wife is with childe full grete, / That makes me nowe sorowe vnsoght" (Beadle, 118).[2] Andreas Capellanus further defines the limits of masculine virility in his popular twelfth-century *De Amore*; Capellanus finds that after sixty, age becomes "a bar" to physical relations: "although one may have intercourse his passion cannot develop into love; because at that age the natural heat begins to lose its force, and the natural moisture is greatly increased, which leads a man into various difficulties and troubles him with various ailments, and there are no consolations in the world for him except food and drink" (32).[3] Giovanni Boccaccio's *Ameto* (1340–41) details the impotence of the older husband married to a youthful nymph, and Eustache Deschamps's ballade 880 relates the intergenerational marriage of January and April.[4] Each of these early examples reveals aging men in weakened positions and inspires literary interest in the possible outcomes of intergenerational desire.

Writing in the late fourteenth century, Chaucer is the most notable medieval writer to take up the theme in English and would have been the most common early source for nineteenth-century British writers adapting the tradition.[5] The hero of Charlotte Smith's *The Old Manor House* (1794) alludes to Chaucer to describe his sister's upcoming marriage to an older man: "one cannot help thinking of January and May!" (294). Older husbands and younger wives are central to three distinct stories in Chaucer's *Canterbury Tales*: "The Wife of Bath's Prologue," "The Miller's Tale," and "The Merchant's Tale." Although the bawdy sexuality and crude schemes displayed by the young wives in these poems could indicate Chaucer's participation in a larger body of anti-feminist literature, these tales support reversals of gendered power. Adapting the fabliau, Chaucer's medieval January–May poems present a world upside down, where the gender hierarchy has not been equalized, but rather set on end. Thus, the older husbands repeatedly emerge as culturally disempowered, while the younger wives, if not matriarchs, at least exploit the male figures in the immediate stories to great effect. Age, sexuality, and wealth form an elaborate system of exchange in these poems and reveal how the younger wives in January–May marriages come out on top in terms of cultural respect, sexual gratification, and economic security.

Alisoun, Chaucer's Wife of Bath, narrates her personal experience of this type of power reversal. Marrying her first husband when she is only twelve, she manipulates a male-dominated economic situation to her advantage; though her first husband purchases his young bride like so much property, it is Alisoun who lives to enjoy the life savings of her husband. Altogether, she successively weds and widows three rich old men and, through their deaths, accrues the small fortune that she exchanges for other social capital in her fourth and fifth husbands. Notably, Alisoun finds that her younger husbands were "badde," while the first three were "goode, and riche, and olde" (197). In these marriages, Alisoun exploits the advantages of her youth to rule her husbands:

> I governed hem so well, after my lawe,
> That ech of hem ful blissful was and fawe
> To bringe me gay thinges fro the faire.
> They were ful glad whan I spak to hem faire,
> For, God it woot, I chidde hem spitously. (219–23)

Alisoun's love-them-to-death approach to marriage could parallel the caricatures of women found in misogynist medieval texts, like her husband Janekyn's book of "wicked wives," but Chaucer presents her with far more complexity and wit than do stock accounts of problematic women. To her husband's disparaging remarks about women, she responds,

> By God, if wommen hadde writen stories,
> As clerkes han withinne hire oratories,
> They wolde han writen of men moore wikked-nesse
> Than al the mark of Adam may redresse. (693–96)

Alisoun is more than a stereotypical portrait of a crass and aggressive woman; she offers a pragmatic perspective about women making the most of a sexist world. While a social system that encourages marriages between twelve-year-old girls and rich old men might fall under Alisoun's understanding of men's "wickedness," she adapts the age-gender-class system to her advantage. By the time of her fourth and fifth marriages, which present their own age-based troubles, she marries men who can satisfy her sexually, the last of whom she "took for love, and no richesse" (526).

Appreciating the Wife of Bath's perspective as a middle-aged woman looking back on her string of January–May marriages helps to clarify the manipulation of power in "The Miller's Tale" and "The Merchant's Tale," which offer portraits of young wives who still expect to benefit from their elderly husbands' deaths. The advantages of such matches would have been transparent to readers in Chaucer's day; young women who managed to marry and to widow older men created uniquely sovereign positions for themselves in the Middle Ages. In her essay, "Widow-To-Be: May in Chaucer's 'The Merchant's

Tale,'" Margaret Hallissy convincingly argues, "When, as in 'The Merchant's Tale,' a healthy young woman marries an older (and richer) man, Chaucer's medieval audience would have seen that marriage as an interlude, as preparation for a longer (and happier) widowhood, if it is managed so as to ensure her well-being in the later 'estaat'" (295). Both May and the young wife in "The Miller's Tale," also named Alisoun, stand to benefit from the economic, social, and legal status that widowhood offers if they can dupe their husbands until death releases them from their contracts.

Subversion of the male-dominated gender system does not have to wait for widowhood to begin. In "The Merchant's Tale" and "The Miller's Tale," the younger wives emasculate their older husbands by affecting traditionally masculine attributes like sexuality, cunning, and control and conversely rendering the husbands impotent, foolish, and powerless. In these poems, the means for this usurping of masculine privilege revolves around sexual desire; thus, while Januarie and John believe they are sating their own sexual fantasies by marrying "som mayde fair and tendre of age," they meet sexual appetites larger than their own and consequently end as cuckolds ("The Merchant's Tale," 1407). In "The Miller's Tale," Alisoun and her lover Nicholas convince John that he needs to prepare for a flood, and while he sleeps in a tub, awaiting the rising waters, Alisoun and Nicholas are free to enjoy one another sexually. Alisoun's challenges to her husband's sexual ability and authority un-man him, and her assumption of an empowered position influences her sexual relations with other men. When Absolon, another suitor, tries to kiss her through a window, he finds too late that she has offered her behind rather than her face, and his attempt to avenge his disgrace by branding her ass with a hot poker only harms Nicholas, who has offered his own bottom to continue the joke. Martin Blum maintains that Alisoun "alone gets away unpunished. She is, it seems, rewarded for being the most successful 'man' of the tale, whereas her male counterparts all receive their individual lessons for failing to fulfill their expected roles as men" (37).

The gender reversal that begins with Alisoun's infidelity would have appeared to some degree "natural" to medieval readers who, unlike John, followed the proverb of Cato:

> That bad man sholde wedde his simylitude.
> Men sholde wedden after hire estaat,
> For youthe and elde is often at debaat. ("The Miller's Tale," 3228–30)

This belief that older husbands should have known better than to wed young, lusty wives mediates the social stigma of their wives' unfaithfulness, allowing the poems room for ribald, amoral fun while legitimizing gender instability as an inevitable component of the marriage of "youthe and elde." John appears to be aware of the dangers that accompany his marriage, but he mistakenly thinks he can prevent his eighteen-year-old wife's adultery:

> Jalous he was, and heeld hire narwe in cage,
> For she was wylde and yong, and he was old
> And demed hymself been lik a cokewold. (3224–26)

But despite his jealousy and attempts to "cage" his wife, he finds, as Chaucer's audience well expects, her abilities circumvent his control. Similarly, in "The Merchant's Tale," Justinus warns his friend Januarie to reconsider marrying a young wife when he is sixty years old. "Trusteth me," cautions Justinus, "Ye shul nat plesen hire fully yeres thre" (1561–62). Indeed, Justinus's prediction comes true, and readers delight at the punishment of such a foolish man.

The Merchant's description of Januarie's perversely humorous lovemaking to May on their wedding night plays on sexual inadequacies associated with old age by portraying the old man as the inept, and rather grotesque, lover, and this depiction of male weakness sanctions the gendered power reversal to come. After Januarie scrapes May's face with the "brustles of his berd unsofte" (1824), he finds that he must work all night to consummate their marriage, whereupon he is so thrilled with his feat that he cries out loud, though "The slakke skyn aboute his nekke shaketh / Whil that he sang, so chaunteth he and craketh" (1849–50). The poem encourages readers to sympathize with May, who has to endure Januarie's roosterlike performance, and foreshadows the likely outcome of Januarie's ineffectual lovemaking:

> But God woot what that May thoughte in hir herte,
> Whan she hym saugh up sittynge in his sherte,
> In his nyght-cappe, and with his nekke lene;
> She preyseth nat his pleyyng worth a bene. (1851–54)

Chaucer's audience anticipates and enjoys Januarie's subsequent disempowerment. When he later loses his eyesight, May makes love with young Damyan in a tree—just above the head of her husband. Though May could be criticized for violating her marriage vows and for appropriating her husband's power, the poem eases readers into an acceptance of the naturalness of the gender and power reversal. And, as in "The Miller's Tale," this reversal extends beyond the January–May couple to same-aged partners. "The Merchant's Tale" is a warning for all men not to ignore their wives' sexual desires or the limitations of their own sexual prowess. By example, Januarie demonstrates for Chaucer's audience what men should not do in romantic relationships, and a marriage market seemingly dependent on male potency and possession backfires to emphasize the power women wield in marriage.

Readers' sympathies guide the subversive qualities of the January–May theme in Chaucer. Few readers mind that the age disparities place the old men in positions of disempowerment or that they disrupt the "Great Chain of Being," because Chaucer stresses that the older husbands act on their own imprudent desires. At times, however, Chaucer reminds his audience that the January–May marriages have created yet another system of gender inequality. The Miller recognizes John's deep affection for his young wife, allowing that he loved Alisoun "moore than his lyf" (3222), and the tale encourages sympathy for John when he suffers injuries from his fall in the tub while those around him "turned al his harm unto a jape" (3842). "The Reeve's Prologue" also gives voice to the older man's perspective, and the Reeve, who has been the butt of the Miller's tale, expresses the frustrations of a man who has had, and lost, the masculine privileges afforded by youth. While these elements remind readers that power inequities continue in power reversals, the hilarity of the fabliau form arises from playful disruption, not social equality.

Rambunctious medieval interest in the January–May marriage wanes slightly during the Renaissance, though the theme continues to operate through shared understandings between author and audience about age, desire, economics, and gender.[6] Ageist stereotypes fulfill readers' expectations in these Renaissance tales; for example, the jest-book *The Sack-full of Newes*, thought to date back to at least 1582, outlines the story of an older master whose young wife enjoys the sexual favors of the servant John.[7] In Shakespeare's *The Taming of the Shrew* (ca. 1590–93), Gremio, a rich and old suitor of the beautiful Bianca, is bested by the young Lucentio. Shakespeare deems Gremio a "pantaloon," and his presence nods to the *commedia dell'arte*, in which Pantaloon, the imprudent older lover in spectacles, slippers, and pantaloons, is a stock figure. Gremio is a "graybeard" whose "love doth freeze" (2.1.335, 402) and the audience delights at how other characters' criticism of his "crafty withered hide" thwarts his proposal to marry Bianca. Yet the threat he poses is not ridiculous. He clearly tempts Bianca's father with a lengthy catalog of his wealth, from his "house within the city" that is "richly furnishèd with plate and gold" to the "sixscore fat oxen standing in my stalls" (2.1.344–45, 356). Gremio advances that his age and imminent death should be viewed as positive qualities, since Bianca, as his widow, will be in control of his estate if she submits for a few years as his bride:

> Myself am struck in years, I must confess,
> And if I die tomorrow, this is hers,
> If whilst I live she will be only mine. (2.1.358–60)

However, unlike Chaucer's young wives, Bianca does not find the prospect of being a wealthy young widow sufficient compensation for marrying an elderly husband. Bianca's father is the only one besides Gremio who considers him a viable husband for Bianca, and her marriage to her young love secures the play's happy ending.

In sonnet 138, Shakespeare provides a more resigned look at the sexual desire and deceit that Chaucer and earlier writers viewed as integral to the January–May theme. In this poem, the aging lover knows his young love "lies" to him and with others, and he chooses to deny both her unfaithfulness and his age: "Oh, love's best habit is in seeming trust, / And age in love loves not to have years told" (11–12). The speaker, "vainly thinking that she thinks me young" (5), realizes he is no "untutored youth" (3) and, moreover, that "she knows my days are past the best" (6), but as she refuses to admit to her lie, the speaker will likewise "not [say] that I am old" (10). The older lover is thus able to preserve, at least superficially, his appearance of youth and his sexual relationship with the young woman, while she manages, like Chaucer's young wives, to do what she likes: "Therefore I lie with her, and she with me, / And in our faults by lies we flattered be" (13–14). The sonnet's cynical older lover thus appears less foolish than Chaucer's oblivious husbands, though it would be difficult to argue that he is more empowered.

In *Othello* (ca. 1603–4), the January–May theme moves even further from the comic tradition to explore the tragic consequences of gender anxiety. Although racial tensions seem to dominate the play, Othello's position as an older husband remains a central issue. His insecurities stemming from generational difference drive his murder of his wife for her supposed adultery.[8] Early in act 1, Iago crassly warns Desdemona's father, "an old black ram / Is tupping your white ewe" (1.1.90–91), and Iago later uses Othello's age to convince Roderigo of Desdemona's love for Cassio. He explains that "there should be . . .

sympathy in years, manners, and beauties—all of which the Moor is defective in" (2.1.229–32). Othello recognizes age as a large part of his sexual anxiety about his wife when he laments "I am declined / Into the vale of years" (3.3.281–82). In this tragic version of the January–May plot, Othello's masculinity suffers not from laughter at his bawdy exploitation, but from the public's offense at his horrific error. Once challenged by the thought of Desdemona's adultery, Othello abuses his power, physically and emotionally destroying his wife; she then becomes a martyr for women through her innocent death. While the play employs conventions of male insecurity, the mutual love between Othello and Desdemona, the absence of real sexual infidelity, and the adaptation of the theme for tragedy rather than comedy, demonstrate the maturation of literary depictions of the January–May marriage.

*Othello* stands, however, as an anomaly in earlier uses of the theme. During the Restoration, numerous playwrights embrace the theme's comic potential for gender trouble, and the bawdier plays of the period celebrate, much like Chaucer's tales, cuckoldry's challenge to normative sexual and gender relations. William Wycherley's *The Country Wife* (1675) uses the January–May theme for subversive purposes: the grasping older husband Pinchwife is cuckolded by his young wife.[9] The play makes it easy to condone the sexual instability initiated by the January–May theme; Pinchwife is a misogynist who ridicules his outspoken sister and other strong London women, and the audience enjoys that his marriage to a "country wife"—whom he believes will be easier to control—leads to his debasement. Pinchwife believes that gender trouble comes from women's corruption in urban society, but the play suggests that the instability of gender originates from the desires and limitations of aged bodies. Through the January–May trope, young Margery Pinchwife's desire proves to be untaught, and the play demonstrates that women only learn the means for actualizing their desires. Eventually, Pinchwife learns that women's submission is not innate, but culturally produced, and that when unrestricted by social mores, women will likely reject traditional gender roles.

Wycherley implies that Pinchwife is less of a man because he cannot sexually please his wife. Though Pinchwife hopes that by importing a wife from the country, he will have a spouse who "will not know the difference betwixt a man of one-and-twenty, and one of forty-[nine]" (1.1.381–82), he discovers that his age disempowers him within his marriage. Failing to satisfy his wife physically, he is likewise unable to reproduce his masculine identity and power theatrically. Thus, the audience and the other characters in the play associate him with the sexually impotent "shadows of men," or "Half-men"—those "old boys, old *beaux garçons*, who like super-annuated stallions are suffered to run, feed, and whinny with the mares as long as they live, though they can do nothing else" (1.1.180–85). Pinchwife's character demonstrates that masculinity is temporal and transitory, and, while recognizing that he was once a young rake, the audience can now take pleasure in the fall from masculine privilege that his age—and his flawed marriage to a much-younger wife—inflicts. Thus, the January–May structure instigates a reconsideration of gender as a stable category from multiple points. As the play emasculates Pinchwife, it conversely endows Horner, feminized through his feigned impotency, with a new masculinity. The play brings into question the perceived masculinity or femininity of all characters when gender emerges as the product of multiple forces that include age—not as a static characteristic of a sexed body.

Women writers also make use of the January–May theme during the Restoration, and Aphra Behn's plays, *The Rover* (1677), *Sir Patient Fancy* (1678) and *The Lucky Chance* (1686), follow the now-familiar motifs of a sexual economy that centers on age.[10] Behn's plays confront cultural values that exchange youthful sexuality for economic gain. In *The Rover*, Florinda rebels against her father's wishes that she marry the wealthy Don Vincentio, who is dubbed "Old Sir Fifty." In response to her brother's advice that she consider the fortune offered by Don Vincentio, she replies, "Let him consider my youth, beauty and fortune, / which ought not to be thrown away on his age and jointure" (1.1.77 78). As with other January figures, Don Vincentio's body is a favorite object for scrutiny—descriptions of his "feeble carcass" invite disgust from the audience and Florinda as they consider the nights she will spend in a "moth-eaten bedchamber" (1.1.110, 104). Yet, in Behn's hands, maneuverings of the January–May theme are at once more explicit and more ambiguous. The audience and characters of her plays share the typical fun with gender that the January–May marriage's power reversal carries, but by the end of the drama, the plays present gender dynamics far more complicated than a Chaucerian world upside down. While Behn, as a female playwright, maintains a vested interest in gender subversion, she is skeptical about the ability of the January–May theme to resolve gender inequalities. In Behn's plays, the January–May theme challenges male authority, but the final curtains close on a world still controlled by masculine power, where women remain the objects, not the agents, of sexual and economic exchange.

In *Sir Patient Fancy*, practical women like the maid Maundy criticize the traffic in young women by older, wealthier men. In this case, beautiful, young Lady Fancy is married to the aging hypochondriac Sir Patient Fancy, and the play centers on the prospect of Lady Fancy's independent widowhood that will come at Sir Patient's death. Lady Fancy masks her extramarital ambitions to ensure her share of his fortune, and Sir Patient believes his wife is true. As Maundy prepares to smuggle a young lover into Lady Fancy's chamber, she explains that infidelity in such marriages should be expected: "to say truth, there's a Conscience to be used in all things, and there's no reason she should languish with an old man when a young man may be had" (3.2.78–80). Appealing to a higher reason, rather than the marriage laws of social contract, Maundy leads the audience to condone her lady's actions. Since Sir Patient is presented as a bumbling fool, absorbed with his own flagging physicality instead of the interests of his wife, he becomes yet another easy object of ridicule like his numerous January predecessors.[11] Thus presented, Lady Fancy's mercenary tactics come across as humorous comedy—the just deserts of a faulty system of exchange—and yet the play's underlying message projects a dark model of agency that simultaneously reflects and critiques existing property law. When Sir Patient fears he is descending to his grave, Lady Fancy's aside, "This is the Musick that I long'd to hear," has already been justified, even as the audience experiences unease at the hypocritical front she maintains to her husband: "[You] Die! Oh that fatal word will kill me—(Weeps) Name it no more if you'd preserve my life" (4.2.71–73). Although this exchange is funny, Behn reveals that Lady Fancy's machinations are no better, nor more moral, than those used by men like her husband to oppress her. Not only does Lady Fancy plan to enjoy her husband's fortune, but she greedily plots to take his daughter's inheritance as well. Encouraged by his nephew, Sir Patient tests and then discloses Lady Fancy's dishonesty to the world. At the end of the play, Lady Fancy loses her power, and Sir Patient reclaims his authority to discipline and to punish. While critical of male-dominated society, Behn is reluctant to replace the gendered hierarchy with another system of gender inequality.

While much of the action in Behn's *The Lucky Chance* continues a theatrical interest in making fun of elderly men, it avoids reductive conclusions concerning the power reversals initiated by youth and age. The two older husbands, Sir Feeble and Sir Cautious, frantically try to maintain control of their wives' sexuality, and the play conveys that "a young wife is able to make any old fellow mad, that's the truth on't" (3.5.42–43). Sir Feeble and Sir Cautious are both ludicrous figures, evoking laughter and contempt from the audience by their unrestrained desires for sex and money, and both men lead to their own undoing. Sir Feeble's baby talk with his wife infantilizes not her, but him, while Sir Cautious makes himself a cuckold by bartering his wife to her lover for three hundred pounds. Behn spares no opportunity to deride these older husbands but treats the young wives, Leticia and Lady Fulbank, sympathetically despite their extramarital affairs. Leticia's flight from her elderly husband into the arms of young Belmour is justified because the two had already sworn themselves to one another before Sir Feeble cheated Belmour of "fame and life, / And then what dearer was, his wife" (3.5.153–54). The play also vindicates Lady Fulbank from full responsibility in her sexual relations with young Gayman, whom she loved before she married Sir Cautious; although she has often teased Gayman sexually, even leading him into her bed, she never consummates their affair until tricked by her own husband into doing so. Technically, she intends to be faithful to her older husband, even though she makes it clear that she longs to be rid of him. But ultimately, the older husbands in *The Lucky Chance* are supplanted, not by their wives, but by the young male rivals whose more traditional masculinity satisfies the desires of the women in the play. Anticipating his death, Sir Cautious promises to leave Lady Fulbank, along with the rest of his property, to Gayman, and the play's ending depicts a system of male-to-male privilege through this sexual inheritance.[12]

Like Shakespeare's *Othello*, Behn's works chronicle January–May marriages' growing complexity in literature, but the theme often follows stereotypical models in the late seventeenth and eighteenth centuries. Playwrights like William Congreve employ January and May figures as stock characters to effect mischievous manipulations of sex, money, and power in plays like *Love for Love* (1694) and *The Old Batchelour* (ca. 1689–93). *Love for Love* uses the foolishness of older lovers for comic purposes through the outcomes of two parallel relationships. Sir Sampson Legend courts the beautiful young Angelica only to lose her love to his own son, yet the audience witnesses the fate Sir Sampson narrowly escapes when the elderly Foresight is cuckolded by his young wife. A similar plot structure arises in *The Old Batchelour*, in which the aging bachelor Heartwell desires to marry the young prostitute Silvia, who is eager to advance her economic position. Fortunately for him, Heartwell never marries, though the audience enjoys the cuckolding of another older man, Fondlewife, by his young wife Laetitia. Older men's desire for young women, even when disassociated from the marriage plot, provides a means for attacking male privilege.

A poem entitled "The Reasons that Induced Dr S to write a Poem call'd the Lady's Dressing room" (ca. 1732–34), Lady Mary Wortley Montagu's response to Jonathan Swift, ties his poetic diatribe against women to his age-based sexual inadequacies. In Montagu's poem, Swift attributes his flawed performance to young Betty's repulsive uncleanliness, but Betty blames his impotence directly on his age: "by God / The blame lyes all in Sixty odd" (74–75). John Cleland's racy *Fanny Hill* (1748) also delights in the explicit details of older men's sexual shortfalls: when an elderly man purchases young Fanny's virginity, her horror of sexual relations with one she describes as "old and ugly," "pestilential," and "hideous" (34–38) dissipates when the sex/rape scene concludes with his premature ejaculation and her escape. Without oversimplifying the intricacies of age and desire in these plots, I find that these narratives gloss age-based powers that other January–May texts explore more fully.[13]

Charlotte Lennox's *The Female Quixote* (1752) indicates that January–May plots were in danger of becoming trite by the mid-eighteenth century. Lennox attributes the January–May marriage of the heroine Arabella's parents to conventional social and sexual motivations—"the Marquis, though now advanced in Years, cast his Eyes on a young Lady, greatly inferior to himself in Quality, but whose Beauty and good Sense promised him an agreeable Companion" (18)—but quickly passes over their relationship, and Arabella's mother dies soon after childbirth. Lennox treats this marriage perfunctorily, but then mocks at length the romantic conventions of older suitors and young women through Arabella's unfounded suspicions of the sexual interests of her suitor's father. From reading too many romances, Arabella believes in a debauched stereotype of older men who cannot control their passions for young women, but in this case, the novel proves her the fool, and not the older man.

Richard Sheridan's *The School for Scandal* (1777) maneuvers a conservative agenda through the January–May motif. The play appears to challenge masculine authority by commenting on the husband's ill-conceived plan to wed a young wife, but the play concludes with a restoration of traditional gender roles. From the opening of the drama, the aging Sir Peter is painfully aware of his weakened position since marrying Lady Teazle, and he bewails,

> When an old bachelor takes a young wife, what is he to expect?—'Tis now six months since Lady Teazle made me the happiest of men—and I have been the miserablest dog ever since that ever committed to wedlock! We tift a little going to church, and came to a quarrel

before the bells were done ringing. I was more than once nearly choked with gall during the honeymoon, and had lost all comfort in life before my friends had done wishing me joy! . . . I am sneered at by my old acquaintance—paragraphed in the newspapers. She dissipates my fortune, and contradicts all my humors; yet the worst of it is, I doubt I love her, or I should never bear all this. (1.2.1–22)

Lady Teazle likewise acknowledges the power that her youth affords while making him even more mindful of his debased condition. To his demanding inquiry, "so a husband is to have no influence, no authority?" she promptly responds, "Authority! No, to be sure—if you wanted authority over me, you should have adopted me, and not married me; I am sure you were old enough" (2.1.11–14). Refusing the submission, respect, and obedience expected of wives, Lady Teazle assumes the command and rights of a self-governing individual.

Like Chaucer's women, Lady Teazle is cognizant of the material advantages she has gained through her marriage and of the economic rewards that widowhood would secure. Although she was the daughter of a simple country squire, "a girl bred wholly in the country, who never knew luxury beyond one silk gown" (1.2.11–12), she has willingly exchanged her youth for wealth and a title. And though, like Wycherley's Pinchwife, Sir Peter expressly chose his young bride "with caution" (1.2.10) by selecting her from outside of the fashionable London circuit, his prudence does not pay, as Lady Teazle refuses to act submissively, or even gratefully, in what she sees as a fair trade of youth and beauty for fortune and prestige. Sir Peter bemoans that her extravagance will be his financial ruin, and she furthers the insult by taunting him with her anticipated liberation at his death. When Sir Peter reminds her of what she has gained through marriage: "you were pleased enough to listen to me—*you* never had such an offer before" (3.2.311–13), Lady Teazle counters that there were other rich suitors who would have made her a widow by now: "No! didn't I refuse Sir Twivy Tarrier, who everybody said would have been a better match—for his estate is just as good as yours—and he has broke his neck since we have been married" (3.2.314–18). Instead of playing the unspoiled, dutiful daughter/wife that Sir Peter had hoped to import from the country, Lady Teazle takes full advantage of the benefits of her age-related power, and she tortures Sir Peter into submission.

Much of this power still arises from the sustained conviction that older husbands cannot please their young wives sexually, and that the young wife has the ability, if not the right, to make her husband a fool in the eyes of society through infidelity. Joseph Surface refers to Lady Teazle's capability of cuckolding her husband as the "only revenge in [her] power" (2.2.287), and though he incorrectly delimits her options to advance his own sexual interest, Surface captures the idea that Lady Teazle's sexual agency adds clout to her position. Lady Teazle thus wields her sexuality over her husband; when he accuses her of an affair with Charles Surface, she pointedly warns, "Take care, Sir Peter! you had better not insinuate any such thing! I'll not be suspected with*out cause*, I promise you" (3.2.325–27). Aware of her ability to make good on her promise, Sir Peter once again acquiesces to her demands. By the fourth act, Sir Peter has given up entirely to Lady Teazle's wishes. She will no longer have to wait for his death for her financial independence, as he resolves to provide her with a separate maintenance of eight hundred pounds a year and to leave her the majority of his wealth on his death. In his conversation with Joseph Surface during the famous screen scene, Sir Peter's deference to Lady Teazle becomes clear; he reasons, "And then, you know, the difference of our ages makes it very improbable that she should have any great affection for me; and if she were to be frail, and I were to make it public, why the town would only laugh at me, the foolish old bachelor who had married a girl" (4.3.199–204). This is an especially self-sacrificial scene, and since the abnegation of self is a traditional mark of feminine virtue, Sir Peter here accepts his new position within the marriage as wife, leaving Lady Teazle to exercise the sexual and financial freedoms normally enjoyed by a husband. Ultimately, Sir Peter accepts the penalty associated with a January–May marriage, and resigns himself to his sentence; after all, as he explains, "the crime carries the punishment along with it" (2.2.113–14).

The reversal of gender roles follows many characteristics of the theme as found in Chaucer—economic gains for the younger wife, the threat of sexual rivals, and public ridicule for the cuckolded husband—but the theme grows more conservative in the late eighteenth century. While *The School for Scandal* continues to play with gender, Sheridan restores a guise of stability through the Teazles' mutual recommitment to their marriage and to normalized gender roles. From behind the screen, Lady Teazle overhears her husband's submission, but his relinquishing of male authority initiates, paradoxically, her return to a feminine position.[14] Having "recovered her senses" (4.3.541), Lady Teazle denounces her intention to take on a lover and reforms herself into the image of the loyal and trustworthy wife that Sir Teazle had originally hoped she would be. After letting her "pine a little" (5.3.309) in remorse of her treatment of him, Sir Peter reclaims his masculine position and his wife, declaring happily, "we may yet be the happiest couple in the country" (5.3.326–27). Importantly, the play never allows for the consummation of Lady Teazle's extramarital exploits, and this nod to sexual etiquette contributes to the play's efforts to reinstall conventional gender roles in the final act. The sentimental conclusion and sexual decorum bolster the play's conservative message, yet the success of that message is questionable, since the final affirmation of gender identities comes only as the result of gender reversals.

As the January–May marriage tradition continues, its ability to restore or disrupt codes of gender and power grows increasingly complex. By the late eighteenth century, the theme carries centuries of established notions of how these marriages work. The reversals that often accompany the marriages support the use of the theme as a tool for social subversion, but the theme's general reliance on narratives of female (in)fidelity and manipulation prevents the message from being fully liberatory. Some of the fun that reigned in Chaucer's use of the theme begins to disappear, and texts increasingly portray younger wives' extramarital desires as sources of real danger, both for their own well-being as well as that of their husbands and children. Nearing the nineteenth century, the literary focus changes, and attention turns to what would be the period after the affair's disclosure; the literature demonstrates an interest in what would be, for example, the consequences after everyone in "The Miller's Tale," including old John, realizes that he has been cuckolded by his wife, or, alternately, what would happen after a young wife realizes she wants to, but dares not, act on her desires. In these later texts, the January–May marriage develops more fully its potential for multiple, and sometimes contradictory, purposes regarding gender identities.

Elizabeth Inchbald's 1791 novel *A Simple Story* demonstrates how much the theme has evolved by the late eighteenth century. Although Miss Milner, who is eighteen, and Dorriforth, who is thirty, do not share the larger age difference that characterizes January–May marriages, the novel's incorporation of other elements of age-based power makes it relevant to a larger overview of the theme.[15] Miss Milner's dying father selects Dorriforth to be her guardian, and she is legally and emotionally his ward before they become husband and wife. From the moment of their first meeting, the difference in their ages and their respective positions as guardian and ward shape their actions toward one another. Miss Milner's youthful beauty overwhelms Dorriforth, giving him "something like a foreboding of disaster" as he greets his ward, who is "lovely beyond description" (13). But Miss Milner is not immune to the effects Dorriforth's age and position have over her;

when she greets him, she bursts into tears, kneels down, and promises "ever to obey him as her father" (13).[16] As their sexual attraction toward one another grows, their age difference affects their negotiations of gender within the relationship, encouraging both their defiance of and submission to gender norms.

Despite Miss Milner's pledge to obey her "deputed father," she struggles with subservience to one whom she also envisions as a potential lover. Dorriforth does not approve of the fashionable lifestyle that she enjoys, and while he attributes his judgments to his religious convictions, they are, in truth, based primarily on his secret fear of exposing her to male rivals, especially the young Lord Frederick, who Inchbald is careful to note is only twenty-three. When "Balls, plays, incessant company, at length rouzed her guardian from that mildness with which he had been accustomed to treat her" (27), Dorriforth summons the powers that he holds as her guardian and commands her to stay at home from an event that she plans to attend. A tense day passes, as no one seems quite sure whether his order will be obeyed or not. Eventually, Miss Milner does submit to his command, and, in turn, Dorriforth releases her to attend the ball. Dorriforth is pleased at the capitulation of his ward, and while he wrestles with his attraction to her, he is nonetheless relieved to believe that she had learned her proper place either as "daughter" or wife.

While Dorriforth's ward, Miss Milner discharges much of her subversive energies toward a surrogate January figure: Mr. Sandford, Dorriforth's advisor.[17] She refuses to submit to his authority and shocks his sensibilities through her liberal understanding of a woman's role in society. Sandford urges Dorriforth to rid himself of her and arrange for "the care of so dangerous a person [to be] given into other hands" (42). Yet Dorriforth, and eventually Sandford, cannot resist Miss Milner's charms. Dorriforth and Miss Milner exchange the bonds of guardian and ward for those of lovers and engage to be wed. Notably, when they openly acknowledge and accept their mutual attraction, the January–May dynamics between them begin anew. Miss Milner explains that she cannot obey him while he is her fiancé, and, in a series of defying actions, she risks their marriage trying to make him submit to her. When he orders her not to attend a masquerade ball, she defies him, dressing "in men's cloaths" (159) to accentuate her assumption of masculine authority. Ignoring his commands and aggravating his unease by flaunting Lord Frederick's continued advances, Miss Milner makes her intentions clear: she explains to her friend Miss Woodley, "instead of stooping to him, I wait in the certain expectation, of his submission to me" (173).

The novel, however, does not fulfill Miss Milner's expectations, and rather than setting up a comical gender reversal, Inchbald's use of age in marriage promotes more complex readings. Miss Milner and Dorriforth (now Lord Elmwood) marry, and he becomes a cuckold when his wife has an affair with Lord Frederick while Dorriforth is away in the West Indies. But Dorriforth is never defeated or feminized to the extent of earlier January figures. His reaction to the affair is violent: "Lord Elmwood's love to his lady had been extravagant—the effect of his hate was extravagant likewise" (197). His wife banishes herself from their home to the most "dreary retreat" (197), and Dorriforth sends away their six-year-old daughter Matilda because she is a constant reminder of her mother, ordering his friend and servants not to mention them in his presence. He also punishes his younger rival: he duels with Lord Frederick and leaves him "so maimed, and defaced with scars, as never again to endanger the honour of a husband" (198). By these exertions of his male power, Dorriforth resists the effects of age on his gender identity, and he soon "regain[s] his usual tranquility" (199) while his wife lingers and dies in guilty seclusion. However, while the novel never endorses the farcical play with gender found in Chaucer, Inchbald steers the novel's conclusion away from an unmitigated affirmation of masculine and feminine constructions. After fulfilling the role of father/lover by rescuing his estranged daughter from a kidnapping and potential rape, Dorriforth submits to female influence—albeit the influence of his biological daughter and not his ward/wife. Inchbald shows Miss Milner, Dorriforth, and Matilda to be the victims of a gendered social order that age can manipulate but not fully overcome, and Inchbald ultimately places much of the blame for the novel's tragedies on the lack of "a proper education" for women.

## THE JANUARY–MAY MARRIAGE IN A NINETEENTH-CENTURY CONTEXT

By the early nineteenth century, the January–May marriage had proven to be an effective plot structure that could evoke a wealth of cultural assumptions concerning male potency, female fidelity, sexual economies, and gender-based power. Able to meet a wide range of objectives, the January–May theme could work subversively or conservatively, through humor or through tragedy. The unique relationship offers a useful tool for authors and readers exploring specifically nineteenth-century concerns regarding gender and sexuality, and the theme resurfaces with newfound energy and intent throughout the period. Without becoming trite, these relationships influence the plots of dozens of canonical nineteenth-century texts. Peculiar circumstances converge to encourage a heightened interest in the theme's potential, and consequently, while January–May marriages pervade British literature, I maintain that the popularity of this theme in the nineteenth century emerges in response to numerous social, industrial, and economic factors that heightened anxieties concerning the identities of men and women.

The last decade of the eighteenth century initiated an increased agitation for public attention regarding the "woman question" and displayed the culminating effects of a century of Enlightenment thought. A prosperous economy and a growing leisure class helped to create a sizeable body of female readers and writers who, as literary consumers and producers, could influence cultural perceptions of masculinity and femininity.[18] By the late 1780s and '90s, women's participation in literary culture grew to have overtly political objectives. Protofeminist arguments like Mary Wollstonecraft's *Thoughts on the Education of Daughters* (1787) and Catherine Macaulay's *Letters on Education* (1790) resonated in subsequent works like Inchbald's aforementioned *A Simple Story*. Moreover, late eighteenth-century women like Wollstonecraft who felt increasingly polarized into separate spheres merged the political philosophy of John Locke with early feminism to argue for women's equality by way of women's rationality. Rejecting established notions of feminine docility, passivity, and sensibility, these women benefited from the intellectual endeavors of earlier Bluestocking women and urged their claims as rational creatures.[19] Assertions for a broader reconsideration of the role of women in society grew alongside the calls for reform that initiated the French Revolution, and Wollstonecraft's demand for "a REVOLUTION in female manners" (192) in her 1792 *A Vindication of the Rights of Woman* aligned the woman question with class oppression and slavery. These broader movements for freedom and equality inspired radical debates over women's rights and brought to the forefront the question: What is the difference between men and women?

Much of this difference was thought to be biological. Physicians and scientists had advocated well into the eighteenth century a "one-sex" model for the human body. Although twenty-first century readers informed by antiessentialist theorists might initially interpret such a unifying system as a progressive method of classification, the one-sex model merely claimed that women were imperfect or underdeveloped specimens of the more complete male anatomy. A biological system of gender hierarchy was already at work in the one-sex model, and women's bodies represented physical lack or, as Freud would later conclude, a castrated male. During the eighteenth century, a different, though still biological, classification of the sexes replaced the one-sex model, and in *Making Sex: Body and Gender from the Greeks to Freud*, Thomas Laqueur describes how the eighteenth century invented our current understanding of sexual and gender distinction: "The reproductive organs went from being paradigmatic sites for displaying hierarchy, resonant throughout the cosmos, to being the foundation of incommensurable difference" (149).[20] Even advocates for the rights of women tended to work within the assumption of essentialized differences between genders and argued for women's rights not as a component of, but as a parallel to, the rights of men. As liberal thinkers further worked for the rights of women, they found that their logical queries returned to questions of innate gender differences. For example, while Mary Hays seems to endorse the idea of gender-based human characteristics, she poses, at the beginning of the chapter "What Women Are" in her *Appeal to the Men of Great Britain in Behalf of Women* (1798): "To say what women *really* are, would be a very difficult task indeed" (67).

The appearance of a two-sex model coincided with an increased need for gender clarity. The agitation for reform regarding the woman question met with a backlash of criticism affirming a political, social, and economic system of male dominance. This conservative movement was fostered by anti-Wollstonecraft sentiment that increased with William Godwin's publication of her posthumous memoirs, which revealed to the public intimate details of her sexual relationships with Godwin and Gilbert Imlay, as well as her two suicide attempts. Yet even the most adamant rejections of Wollstonecraft's theories reveal that social perceptions of gender were in flux, and many of the advocates for traditional gender roles disclose their own fears and anxieties about gender identities. Responses to Wollstonecraft and the woman question such as Thomas Taylor's *Vindication of the Rights of Brutes* (1792) and Richard Polwhele's *The Unsex'd Females* (1798) convey a frantic scurrying to reinstate codes of natural law that privileged physical and psychic differences between the sexes. Polwhele expresses his vision of anarchic women presuming rights in a footnote to his poem: "Nature is the grand basis of all laws human and divine: and the woman, who has no regard to nature, either in the decoration of her person, or the culture of her mind, will soon 'walk after the flesh, in the lust of uncleanness, and despise government'" (6). Subversive and conservative forces struggled throughout the early nineteenth century to make sense of the ongoing debate, encouraging, for vastly different reasons, a social reconsideration of gender.

Moves toward gender equality begun across the Channel in France contributed to British interests in reforming or reinstating laws regarding women's access to property and divorce. In 1789, the French Revolution abolished primogeniture and declared all children, including females, equal inheritors of their parents' estates—an important change that Patricia Mainardi connects to the nineteenth-century French fascination with marital infidelity in art and literature because of its implications regarding the passing of property to illegitimate children. The postrevolutionary French government also made divorce an accessible option for failed or failing marriages (Mainardi, 1–12). While these radical developments were not immediately embraced in Britain, and were reversed or reduced in France in the following decade, their temporary enactment inspired hopes and fears in Britain and indicate the volatility of early nineteenth-century solutions regarding gender, marriage, and the law.

By the mid-1840s, the increasing effects of industrialism and capitalism coincided with processes that undermined and reinstated gender identities.[21] In her influential *Women, Power, and Subversion*, Judith Lowder Newton examines the division of the nineteenth-century labor force, claiming that the rise of factory production led to the decline of home industry and therefore to the rise of "separate spheres" (18–21) for masculine and feminine work. Yet these gendered realms of labor were inextricably bound with class economics; rather than experiencing a dramatic division of a masculine workplace and feminine domesticity, working-class laborers witnessed an increased blurring of gender division by the mid-1840s. Agrarian notions of men and women's work dissolved as the growing industrial economy used both men and women.[22] The corresponding polarization of male and female realms within the middle class emerged from the instability of working-class gender roles in the new social framework. For example, in 1843, Charlotte Elizabeth Tonna published a study on the British working class: *The Perils of the Nation: An Appeal to the Legislature, the Clergy, and the Higher and Middle Classes*. Tonna examines the lack of gender identities among the mining poor, lamenting at length the sinful licentiousness that pervades the mine, this "scene of deepened gloom" (54). Men, women, and children worked in mixed company in the mines, wearing little clothing because of the heat, and created an androgynous workplace where the notion of separate spheres and often gender differences themselves did not exist. She writes, "The dress of these young labourers of both sexes is the same: from seven or eight years of age to twenty and upwards they may be seen, naked to the waist, and having a loose pair of ragged trowsers, frequently worn to tatters by the constant friction of the chain" (47). Tonna writes repeatedly, almost obsessively, of the virtually "naked" bodies sweating and writhing in the dark tunnels of the mines and concludes, "No circumstances can possibly be conceived more inevitably tending to general profligacy; and that the most abandoned vice does reign in the mines, transforming the female character into something so depraved that their language and conduct are described as being far worse than the men's, is but too well attested" (56). The gender ambiguities of the miners clearly offended Tonna, and she warns her reader that the deviancies of the poor have widespread ramifications as these androgynous figures are reborn from the mines into society: "Indeed, the transfer to the surface, of a body of females so utterly hardened in the gross depravities of the mines, must, for a time, spread contamination on all sides" (54).

This language highlights a middle-class fear that the androgyny of the working class was infectious. Tonna's simultaneous reluctance and willingness to talk about the lack of gender affiliation in mining work reveals middle-class anxieties of gender multiplicities, and the threat of gender disruption forms a core component of the "perils" facing British society. For social reformers, the lack of gender division among the working class justified a cultural imperialism that attempted to inscribe morals and identities on working-class bodies in exchange for physical necessities like healthy food and air. Tonna's work certainly demonstrates a concern for the well-being of the working poor, yet the need for reform that Tonna advocates coincides with explicitly middle-class interests. Tonna capitalizes on the middle-class fear that the workers will spread their androgynous identities outside their social context and therefore motivates social philanthropy through class interest in gender stability.

Like Tonna, Friedrich Engels makes similar observations of class-based gender ambiguities in *The Condition of the Working Class in England* (1845); concerned here with factory labor, he writes of a "condition, which unsexes the man and takes from the woman all womanliness without being able to bestow upon the man true womanliness, or the woman true manliness—this condition which degrades, in the most shameful way, both sexes, and through them, Humanity" (184). Again, the social reforms address the welfare of the poor in conjunction with the larger interests of the middle class to reinscribe clear gender divisions, and Engels, typically an advocate for the working class, speaks for the bourgeoisie.

Perhaps even more threatening than Tonna's examples, here gender roles are not androgynous, but, as in Chaucer's upside-down world, sexually reversed. Quoting from a letter from a working-class man, Engels describes a husband sitting by a fireside mending stockings with a bodkin while his wife works at the factory. Regretfully pining for the separation of spheres that his class position no longer affords, the male-wife complains to his friend that "she has been the man in the house and I the woman" (183). Rousing fervor for social change, Engels prompts his middle-class audience's likely response: "Can any one imagine a more insane state of things than that described in this letter?" (184). The "perilous" condition of Tonna's mine workers and the "insane state" of Engels's factory family indicate an equally dangerous position for the middle class, who, seeking to help the working class with basic economic concerns, also try to resolve their own basic gender concerns by establishing a natural hierarchy of gender by way of labor relations.

Legislative reforms attempted to address many of the century's multiplying sources of gender anxiety. Parliament demonstrated that it was more likely to advance legal changes, such as the 1839 Infant Custody Act, that supported women in their traditional roles as mothers and wives, but even these limited changes worked to improve a long-established code of justice that endorsed male privilege. Later reforms indicate a slow but continued effort to empower women within their marriages by giving them more rights to their property and children, as well as the ability to terminate marriage contracts without the financial expense and legal maneuverings of an act of Parliament, as had been earlier required.[23] Conservative legislation often sought to mitigate the effects of these strides toward female equality. The Contagious Disease Acts of the 1860s singled out women thought to be prostitutes, but not their male partners, for examination and detention, and as a "protective" measure, the Factory Acts of the 1870s limited the hours women, who often worked for lower wages than men, could be employed in the factories. Both laws treated women unequally while claiming to protect them. Failed legislation also provides insight into nineteenth-century gender issues: John Stuart Mill added an amendment for women's suffrage to the Second Reform Act of 1867, and although he met wide ridicule for his stance, his agitation suggested that social change would eventually come and encouraged the creation of women's suffrage groups in major British cities.

The diverse literature of the nineteenth century reflects the changing ways men and women viewed themselves and one another, and many texts attempt to make sense of the shifting gender roles that individuals encountered in real life. Some works didactically push social thought toward specific outcomes, endorsing new extremes of gender identities like the now-notorious "angel in the house" of Coventry Patmore's 1854 poem. The necessity to install clear boundaries between masculine and feminine labor thus surfaces in Victorian literary creations directed toward middle-class audiences like Tennyson's *The Princess* (1847). Though Tennyson tempers the King's gender proclamation through the perspectives of the Prince and Princess, the King's reactionary call for strict gender codes records a social backlash against gender unrest:

> Man for the field and woman for the hearth:
> Man for the sword and for the needle she:
> Man with the head and woman with the heart:
> Man to command and woman to obey;
> All else confusion. (5:437–41)

Appearing only two years after Engels's description of the domesticated factory worker, the poem responds to confusing social realities. Tennyson intends *The Princess*, however, as a work advocating women's rights, and he shares concerns with other mid-Victorian authors like Elizabeth Barrett Browning, whose *Aurora Leigh* (1856) promotes gender equality.[24] For example, coming on the heels of Mill's call for women's suffrage and his feminist treaty *The Subjection of Women* (1869), Anthony Trollope's novel *He Knew He Was Right* (1869) details social and legal structures that deprive a woman of her child when her husband goes mad from sexual jealousy. Gender surfaces as an imperative topic for writers of the day, and questions about how designations like "male" and "female" relate to distributions of power permeated nineteenth-century texts. This unique cultural uncertainty created fertile ground for the January–May marriage in literature, and the theme blossoms, incorporating some tropes of the tradition but adapting its characteristics to respond to the contemporary gender crises.

I conclude this chapter with Canto I of Byron's *Don Juan* (1818), because it demonstrates the basic premises of triangular romances and gender parody that are fundamental to the January–May literary tradition. While Byron's poem captures the essential dynamics and gender anxieties that the theme addresses, in many ways, *Don Juan* serves as a bridge between early manifestations of the theme and those of the nineteenth century. Whereas *Don Juan* shares with most of its January–May predecessors an interest in the overt cuckolding of the older husband, most nineteenth-century texts revise this expression of consummated adultery into an obsession with the mere threat of adulterous behavior; the triangular pattern persists but rarely is the husband a victim of an extramarital affair. Though parody remains an important element of the theme throughout the century, January–May marriages take on subtler and more complex methods for probing identity, suggesting that anxieties about gender and age have perhaps become too fragile and too visible for such ribald play. Moreover, while I generally try to avoid authors' biographies as a method of exploring the literature, I indulge the practice in this instance as a means of suggesting how nineteenth-century contexts, both private and public, inspired interest in the way age affects gendered power. As a literary sensation, *Don Juan* established the importance of January–May marriages throughout the century, and it offers a starting point for considering the period's fascination with the age and gender nexus.

## "She thought of her own strength, and Juan's youth": Age and Gender in *Don Juan*

Byron's *Don Juan* provides an interesting case study of the dynamics of the nineteenth-century January–May marriage. From the first canto, Byron establishes age as an essential component of gendered power relationships, and this quality is responsible for much of the fun in the poem. Like cross-dressing, homosexual innuendoes, extramarital affairs, and other efforts to play with gender in the poem, age raises questions regarding the stability and legitimacy of sexual identities. From the youth of Juan to the maturity of Catherine the Great, *Don Juan* uses age as yet another guidepost in its wandering navigation of gender.

Juan, of course, is consistently—and considerably—younger than most of his female sexual partners. While youth can be read as a feminizing characteristic for men, as in the case of Juan's relationship with Catherine, the ages of the poem's sexual partners manipulate gender in different ways. Byron delights in the complexities age affords, and he begins the poem by evoking the larger January–May marriage tradition. Byron's interest, then, is not in just the power dynamics of younger men's relations with older women, but also in those between older men and younger women, as he evidences through the Alfonso-Julia-Juan triangle of Canto I. The January–May marriage theme provides a narrative structure that both deconstructs and reifies masculine and feminine identities, and a close reading of Byron's initial subject matter is an important foundation for understanding any subversions or affirmations of gender that the poem posits in later cantos.

Byron's own position in this growing debate over men and women proves to be as ambivalent and varied as that of the larger British population. Even when placing his stances within a historical context, it would be difficult to label Byron's views on women as "feminist." His distaste for the increasing intellectualism of women finds voice throughout his letters and recorded conversations, as well as in his satirical *The Blues* and repeated jabs in *Don Juan* at the Bluestockings. The general chauvinist tendencies he directs toward his mother Catherine Byron, his wife Annabella Milbanke, and ex-lovers like Claire Clairmont are well documented.[25] Notoriously, he is quoted by Thomas Medwin as saying, "Give a woman a looking-glass and a few sugar-plums, and she will be satisfied. I have suffered from the other sex ever since I can remember any thing. I began by being jilted, and ended by being unwived. Those are wisest who make no connexion of wife or mistress" (73). Yet such rantings fail to paint a complete picture of Byron's complex fascination with and repulsion from women. While his statement provides a glimpse into his rationale of heterosexual, and even heterosocial relationships, Byron did not live up to his ideal of the "wisest" who refrain from involvement with women.[26]

Biographical insights into Byron's treatment of gender in *Don Juan* are certainly limited, but a brief analysis of the power structures of his relationships, especially the Alessandro Guiccioli–Teresa Guiccioli–Byron triangle, provides an important foundation for my reading of the poem.[27] Although Byron and Teresa's sexual relationship did not begin until April 1819—after Canto I had been mailed to John Murray, Byron's interest in the Italian concept of the *cavaliere servente*, a lover of a married woman who often committed to the relationship for life, was already well formed. In 1817 and 1818, similar triangles inspired *Beppo* and *Mazeppa*, which can be seen as precursors to *Don Juan* in form and theme.[28] The power dynamics of such relationships intrigued Byron, and he reflects in a letter to John Hobhouse dated April 6, 1819, on his earlier observations of Alessandro's jealousy: "[he] does not seem so jealous this year as he did last—when he stuck close to her side even at the Governor's.—She is pretty" (*Byron's Letters and Journals* [hereafter, *BLJ*], 6:107). Byron had met the Guiccioolis in January of 1818 and in the same letter to Hobhouse conveys, "I knew her a little last year at her starting" (*BLJ*, 6:107). As the parties circulated within the same Venetian *conversazioni*, it is possible that Byron was already thinking of the Guiccioli marriage when he began Canto I in July of 1818.[29] The problematic intergenerational structure of the January–May relationship seemed apparent to Byron; speaking of the Guiccioli marriage, he quips, "What happiness is to be expected, or constancy, from such a *liaison*? Is it not natural . . . she should find somebody to like better, and who likes her better. . . . young women, and your Italian ones too, are not satisfied with your good old men" (Medwin, 22–23).

Often, the similarities between the art of *Don Juan* and Byron's and Teresa's lives were exceptionally close. As Byron relates in a letter to John Murray, "Tonight as Countess G[uiccioli] observed me poring over 'Don Juan' she stumbled . . . on the 138th Stanza of the first Canto—and asked me what it meant—I told her—nothing but 'your husband is coming' as I said this in Italian with some emphasis—she started up in a fright—and said '*Oh My God—is* he *coming*?' thinking it was *her own*" (*BLJ*, 6:239). As his letters and journals from the early months of their affair show, Byron liked the correlation between his life and *Don Juan* and seems to have gained as much pleasure from enacting his artistic creation as from the affair itself.

Even more compelling than the affinities of the situations are Byron's struggles with age-based power within the Guiccioli triangle, which Byron ultimately found as disturbing in real life as in fiction. In many respects, the age difference of the Guiccioli marriage exaggerated typical early nineteenth-century gender characteristics, as Alessandro assumed a heightened position as domineering, fatherly authority and Teresa a position of childlike docility. In several letters to different people, Byron depicts Teresa as a "pretty fair-haired Girl last year out of a Convent" (6:107) and emphasizes her youth by repeated references to her age of "nineteen years" (6:113–14) in contrast to the Count's age of "sixty" (6:215–16).[30] Byron often presents Alessandro as a particularly sinister character, whose reputation hints at his involvement in several murders (6:144), and Iris Origo and many others have suggested he might have killed his first wife (26–27). At other times, Alessandro appears to be entirely under the control of Teresa. Byron describes how the Count came to him crying on discovering Teresa's infidelity (*BLJ*, 6:244). Moreover, Teresa is very much in power in her relationship with Byron, especially in its early stages. Calling Byron "the greatest trophy of the age," biographer Fiona MacCarthy relegates Byron to the position of trophy "wife" and debunks assumptions about Teresa's powerlessness as a child bride (356). These reversals of gender stereotypes afforded by the January–May marriage structure fascinated Byron, who at first indulged himself by taking a feminine role in the triangle; however, as the novelty of this position wore off, Byron felt increasingly uncomfortable in his role as *cavaliere servente*. In June 1819, he writes rather proudly to Richard Hoppner, "he is completely *governed* by her—for that matter—so am I," but by October he suggests a change in his perception in a letter to John Hobhouse: "I can't say that I don't feel the degradation. . . . here the *polygamy* is all on the female side. —I have been an intriguer, a husband, and now I am a Cavalier Servente. —by the holy!—it is a strange sensation" (*BLJ*, 6:164, 226). Byron's "strange sensation" is indicative of early nineteenth-century ambivalence about the access of men and women to power. To some extent, Byron enjoys Teresa's control within the triangle, and in *Don Juan* he celebrates the reversal of traditional power through the January–May marriage of Julia and Alfonso.

Sexuality serves not only as a means of repression in the poem, but also as a vehicle of exerting power, and both Juan and Alfonso are temporarily feminized through Julia's sexual maneuverings. Classifying characters by their sexual abilities, the narrator quickly recognizes Julia's prowess, while mocking Alfonso for both his impotence and familiarity:

> Wedded she was some years, and to a man
> Of fifty, and such husbands are in plenty;
> And yet, I think, instead of such a ONE
> 'Twere better to have TWO of five and twenty. (1.62.489–92)

Julia's sexuality, while in many ways affirming the notion that women—especially darker women—were innately more physical and more licentious than men, nevertheless provides a means to power. In this light, Mary Hays's 1798 argument in defense of coquetry becomes more subversive than it might appear on a first reading: "And if indeed, women do avail themselves of the only weapons they are permitted to wield, can they be blamed? Undoubtedly not; since they are compelled to it by the injustice and impolicy of men" (91). As in earlier January–May texts, *Don Juan* foregrounds the naturalness of Julia's sexual desire, and through her desire, she comes to control her husband by renaming him as a cuckold.

Juan's youth enables the gender reversal in much the same manner as boys were feminized within Greek society in homosexual encounters and in Turkish performances of boys dancing as girls, both customs of interest to Byron as revealed in Louis Crompton's *Byron and Greek Love*. Consequently, Byron describes how society deems Juan at sixteen as "almost man" (1.54.429), which causes his mother to fly into a rage and bite her lip to keep from screaming. Though Donna Inez's reaction indicates a fear of her son's growing masculinity, Byron phrases the description to imply, also, her distaste with Juan's youthful femininity. Later, Antonia criticizes her mistress's lover as a "pretty gentleman" (1.170.1360) with a "half-girlish face" (1.171.1378), and deems him unworthy of the risks imposed to Julia's marriage and her job: "'Had it but been for a stout cavalier . . . But for a child . . . I really, madam, wonder at your taste'" (1.172.1368–71). From the initial stages of the affair until the violent scene of its disclosure, Juan's passivity advances his feminine position with Julia. Within the pair, Julia assumes the conventionally masculine role of instructing her young lover. Dreaming of the day her husband will die "even seven years hence," Julia envisions teaching Juan "the rudiments of love"(1.85.676, 679) and raising Juan as her sexual partner. When their affair begins, she places her hand on Juan's and leans onto him, controlling him physically: "The hand which still held Juan's, by degrees / Gently, but palpably confirm'd its grasp" (1.111.881–82). As with Horner in *The Country Wife*, Juan's lack of masculinity facilitates his access to women, and Juan's young body links him to an objective feminine position.

Interestingly, age works in much the same way for Alfonso; his "fifty, or sixty" (1.146.1164) years remove him from the height of masculine privilege just as Juan's age emasculates through youth. Echoing the narrator's early remark about men "five and twenty," Antonia indicates that a cavalier "Of twenty-five or thirty" embodies her ideal of manliness, and the narrator of the poem scathingly attacks Alfonso through his age:

> She thought of her own strength, and Juan's youth,
> And of the folly of all prudish fears,
> Victorious virtue, and domestic truth,
> And then of Don Alfonso's fifty years;
> I wish these last had not occurr'd, in sooth,
> Because that number rarely much endears,
> And through all climes, the snowy and the sunny,
> Sounds ill in love, whate'er it may in money. (1.107.849–56)

The narrator's description of Alfonso as "A man well looking" is qualified by the phrase "for his years" (1.65.514), and Byron allows Julia to exaggerate his age even further: "you have threescore, / Fifty, or sixty—it is all the same" (1.146.1163–64). Thus, although he maintains the façade of manly power, Alfonso is acutely aware of the ways age threatens his sexual power; Byron writes, "he was jealous, though he did not show it, / For jealousy dislikes the world to know it" (1.65.519–20).[31] The poem suggests Alfonso's age likewise defiles his virility, and after a verbal battering from Julia that lasts thirteen stanzas and a "half-hour," Alfonso appears a "foolish figure" (1.161.1282). When he returns from his expulsion from Julia's bedroom, she has maintained her ability "to turn the tables" (1.175.1396) of gender and dominate the relationship. The power associated with the male is firmly in Julia's hands as she "laid conditions, he thought, very hard on, / Denying several little things he wanted" (1.180.1435–36).

While Juan and Alfonso are feminized, signifiers of gender construct Julia's masculinity. Even before the affair, Julia's eyes are "handsome" and full of fire and her "stature tall" (1.60.473, 1.61.488), and the shift in power brought about by her affair nurtures her masculinity. She discards the voicelessness of traditional femininity under the threat of her affair's disclosure and gains masculine voice. Though Byron rebukes her hypocrisy—"Oh shame! / Oh sin! Oh sorrow! and Oh womankind! / How can you do such things and keep your fame" (1.165.1313–15)—he presents her critique of her marriage and sexual dissatisfaction with such wit that the reader is amused at Alfonso's embarrassment. In her thirteen-stanza tirade, she threatens not only Alfonso, but the other men of the *posse comitatus* as well. Julia harshly ridicules Alfonso's impotence, advancing her own masculinity by publicly stripping his; sarcastically mocking Alfonso's age, she hopes the man they are searching for "has not sixty years, / At that age he would be too old for slaughter, / Or for so young a husband's jealous fears" (1.155.1233–35). Flaunting her sexual agency, she runs through a litany of young suitors she could have selected as lovers, reminding the married men of their wives' power to humiliate them. She even transcends the realm of domesticity by publicly challenging the lawyer's business practices. Yet whereas Juan's and Alfonso's feminized positions call for humor and readers laugh at their diminished manhood, Julia's newfound masculinity simultaneously evokes the reader's compassion for her plight and a heightened social anxiety due to her newly liberated status.

The January–May marriage enables gendered power to be redistributed, yet the shift does not exchange identities completely. *Don Juan* demonstrates how age works to reverse the gender binary in regard to sexual power, but the poem shows how it can also work, in the same context, to exaggerate conventional systems of male-female power. In the January–May theme, the wife who finds herself infantilized by nineteenth-century culture can be further relegated to a childlike position in contrast with her even more fatherly, oppressive husband. A basic materialist feminist reading of any such relationship would argue that an older male has more opportunity than his younger female counterpart to amass wealth, power, and experience. Young men likewise could exhibit more intense masculinity as a result of raging hormones, role-playing, and cultural pressure. Juan and Alfonso, however feminized, cling to the concept of manhood, while the empowered Julia remains bound to feminine constructions. Paradoxically, at the same time Julia adopts masculine characteristics, she exudes an exaggerated femininity, and while Juan and Alfonso take on feminine guises, they show excesses of masculinity.[32] By analyzing the manuscripts for clues to the revision process, T. G. Steffan, in articles such as "Byron at Work on Canto I of *Don Juan*," documents the numerous places in the canto where Byron revised specifically for an embellished effect. For example, Alfonso originally was to arrive with only half his "household," not half the city at his back, and Julia's desirability is revised to merit not one, but two bishops' devotion in the final version. Fully aware of the power of parody, Byron alters the manuscript to heighten already inflated markers of gender. These excesses themselves have subversive qualities and form a more complex attack on masculine and feminine identities. The theatricality and parody of the January–May theme draw attention to the instability of any notion of a gendered original that the parody is replicating. By overstating the way power is coded and demonstrated by "men" and "women," the January–May marriage theme unhinges existing gender roles.

Donna Julia, especially before her love affair with Juan, exudes a childlike feminine excess that parodies the characteristics culturally ascribed to women. Though on the surface the descriptions of Julia seem little more than Byron's creation of his "*beau ideal*," they express ulterior motives. Byron chooses to portray the young wife Julia as so much woman that she becomes no woman, thereby challenging fundamentals of gender identification. The narrator introduces her:

> There was the Donna Julia, whom to call
> Pretty were but to give a feeble notion
> Of many charms in her as natural
> As sweetness to the flower, or salt to ocean,
> Her zone to Venus, or his bow to Cupid,
> (But this last simile is trite and stupid). (1.55.435–40)

Byron plays on the conventional tendency to naturalize a woman's feminine qualities, but self-reflexively unveils the error of his last allusion and concedes the problems of essentializing femininity. Julia embodies both plentitude and lack when she initially denies her longings for sexual pleasure—fulfilling extremes of opposites, both "sweetness" and "salt." The poem demonstrates how the repressive structure of sexual codes leads to further excessive displays of feminine virtue, which are complementary moves in this gender spectacle. She acts

> As if her heart had deeper thoughts in store
> She must not own, but cherish'd more the while,
> For that compression in its burning core. (1.72.571–73)

Julia's initial commitment to a wife's faithfulness is so extreme that it suggests childlike naïveté more than hypocrisy, yet she feels herself so capable of fidelity that she puts herself to the test. After all, as "a virtuous woman," she believes she "Should rather face and overcome temptation," and "That flight was base and dastardly" (1.77.609–11). But Julia's performance of feminine virtue is transparent both to the reader and to the narrator, who, knowing the likely results of her repressed desires, urges for his own sexual benefit, "young ladies to make trial" (1.78.624). Byron encourages parodic representations of masculinity and femininity with keen awareness of their disruptive consequences.

As a parody of patriarchal law, Alfonso appears with all the social props of male authority, and he arrives to confront Julia with "more than half the city at his back" (1.137.1090). While the investigation of Julia's room is invasive, the display of masculine excess is farcical. His age, which should convey a public mark of dignity and respect, causes Julia to question if the attack is "worthy of your years?" (1.146.1163). Alfonso is flocked with "torches, friends, and servants in great number" privileging him with manly reason, social custom, and class advantage. The legal representative who accompanies Alfonso proves to be little more than authority for hire. Even Alfonso's use of weapons, the phallic signifiers of male power, is so excessive that it is ridiculous. Julia chides, "Oh, valiant man! with sword drawn and cock'd trigger, / Now, tell me, don't you cut a pretty figure?" (1.150.1199–1200). Byron's parody of the patriarchal husband becomes even more scathing in light of Alfonso's affair with Donna Inez. Patriarchal authority in its excess reveals itself to be so hypocritical, and so theatrical, that its validity disintegrates.

Byron conveys Juan's romantic, youthful masculinity with such plentitude and humor that it too loses all pretense of legitimacy. Evoking Wordsworth and Coleridge as the whipping boys of manly sentiment, Byron mocks the high seriousness associated with masculine romanticism:

> He, Juan, (and not Wordsworth) so pursued
> His self-communion with his own high soul,
> Until his mighty heart, in its great mood,
> Had mitigated part, though not the whole
> Of its disease; he did the best he could
> With things not very subject to control,
> And turn'd, without perceiving his condition,
> Like Coleridge, into a metaphysician. (1.91.721–28)

Here, Byron strikes at common signifiers of masculinity by showing Juan's pubescent abundance of sexual desire. As Juan dwells on the significance of the stars and other natural phenomena, the narrator reminds the reader, "If *you* think 'twas philosophy that this did, / I can't help thinking puberty assisted" (1.93.743–44). The poem suggests Juan's stargazing is inspired by his reclined position, likely to facilitate his masturbation, while thinking of the "boundless skies" and "Donna Julia's eyes" (1.92.735–36). Juan orgasmically "pored upon the leaves, and on the flowers" (1.94.745), losing himself in his pleasures until he finds he has missed his dinner. The "lonely walks" and "lengthening reveries" coded by Romanticism as manly poet-visionary characteristics are exaggerated with other youthful, masculine objectives into witty parodies of gender excess.

Through the reversal of power within the triangle and the age-based parody of masculine and feminine constructions, Byron criticizes normative gender identities and their power. By highlighting how age influences readings of gender, the January–May construction forces a reconsideration of gender as a self-contained marker of identification, and gender emerges as a composite of multiple elements that include race, class, and age. Byron reflects the lack of a coherent understanding of gendered identity: "Man's a phenomenon, one knows not what" (1.133.1057). The excesses of gender traits expressed in age-disparate marriages do subvert masculine and feminine norms in their treatment of the subject, but in their satirical play, they also recreate the very notions they attempt to dismantle. The January–May marriage serves a dual purpose that suits Byron's complex attitudes toward the woman question. After numerous complex challenges to traditional gender, Canto I concludes with a more outright attempt to reaffirm masculine and feminine norms, which should inform readings of gender throughout the rest of the poem.

Byron's literary attacks on conventions of gender reveal his interest in dismantling such restrictive identities, perhaps for personal reasons motivated by both his heterosexual and homosexual desires, several of which were considered prosecutable by law in Regency society. However, parody, in reproducing to excess the codes of gender it challenges, ironically must participate in their reconstruction. Arguably, this fits Byron's own investment in heterosexual male domination, even as he suffers from its effects. As Susan Wolfson notes, "Even granting the notoriously adept ironies of *Don Juan*, its politics of sexual difference prove remarkably complex and unstable. At times they are governed by the general satirical perspective of the poem; at other times they clash with Byron's pronounced liberal politics; and at still others they appear scarcely fixed" (585). Age provides Byron with a way to navigate these instabilities meaningfully, and the January–May theme offers a vehicle that encompasses Byron's contrary personal motives. For example, when his affair with Teresa Guiccioli becomes known to her husband, Byron takes a decidedly conservative, and unusually self-sacrificial, approach in recommending she stay with her husband: "[I] persuaded her with the greatest difficulty to return with her husband to Ravenna" (*BLJ*, 6:241). Here, Byron's inconsistent display of respect for his elder counterpart and the institution of marriage conveniently allows Byron to disengage from a relationship no longer very exciting.

But Byron's most obvious biographical display of his interest in manipulating and advocating gender roles comes when he denies Claire Clairmont access to her daughter Allegra despite the pleas of both the Shelleys. Until the 1839 Custody of Infants Act that was fueled by the famous Caroline Norton case, a mother did not have equal rights under English law to her children (Caine, 67).[33] He writes, in a letter to Richard Hoppner in September 1820, "Clare writes to me the most insolent letters about Allegra—see what a man gets for taking care of natural children! . . . If Clare thinks that she shall ever interfere with the child's morals or education—she mistakes—she never shall— The girl shall be a Christian and a married woman—if possible. . . . To express it delicately—I think Madame Clare is a damned bitch" (*BLJ*, 7:174–75). While in works like *Don Juan* and *Sardanapalus* (1822) Byron displays a desire to subvert gender, he is not above using tradition to his practical advantage to keep his ex-lover and daughter in submissive positions. Fortunately for him, he can manipulate age, like other characteristics that can be used to reground or subvert gender, at any time in favor of his identity as father and man.

Byron reminds the reader of his ambivalent stance on the rights-of-woman issue. Though the narrator often champions the naturalness of Donna Julia's sexual desire for a younger man, he chastises her for her infidelity by appealing to religious tradition when it benefits him:

> For instance—gentlemen, whose ladies take
> Leave to o'erstep the written rights of woman,
> And break the—Which commandment is't they break?
> (1.98.778–80)

If the "written rights of women" are grounded in Christian theology, Byron can use religious tradition to contradict his more rational arguments regarding the naturalness of Julia's desire, which he can now read as adultery—a crime to both the state and the church. Moreover, Wolfson notes how "a feminized Juan always invites death into the poem, whether in the form of threats to his own life or to the lives of those implicated in his travesties" (601), and thereby warns of clear physical ramifications for gender deviancy. Arguably, Byron senses the consequences of his gender bending to his own male privilege and quells his gender anxiety through an affirmation of gender norms.

The gender reversals initiated by the January–May marriage come crashing down through a seemingly insignificant marker of maleness—a pair of shoes. After chronicling Julia's sexual exploits and building expectations that Julia and Juan might escape, Byron reinstalls male power. Just when Alfonso finds his control most diminished and the searchers of Julia's bedroom are about to leave, having found no evidence of infidelity, Byron allows him to find

> A pair of shoes!—what then? not much, if they
> Are such a fit with lady's feet, but these
> (No one can tell how much I grieve to say)
> Were masculine; to see them, and to seize,
> Was but a moment's act.—Ah! Well-a-day! (1.181.1441–45)

Society inscribes the stylistic differences between male and female shoes; their gendering is not essential or biological. As such, the shoes remain a subversive element of the poem because of their arbitrariness though they nevertheless indicate gender.[34] The "seeing" and "seizing" of the shoes mark the shift in the canto toward a return to gender norms. The reversal of gendered power comes to an end, and the return to masculine domination begins.

Despite the comic cheekiness of the shoes' phallic symbolism, the shoes become an important gender signifier in the poem, and Juan gains a noble male virility that he has lacked thus far in the poem. Rejecting the feminine passivity that has characterized him heretofore, he actively wrestles with Alfonso in heated battle and adopts the dangerous qualities of masculine power: though his voice remains "an octave higher" than Alfonso's, he blasphemes, his "blood was up" (1.184.1470, 1471), and he loses his temper—all actions proper for men, but not for women in the nineteenth century. Juan is now menacing, and the narrator describes Alfonso as lucky: if Juan had seized the dropped sword, "Alfonso's days had not been in the land / Much longer" (1.185.1478–79). Juan throttles Alfonso and causes his nose to bleed before losing his only clothing, revealing his body in further support of his manliness. Furthermore, the discovery of his shoes indirectly leads to his adventurous travels, advancing his association with the youthful masculinity of the Romantic quest and carrying him through the rest of the poem.

The end of Canto I also restores Alfonso to a secure place of male privilege within the law, which pays the customary respect to his age, gender, and authority. Whereas the moment before he discovers the shoes, he is in exile "like Adam lingering near his garden" (1.180.1437) begging forgiveness from a godlike Julia, his detection of the masculine shoes gives him evidence of gender (albeit not *of* the body but worn *on* the body) that is sufficient to reinvigorate his male potency. Appropriately, he leaves the room to regain another phallic object, his sword, and on returning, "threaten'd death" (1.183.1464). Although he does not kill anyone, Alfonso manages to inflict injury through the law, likewise restored to its former prestige, and Alfonso sues for divorce, enforcing the sexual double standard that condones his affair with Donna Inez but punishes Julia's infidelity. The end of Canto I vindicates Alfonso's age and gender, and he returns to a respected position as a senior patriarch.

Julia, in contrast, becomes once again a child, "sent into a nunnery" where numerous girls, including Byron's daughter Allegra, were directed for their educations. In choosing to punish Julia, Byron follows the mob's rationale for storming her room, "Were *one* not punish'd, *all* would be outrageous" (1.138.1104), and reinstates gender identity and subsequent female repression by men. Julia loses her adult status as a sexual individual and her agency as a young wife and becomes a passive victim both of Alfonso and of Juan. Her letter to Juan expresses her assumption of the traditional codes of the female gender: "I have no further claim on your young heart, / Mine was the victim, and would be again" (1.192.1531–32). Byron vents his views on essential gender difference, superficially sympathetic, through Julia's letter:

> 'Man's love is of his life a thing apart,
> 'Tis woman's whole existence; man may range
> The court, camp, church, the vessel, and the mart,
> Sword, gown, gain, glory, offer in exchange
> Pride, fame, ambition, to fill up his heart,
> And few there are whom these can not estrange;
> Man has all these resources, we but one,
> To love again, and be again undone.' (1.194.1545–52)

Julia's newfound commitment to gender norms shapes her letter. She grieves that her "breast has been all weakness" and that her "brain is feminine" (1.195.1553, 1557). While these self-deprecatory remarks do not fit the woman who publicly belittled her husband with strength and wit, they correspond with Byron's need to reestablish feminine subjection. Julia confirms the sexual double standard again as she accepts that Juan "will proceed in beauty, and in pride, / Beloved and loving many" while in contrast, she envisions "all is o'er" for her life "except some years to hide / My shame and sorrow deep in my heart's core" (1.196.1561–64). Indeed, the poem sadistically fulfills her prophecy, when Juan, in Canto II, quickly forgets her love for that of Haidée.

Byron continues to play this "come here/go away" game with gender identities for the remainder of *Don Juan*, cyclically undermining masculine and feminine norms only to reinstall them with force. In Canto IV, Haidée's father overthrows her matriarchal rule of paradise. Juan's sexual subordination to powerful female figures like the Sultana Gulbeyaz is countered by his manly sack of Ismail. And, of course, Juan's sexual exploits have their own way of reifying a masculine identity. While traditional gender identities surface throughout the poem, these repetitive motions that reestablish gender point not only to Byron's apparent personal confusion but also to nineteenth-century society's inability to feel comfortable with gender. If age can demarcate social divisions of power, then using gender as a basis of a sex-class system appears all too erroneous, and yet the restoration of traditional masculine and feminine identities is the necessary effect of gender's failure to hold up under Byron's scrutiny.

Allowing for such repetition and yet disrupting gendered distributions of power, the January–May marriage theme in Canto I lays a foundation for gender presentations in all of *Don Juan*. Byron repeatedly feminizes Juan only to restore him to positions of male privilege.[35] Furthermore, as gender binaries become more polarized during the nineteenth century, *Don Juan* initiates a literary attraction to the January–May marriage's varied implications for masculine and feminine identities in the Victorian period. Although, in its emphasis on age-based power imbalances, the January–May marriage forces readers to reconsider gender's vitality as a social category, its subversion is much more complex, and more troublesome, than perhaps even Byron could grasp or control.

## Chapter 2

# "Old Enough to Be Her Father"

## Incest Narratives in Dickens

Analogies between January–May marriages and father-daughter relationships surface in numerous nineteenth-century texts, highlighting marriage as a venue for traditional patriarchal authority as well as a cover for overtly disruptive sexualities. In her chapter on "Dickens' Little Women" in *Dissenting Women in Dickens' Novels: The Subversion of Domestic Ideology*, Brenda Ayres includes a paragraph on "the December/May relationships that often occur in Dickens' novels." According to Ayres, "Usually the text depicts the father as a good patriarch and the woman as a true beneficiary. Marrying a father figure facilitates transfer of patriarchal power. The female is to respect not only gender, but age as well. Having submitted to the authority of the father since birth, she also will submit to a man who reminds her of her father. Although perhaps fortifying the bastions of patriarchy, such a practice blisters with incestuous implications" (71). Ayres is right. It is difficult to miss the "incestuous implications" or the power inequities in Dickens's intergenerational marriages. For example, Annie Strong passionately entreats her elderly husband Doctor Strong, "Oh, my husband and father, break this long silence" (606). This blurring of romantic and biological claims is disturbing to a twenty-first-century audience, and it would have troubled nineteenth-century readers, too. On the surface, Annie's words strengthen male familial roles as Ayres describes—after all, Annie is trying to save her marriage—but because those roles collapse, the taint of incest spoils what should be comfortable.

Even in the twenty-first century, objections to January–May relationships often begin with the line, "He's old enough to be her father," and the incestuous daddy-daughter component of these relationships is difficult to ignore in nineteenth-century literature. *Jane Eyre*'s Mrs. Fairfax blurts, "He might almost be your father" (263) in response to Jane's announcement of her engagement to Rochester; Phillotson in *Jude the Obscure* is "old enough to be the girl's father" (86); and in *Middlemarch* Dorothea Brooke proclaims that a "really delightful marriage must be that where your husband was a sort of father, and could teach you even Hebrew, if you wished it" (7). In Sarah Grand's *The Heavenly Twins* (1893), Angelica emphasizes the slippery roles within January–May marriages by calling her older husband "Daddy" throughout their marriage. Other novels, such as Austen's *Emma* and Charlotte Brontë's *Villette* (1853), emphasize the paternal role of the husband-to-be, who gently but firmly disciplines his rebellious "daughter" before taking her as a wife. Such marriages exaggerate the imbalance of power among men and women in the nineteenth century by giving the husband the additional authority of parent, and conservative writers adopt the January–May theme to illustrate the husband's consolidation of gender and generational power. In this line of interpretation, January–May marriages also extol the virtues of a patriarchal society by demonstrating women's desire for male leadership, instruction, and control. Marriage becomes an extension of women's childhood and keeps husbands in an idealized state of knowledge and ability.

But there is more. Just as January–May marriages served multiple objectives in nineteenth-century literature, the theme's connotations of incest between older husbands and younger wives make difficult and sometimes contradictory statements about age, gender, and power. As Ayres points out, associating husband with father doubles the masculine power base within the family. The incestuous dimensions of January–May marriages can also be a part of a larger social indictment against sexual deviance and gender instability, and if texts present these incestuous relationships as horrific, they fulfill an Oedipal pattern that rejects incest in favor of normative, exogamic heterosexuality.[1] But there is something provocative about the role of incest in the development of "normal" gender identification and sexuality. Reading intergenerational marriage as an "almost"-incest narrative can challenge traditional structures of gender and power.[2] Rather than advocating presumptive heterosexuality or binary gender identification, the January–May marriage's incestuous overtones suggest radical revisions of kinship structures and sexuality by collapsing normalizing (marriage) institutions and disturbing (incestuous) desires.

The subversive potential of incest arises from specific dynamics within the January–May marriage theme. Since many same-age nineteenth-century marriages maintained women's submission to their husbands as patriarchal figures, the foregrounding of generational gaps in January–May marriages allowed for parodic critiques of men's paternal power. Entering into second childhoods, these older husbands underscore the pliability of gendered and aged constructions and make conventional power distinctions impossible. Moreover, if the Oedipal stage is a compulsory process that leads to gender identification, then incestuous desire ironically is vital to social and gender stability, though the desire must be continuously inspected and restrained to prevent the tragic consequences of *Oedipus Rex*.[3] Paul Kelleher theorizes that Freud's "counterintuitive" interpretation of incest concludes that "normal sexual development entails a necessary deviance that precedes normality" (157). Deviant, incestuous, or queer desire proves necessary for heterosexual identification, and this interdependence of standard and abnormal sexualities undermines the binary logic of what is subversive and what is conservative. When January–May marriages offer the collapsed roles of father and lover, daughter and wife, as ideal rather than as violation, they on the one hand uphold patriarchy, but on the other, shatter heterosexual norms. Many January–May texts present intergenerational romances between figurative fathers and daughters who are happily married, rewriting the horror of Oedipus as a plausible ideal and removing the apparent need to move from deviant to normal behavior. Because the incest theme also negotiates female Oedipal desire, it legitimizes feminine sexuality by equating it with familial love. Even if daughterly desire were evidence of the monolithic power of the heterosexual rubric, her desire challenges gender constructions by emphasizing feminine subjectivity. And incest raises other subversive prospects. Since the January–May marriage's triangular structure prompts a male Oedipal struggle, women join forces with young men who have also been objectified by male power to strike at father figures. Additionally, texts that introduce the January–May marriage only to reject its consummation teasingly perpetuate the incest theme by prolonging the fulfillment of (pseudo)incestuous desire.[4]

Incest also has the radical potential to debunk marriage as a social institution. If, as Foucault asserts in *The History of Sexuality*, an

*Introduction: Volume 1*, the family offers a system of alliance built on two fundamental relationships, those between parents and children and husbands and wives, the disintegration of boundaries between these two axes of power fostered by incest narratives challenges the basic organizational structures of society (108). In the January–May theme, this disintegration is not merely figurative. Since paternity was difficult to establish in this period, these marriages toy with a literal potential for incest, and a young woman marrying a man "old enough to be her father" could, in fact, be marrying her father. Scores of nineteenth-century texts, including Dickens's *Bleak House* and Hardy's *The Mayor of Casterbridge* (1886), structure their plots around the uncertain paternity of young and beautiful heroines. For example, in George Bernard Shaw's *Mrs Warren's Profession*, Sir George Crofts, a longtime friend, lover, and business partner of the prostitute-turned-madam Mrs. Warren, hopes to marry her daughter Vivie, whose father remains unidentified throughout the play. Crofts admits, "Why, for all I know, *I* might be her father" (43). Finding no physical resemblance between himself and Vivie, Crofts unsuccessfully attempts to draw the mystery of Vivie's parentage from her mother. Admitting that he is "thoroughly uncomfortable about" (44) the possibility that Vivie could be his biological daughter, Crofts nevertheless indulges his sexual attraction and proposes marriage. In Shaw's original manuscript, the possibility of incest increases Crofts's desire. To Mrs. Warren's objection, "How do you know that the girl maynt be your own daughter, eh?" Crofts counters, "How do you know that that maynt be one of the fascinations of the thing? What harm if she is?" (Conolly, 56–57). Though Vivie declines Crofts's offer, the incestuous elements of their proposed marriage contribute to the play's indictment of gender inequalities in marriage.[5]

As I have suggested, authors did not always manipulate the January–May theme's associations with incest for a progressive agenda, and nineteenth-century writers enjoyed the varied interpretations that incest made possible. Often the daughter's "seduction" solicits sympathy for her plight, and as victim of pedophilic desire, the younger wife emerges as martyr. In these versions of the incest narrative, the older husband often appears as the stereotypical "dirty old man" whose perverse passion deserves public scorn and demands surveillance and control. In these scenarios, the young male suitor of the molested young wife can free her from the taint of an incestuous relationship and restore masculinity and femininity to the realms of normative heterosexuality. Texts can also elicit sympathy for masculinity by venerating the older husband as a kind and gentle patriarch, lovingly (and seemingly platonically) guarding his child wife. Younger wives in these stories seem to enjoy having another father, and conventional views of husband as guide and protector endorse the narrative sleight of hand substituting spousal for fatherly authority. Several of these January–May narratives suggest that women prefer domination to equality, though the pat equation of father with husband must remain troubling. While the January–May theme may often appear to promote traditional gender roles in marriage, its incestuous connotations ensure that it can never be completely successful in advocating its conservative agenda.

For nineteenth-century writers, these incestuous elements offered a convenient method of integrating both subversive and normative approaches to gendered power into popular discourse under the guise of a legitimized, heterosexual union.[6] Later in the century, more texts take up the January–May theme as the literature moved away from the Romantic period's more explicit tales of incestuous relationships. There is little to compare with the openly incestuous narratives in Percy Shelley's *The Cenci* or Mary Shelley's *Mathilda* during the Victorian period, and the prevalence of texts dating from the late 1830s about older husbands and younger wives indicates that these marriages served as an acceptably disguised outlet for exploring dynamics of incest. In his influential *The Incest Theme in Literature and Legend*, Otto Rank describes the way the incest theme has been masked within standard storylines to vent socially inappropriate subjects: "we observe continually increasing repression of the attraction between father and daughter, expressed in the increasing obscurity and delicacy with which this incestuous relationship is depicted" (330).[7] In a fictional January–May marriage, incest is titillating but controlled, dangerous yet safe, and it is therefore no wonder that the theme surfaces in the works of canonical Victorian authors.

For Charles Dickens, the incestuous marriage afforded a perfect situation for reconsidering gender and power. While other nineteenth-century writers draw attention to these unions as disguised incest narratives, more than any other author, Dickens obsessively returns to the theme as a means of rewriting these differing implications of incest, repeatedly evoking the dynamics of father-daughter love to destroy and rebuild the roles of husband and wife. Each of the incestuous scenarios that I have described as possible in January–May marriages occurs in Dickens's works. A thorough examination of Dickens's diverse portrayals provides valuable models for theorizing about how other authors engage the deviancies of intergenerational romances in their works.

Dickens's novels make it difficult to ignore the frequent and anything-but-subtle exchanges of affection between mothers and sons, fathers and daughters, sisters and brothers. A rich critical heritage exists that probes the Oedipal and Freudian dimensions within his larger corpus of works.[8] Over the last decade, Robert Polhemus has offered some of the most provocative interpretations of older men and younger women relationships in Dickens. He expands his readings of incest in *Lot's Daughters*, in which he reinterprets incest through the biblical tale and the surrounding events of the destruction of Sodom and Gomorrah. Revising the Oedipus complex as the "Lot complex," Polhemus charges, "Dickens had a Lot complex that shaped his outlook, his relations with women, and his hugely influential fiction. A sanitized Lot theme featuring the benevolent embrace of daughterly figures by men and of paternal figures by very young women appealed to him, and he used it again and again" (29).[9]

Other critics describe Dickens's incest narratives in more explicitly Freudian terms. Dianne Sadoff argues, in *Monsters of Affection: Dickens, Eliot and Bronte on Fatherhood*, "Charles Dickens's narrative project . . . takes as its central metaphor the primal scene. His novels track down the father's sexual and violent rape or wrong as narrative origin, deny the hero could have been conceived by that sinful figure, structurally and surreptitiously kill the father, and proceed to engender the hero as subject with language; the figure of the daughter serves to efface these sonly activities" (3). For Sadoff, Dickens's fathers are frightful figures who threaten rape and castration to their children, and I agree that this characterization is sometimes accurate. However, this chapter at once widens and focuses the current conversation about incest in Dickens. Instead of revisiting David Copperfield's frustrated longing for his mother or the urge to supplant a dead father in *Great Expectations*, I stress the importance of reading the January–May marriage as father-daughter incest narrative and consider the development of this theme throughout Dickens's works. The January–May theme emerges in so many of Dickens's novels, including *Nicholas Nickleby*, *The Old Curiosity Shop*, *The Cricket on the Hearth*, *David Copperfield*, *Bleak House*, *Hard Times*, and *Little Dorrit*, it forms an integral part of Dickens's larger wrestling with gendered identities and familial relationships. Incest is not the only element of the January–May marriage at play in Dickens's use of the theme—work remains to be done on how Dickens's narratives of intergenerational relationships incorporate other January–May concerns—but incestuous nuances unify his long and varied treatment of the family romance, even when those incestuous elements emerge in contradictory ways.[10]

From a psychoanalytical perspective, what Dickens does with the incest theme is quite complex. By presenting both successful and unsuccessful January–May romances, Dickens manages alternately to preserve and to overturn the incest taboo. The effects of aging further muddle divisions of gender and the ordering of kinship bonds; as children serve as parents and parents as children in Oedipal revisions, it is difficult to say who is killing whom. After all, as sexual identities become threatened through rumors of female infidelity and myths of women's sexual prowess, it seems as if the older men, and not the infants, would suffer most from a castration complex.[11] And the solutions that Dickens offers to struggling, emergent identities are remarkably fresh—and at times startlingly provocative. Though critics have often noted the predictable pattern of Oedipal aggression in Dickens's works, they have overlooked his attempts to resolve that struggle nonviolently. Although Dianne Sadoff chooses to highlight a pattern in which "the son must continue symbolically to vengefully murder the father in an effort to transform him into the dead father" ("The Dead Father," 45), Dickens often presents not the murdering of father, but the marrying of father as a restorative ideal. Furthermore, when incestuous January–May ties do not form, incestuous desire proliferates, often redirecting the familial love that has been displaced outside the family back into biological parent-child venues.

I structure this discussion of Dickens chronologically because I believe that Dickens comes to realize the greater potential of the January May marriage as incest narrative only after early, somewhat predictable, endorsements of the social taboo, and because I want to emphasize the trajectory Dickens follows as he connects his wide-ranging depictions of incest to his concerns with marital stability and with gendered power. *Nicholas Nickleby* and *The Old Curiosity Shop* outwardly accept the incest taboo, and as a consequence, their plots adopt threats of incest that tacitly inspire readers' fear and disgust. Adding to the horror of potential incest, husbands and fathers in these early works are selfish and corrupt, if not outright sinister, and, abusing power they garner through age and gender, they introduce the young women in their care to danger rather than providing patriarchal protection. Through these early novels, Dickens upholds same-age heterosexuality as the ideal and stresses the necessity for the incest taboo, but because his claim for normalcy develops from incestuous desire, it is weak at best. Moreover, because these novels imply that marriage itself can be somewhat incestuous and that marriage can be abused by "bad" men, they challenge marriage and masculinity as sources of social constancy.

These early works make provocative claims about the January–May marriage and incest by themselves, but Dickens complicates his first renditions in later revisions of the theme. It would be reductive to say that Dickens moves from an early approval of the incest taboo to a later sanction of incest, but his works reveal his increasing awareness of the light incest sheds on gender and power. In *The Cricket on the Hearth*, Dickens creates several January–May romances that inspire different conclusions. In this work and in subsequent novels like *David Copperfield* and *Bleak House*, incestuous dynamics further destabilize traditional marriage when the "horror" of intergenerational romance is recast as idealized incest and fatherly older husbands become sympathetic figures who are desired by their young brides. Not only do these texts foreground female agency, but they also disclose problems with masculine authority without demonizing it or suggesting it is beyond repair. By encouraging the reader to feel sorry for these father figures, Dickens eventually crafts narratives in which incestuous love has the potential to reform "bad" masculinity, as in *Hard Times* and *Little Dorrit*. Unlike *Nicholas Nickleby*, these later January–May plots boast no heroic young savior who will rescue the young bride from legitimized incest, and there is little pretense that gender and power are stable forces in marriage. But to get to these depictions of January–May marriages in his later works, Dickens must begin by invoking the incest taboo as psychological horror.

## The Horror of Incest in *Nicholas Nickleby* and *The Old Curiosity Shop*

Dickens's *Nicholas Nickleby* offers one of the earliest Victorian treatments of the January–May theme, and its incestuous subtext advances the central romance plot. Madeline Bray's unquestioning devotion to her father Walter initiates her betrothal to Arthur Gride, more than fifty years her senior. Both relationships suggest the destructive implications of daddy-daughter love, and, ultimately, Nicholas, the representative of normative heterosexuality, revalidates the incest taboo. In *Nicholas Nickleby*, incest is never idealized or actualized; it appears as a terrifying possibility that haunts the heroine and the reader, who are saved from witnessing its realization, even though both have ample time to reflect on its fulfillment. The quasi-incestuous relationship between Walter and Madeline Bray prepares the reader for the reciprocal January–May arrangement, and suggestions of incest undermine familial bonds in both relationships. Increasing the horror of incest, the novel reveals a larger fear of aging and abusive male power, and Dickens thrills his audience with both social and sexual perils.

The narrator describes Walter Bray as "an unnatural scoundrel" (692); this initial description casts him as one who had "something of the old fire in the large sunken eye notwithstanding, and it seemed to kindle afresh as he struck a thick stick, with which he seemed to have supported himself in his seat, impatiently on the floor twice or thrice, and called his daughter by name" (698). Violently phallic, Walter Bray's actions dominate Madeline, a "young and beautiful creature" (716) who eerily resembles her dead mother, yet Madeline refuses to abandon him. Dickens presents Walter Bray as a sick figure, furiously compensating for his lack of economic, physical, and social power through his exertions over his daughter. He expects her to be a "slave to [his] every wish" yet protests against the notion "that there is anything in what she has done for me but duty" (709, 714). He knows that he is in control of Madeline's will and her body, and while his decision that she marry Gride hinges on economic benefits, he enjoys the gratification of his paternal right to his daughter's body.[12] To the suggestion that he drop a "hint" about his choice of bridegroom for Madeline, Walter Bray boldly responds, "To hint a wish, sir! I am her father, am I not? Why should I hint, and beat about the bush?" (714). Literally and figuratively, Bray drives his point home. His domination is so overtly abusive that characters in the novel pragmatically suggest that the economic and sexual liberation Madeline can expect on the death of her much-older husband would displace her pent-up resentment toward her father. Ralph Nickleby cunningly advises, "If she profits by anybody's death . . . let it be by her husband's—don't let her have to look back to yours, as the event from which to date a happier life" (716). Heeding the truth of Ralph's suggestion, Walter Bray accepts Gride's proposition. Though he delays revealing his intentions to Madeline, jumping up to silence the discussion with "a gleam of conscience in the shame and terror of this hasty action" (716), Bray does insist on the marriage of his eighteen-year-old daughter to the seventy-something Arthur Gride, replacing the novel's insinuations of destructive father-daughter love with the substitute of (grand)father-daughter marriage.

The novel capitalizes rhetorically on the "perverse" sexuality that this marriage would make possible. Stressing the lecherous motivations of Gride, the novel ensures that readers can vividly imagine the consummation of conjugal rights so that they can fully enjoy the perverse before its possibility is eliminated. When Madeline caresses her father after he experiences a spasm, the novel allows the reader to fall into Gride's lustful fantasies. Though Dickens claims that even "a very hard and worldly heart" would have pitied Madeline as she held her father and "pour[ed] forth words of tender sympathy and love," Gride's "bleared eyes gloated only over the outward beauties, and were blind to the spirit which reigned within, evinced—a fantastic kind of warmth certainly, but not exactly that kind of warmth of feeling which the contemplation of virtue usually inspires" (716–17). Put simply, Madeline is "hot," she makes Gride hot, and yet the text clearly intends for this glimpse into sexual fantasy inspired by a father-daughter embrace to give readers the chills. Manipulating incestuous and intergenerational taboos, the text conjures images of "unnatural" sexual relations and lingers on moments when this damsel-in-distress is in sexual danger. When Bray instructs her to shake Gride's hand, "Madeline shrunk involuntarily from the goblin figure, but she placed the tips of her fingers in his hand" (717). After the handshake, Gride displays "many amorous distortions of visage" and, overcome with desire, resorts to kissing his own fingers. As he excitedly anticipates his wedding day, the novel leaves the reader to conjecture about the unrestrained release of Gride's sexual appetite on Madeline's body. Dickens intends the thought of sexual relations between Madeline and her (grand)father-husband to elicit widespread revulsion, though a degree of pleasure is evident in the cathartic invocation and imagining of the deviant.

Bray's timely death on Madeline's wedding day saves her from this incestuous marriage, and the novel ultimately commands the reader's respect and gratitude for the incest taboo that has averted sexual tragedy. Because the novel does not sympathize with Walter Bray or Arthur Gride, Bray's death and Gride's rejection appear just—even natural. While the novel remains a critique of paternal authority, it clarifies the dependence of social and sexual stability on the incest taboo. Importantly, the incestuous threat comes before the younger masculine power (Nicholas) can restore a traditional family structure, thus making the normative, same-age marriage of Nicholas and Madeline dependent on a primary narrative of incest.

\* \* \* \* \*

The January–May incest plot of Madeline Bray and Arthur Gride proves so thematically successful in *Nicholas Nickleby* that Dickens recycles it in his next novel, *The Old Curiosity Shop*. In this retelling, Nell, like Madeline, suffers from the poor decisions and injurious habits of her guardian, who exposes her to the libidinous wishes and

January–May proposal of a much-older man. Dickens sensationalizes many of the details from the Bray-Gride plot, which had already seemed exaggerated, to grotesque effect.[13] At thirteen, Nell is even younger than Madeline, and the destructively close familial relationship exists between Nell and her grandfather rather than her father, who is dead.

Thus, outreaching Madeline, Nell resembles not only her beautiful dead mother, but also her dead grandmother, and thus links granddaughter, daughter, and wife as one.[14] Already married, Quilp is "an elderly man," and although not as old as Gride, he is even more physically repulsive, as Dickens advances his more overtly ageist attacks in *Nicholas Nickleby* through Quilp's exponentially problematic body (29). As one of his wife's friends puts it nicely, Quilp is "not quite . . . what one calls a handsome man, nor quite a young man neither" (38), and the narrator describes him less tactfully as a "panting dog" whose animalistic "ghastly smile" displayed "the few discoloured fangs that were yet scattered in his mouth" (29). When Quilp proposes to Nell that she "be my wife, my little cherry-cheeked, red-lipped wife" (53), he brings to the fore the implied incest of the January–May marriage—paired this time with pedophilia, bigamy, and bestiality—for readers' sublimely intertwined horror and delight.

Though the marriage proposal is relatively brief and never seriously entertained by anyone but Quilp, its early interjection in the novel drives the plot by prompting the flight and exhausting travels of Nell and her grandfather.[15] As Hilary Schor describes, "The spectacle of *The Old Curiosity Shop* is organized around the alternate veiling and discovering of Nell's sexual vulnerability. Nell is a kind of pornographic object" (34). Shockingly, Quilp details his lecherous intentions with particular reference to their age difference: "Say Mrs Quilp lives five years, or only four, you'll be just the proper age for me. Ha, ha! Be a good girl, Nelly, a very good girl, and see if one of these days you don't come to be Mrs Quilp of Tower Hill" (53). To Nell, the proposal that she become Quilp's "number two" is hard to comprehend, but she quickly internalizes the dreadfulness of his request, and her terror prompts her to action. While his proposal is to be delayed until his wife's death, the sexual threat Quilp poses is imminent. Several critics, including Polhemus, have noted both the narrator's and Quilp's fascination with Nell's bed, and, coming shortly after his indecent proposal, his request to give Nell a kiss on her cheek stimulates her revulsion.[16] When Nell obliges, he praises "what a nice kiss that was—just upon the rosy part. What a capital kiss!" and leeringly admires her body, "so small, so compact, so beautifully modeled, so fair, with such blue veins and such a transparent skin, and such little feet" (81). He later urges Nell to "sit upon Quilp's knee" (94). Though such talk makes Nell's grandfather nervous, Quilp avoids addressing his offer to Nell's guardian, and so, conveniently, Dickens avoids the question of whether the grandfather's blinding greed and gambling addiction would lead him to follow Walter Bray's example and sell the sexual rights to Nell's body.

Quilp's offer of marriage shifts attention from the threat of the grandfather, whose abuse of Nell's body leads to her death, and from the gender instability of a precocious child caring for a childish adult. The proposed January–May marriage isolates incestuous desire and suggests that it is something that one can flee from, escape, and overcome. Each time Nell manages to give Quilp the slip, the novel legitimizes the incest taboo, and the disruption of expected gender and age roles caused by Nell and her grandfather lapses into comfortable Victorian notions of the dutiful daughter. The death of Quilp removes the pressing threat of a January–May marriage for Nell, and the narrative restores the relationship of grandfather and granddaughter to familial normalcy just before their deaths, so that the reader can accept that in their graves "the child and the old man slept together" (548).

Thus far, Dickens uses the incestuous connotations of the (failed) January–May marriage theme to advocate presumptive heterosexuality. The propositions in *Nicholas Nickleby* and *The Old Curiosity Shop* provide the reader with the opportunity to fear the dissolution of the incest taboo before having the taboo, and gender stasis, neatly reinstated. But this pattern of disruption and stabilization does not explain fully how age reworks the incest narrative because age complicates the characters' identities. Throughout *The Old Curiosity Shop*, Nell plays the parent to her childish grandfather, and although she evokes traditional images of mothering women, she also enters into socially inscribed male territory. While her grandfather's gambling fails to secure Nell's future fortune, she assumes the real breadwinning position within their family, taking on a number of odd jobs along their journey to provide their food and lodging. She directs their travels—as the grandfather relates, "she walked behind me, sir, that I might not see how lame she was—but yet she had my hand in hers, and seemed to lead me still" (535)—and she negotiates the necessities for their survival on a daily basis. James Kincaid asserts, "Nell is precocious, more the adult than her own grandfather" (*Child-Loving*, 238).[17] This age and gender reversal changes the implications of the incest taboo. If father and daughter are no longer affixed to conventional gender restraints, then the incest taboo loses its power to impose normative heterosexuality. Moreover, if the narrative displaces incestuous desire onto January–May marriage, then it places the deviant within the socially and religiously sanctioned venue of marriage. Does this merger of the deviant with the normative weaken heterosexual marriage and its gender identifications, or does it weaken the taboo against incest? Or does it weaken both? If the incest taboo is violated, then is the drive to gender identity and heterosexuality interrupted? Consciously or unconsciously, Dickens grasps this potential for gender trouble after writing through these first two January–May scenarios, and other January–May dynamics in *The Old Curiosity Shop* indicate that Dickens begins to revise his conception of the January–May plot. While the age difference between Dick Swiveller and the Marchioness is not as extreme as that between Madeline Bray and Arthur Gride or between Nell and Quilp, their ages and their intermingling of parental and spousal roles push Dickens's use of the January–May marriage theme and incest in new directions.

Dickens does not disclose the exact ages of Dick Swiveller or the Marchioness. In response to his question, "Why, how old are you?" she replies, "I don't know" (430). Yet Dickens confirms her position as a child by repeatedly describing her as "the child," "the girl," and "the small servant," and, in the final chapter, the narrator explains that after six years of schooling, the Marchioness is "at a moderate guess, full nineteen years of age" (552).[18] Though the details are more estimation than fact, the Marchioness is nevertheless very young, and her relationship with Dick Swiveller demonstrates that January–May marriages can blur the boundaries between incest and marriage while answering audience expectations of a predictably sentimental ending. If the reader applies Dickens's approximation of her age in the final chapter to previous chapters, the Marchioness is about thirteen years old when she first meets Dick Swiveller, who coaxes the half-starved waif into his confidence through food and drink.[19] She is thirteen when she flees her situation with Sally Brass to live with and care for Dick Swiveller during his illness, after which he wakes to find himself undressed without "so much as a waistcoat" because the Marchioness has had to sell his clothes for food (surely an occasion for Victorian audiences to question the propriety of their arrangement). Later, Dick Swiveller supports the Marchioness from his annuity, becoming the unofficial guardian of the parentless child, and sends her to boarding school. While he visits her, he reflects on his dual role as parent and as lover, and the reader learns what he already knows: "it occurred to him, *but not for the first time*, that if she would marry him, how comfortable they might be!" (552, emphasis added). Dick Swiveller has raised his own wife, and although he waits for her to be of age to propose, the marriage's associations with incest and pedophilia are too blatant to ignore.[20]

This relationship, forming one of the novel's several romantic subplots, is important because it foreshadows Dickens's more nuanced treatment of the January–May theme in later works. Even though the ages of Dick Swiveller and the Marchioness are not dramatically different—perhaps only ten or fifteen years—in recognizing the guardian-child marriage as a normative, indeed "comfortable," ideal, Dickens reshapes his former depiction of incest as a tragedy to be avoided at all costs. Prior to the Swiveller-Marchioness relationship, even death was preferable to a January–May marriage (the deaths of Madeline's father and of Nell prevent the other nuptials); after the Swiveller-Marchioness marriage, the January–May plot, and even its incestuous connotations, are not so horrific. Together, the Swivellers extend a picture of matrimonial bliss, as the Marchioness becomes "a most cheerful, affectionate, and provident wife" and Swiveller "an attached and domesticated husband" (553).[21]

## Good Daddy/Bad Daddy: Revisions of Incest in *The Cricket on the Hearth*

In the first of his Christmas stories, *The Cricket on the Hearth*, Dickens draws on incest to make different arguments about gender. To facilitate these multiple readings, *The Cricket on the Hearth* contains several potential January–May marriages, each with incestuous components. First, there is the central January–May couple of John the Carrier and his wife Dot, who, like Dick Swiveller and the Marchioness, present intergenerational marriage as a plausible success. The text includes repeated references to their ages at the beginning of the story—"fair she was, and young"; "a man, much taller and much older than herself"; "I was very young"; "I being such a child"—but, in case the reader has ignored these pointed designations, in the text Dickens calls attention to the potential for misinterpreting. The figure of the visiting Stranger, who affects deafness, demands clear speaking about their relationship, but what is clarified is not the normalcy of their marriage, but rather its disruptive potential:

> "Your daughter, my good friend?"
> "Wife," returned John.
> "Niece?" said the Stranger.
> "Wife," roared John.
> "Indeed?" observed the Stranger. "Surely? Very young!" (177)

The repetitive "wife" emphasizes the Stranger's and the reader's difficulty in recognizing normative heterosexual marriage because of the age difference between John and Dot. To clarify the familial arrangement, the Stranger must check again with "Indeed?" and "Surely?" and Dickens plays with the mingled discomfort and delight "wife" brings John and the reader. Confirming the sexual relations between this older man and "very young" woman, the story then provides physical evidence of their coupling: the baby. "Baby, yours?" questions the Stranger. Dickens explains that "John gave him a gigantic nod; equivalent to an answer in the affirmative, delivered through a speaking trumpet" (177). While the Stranger's question about paternity winks at expectations of sexual unrest within intergenerational marriages, the baby stands as signifying product of John and Dot's success in intertwining the roles of child, wife, mother, father, and husband.

The Stranger is not the only character attuned to the incestuous possibilities in their relationship. The plot turns on Dot's perception of their marriage, and though she affirms her feelings for John early in the story, she confirms her awareness of the oddity of their arrangement, confessing, "I did fear once, John, I was very young, you know—that ours might prove an ill-assorted marriage, I being such a child, and you more like my guardian than my husband" (173). She tells John how she had previously worried that he might not "learn to love me, as [he] hoped and prayed [he] might" (173). But he affirms their mutual desire. Admitting to have "learnt that, long before I brought you here," John, like Dick Swiveller, pushes the January–May relationship even further into pedophilic fantasy by dating his attraction further into Dot's youth. John does not permit himself to acknowledge his child-loving consciously, but when Dot speaks of being a girl at school, Dickens allows that "He might have been thinking of her, or nearly thinking of her, perhaps, as she was in that same school time" (174).[22] Despite the unspeakable motivations of their desire, the parent-child romance remains a fantasy that both indulge in, and both jubilantly fulfill. While encouraging the reader's not thinking but "nearly thinking" of the incestuous insinuations of the relationship, the story depicts the January–May marriage as a model of domesticity. As an infantilized Dot tends to the kettle, fills John's pipe, sits on a stool at his feet, and performs other wifely duties, the text lulls the reader into a complacent acceptance of the normalcy, even the perfection, of their relationship.

Ironically, tensions develop within the story when this incestuous model becomes threatened by what is, on one level, the possibility of cuckoldry typical of January–May romances, and on another level, a father's possessiveness of his daughter. With the introduction of the young Edward Plummer disguised as the old Stranger, Dot's fidelity becomes suspect, and John and those close to the couple are quick to presume Dot's inclination toward a same-age sexual encounter. Dickens loads the story with apprehensive references to Dot's potential adultery, purposefully misleading the reader with numerous allusions to the "shadow" that haunts their happy hearth. When John's friend Tackleton exposes Dot's suspicious conduct, he voices social expectations that prescribe same-age, nonfamilial desire. Tackleton prepares John for the revelation of his wife's betrayal: "I am sorry for this. I am indeed. I have been afraid of it. I have expected it from the first" (212). Here, adultery is normative, and it threatens the idealized incest embedded within the January–May marriage. Dickens provides a visual denouement. As John and Tackleton peer in the lighted window at the suspected lovers, Edward, who had been dressed as an old man, holds the white wig of his disguise in his hand, and same-age heterosexual desire appears a shockingly dirty secret, concealed by the more legitimate, albeit incestuous, intergenerational masquerade.[23]

As is typical in revelations of adultery, John reacts violently per conventional masculinity to what he has seen, brooding through the night about his urge to murder the young lover and likewise avowing his longing to seek revenge on his wife.[24] Both the possibility and progeny of their marital bliss disintegrate, and Dickens reveals that John "could have better borne to see her lying prematurely dead before him with their little child upon her breast" (215) than to realize her infidelity. But John's predictable response does not last through the night, and the story suggests that the incest narrative has destabilized gender roles within the marriage to a remarkable degree. John and Dot's idealized incest derails the "normal" trajectory toward traditional gender identification and heterosexual desire; that is, if the incest taboo is what initiates the process, then disregard for the taboo provides for a reformulation of gendered identities. Guided by the home's Cricket and household Fairies, John reconsiders his role as man and husband. Vindicating Dot's power to her accuser Tackleton, John praises his wife, whom he had watched "grow up, from a child, in her father's house" and condemns himself: "I had not—I feel it now—sufficiently considered her" (222). He rhetorically asks, "Did I consider that I took her—at her age, and with her beauty—from her young companions?" (223). John scorns himself for selfishly marrying a woman young enough to be his daughter and concludes that he is a "wearisome" husband who does not deserve his wife.

While Tackleton stares wide-eyed at John's conscious resignation of power to his wife, John actually praises his wife's deceit: "Heaven bless her . . . for the cheerful constancy with which she tried to keep the knowledge of this from me!" (223). He announces his sacrificial intention to give Dot "the best reparation" that he can, and "release her from the daily pain of an unequal marriage" (223–24).[25] Pledging his undying love, John validates female sexuality and the "natural" heterosexuality of same-age unions. Humbly and nonviolently succumbing to both the subversive effects of female desire and to the conservative forces of normative, same-age sexuality, John announces his plan to step aside.

The inherent contradiction in Dickens's sentimental ending is that in clearing Dot of the charge of adultery and restoring monogamous marriage to a central place, the story sustains a reading of idealized incest that challenges traditional gender identities. After the supposed affair, Dot's sexual desire is a recognized force in the marriage, though the spouses' sentimentalized reconciliation affirms her attraction to John. Dot explains, "at first I did not love you quite as dearly as I do now . . . when I first came home here, I was half afraid I mightn't learn to love you . . . being so very young, John! But, dear John, every day and hour I loved you more and more" (235). Dot makes it clear that their desire is mutual, and she resumes her role as daughterly wife with the authority of a sexually empowered individual. Having just overheard John's relinquishing of authority, Dot is aware of her power over John, whether she is cast as faithful or adulterous. Consequently, she puts off the physical embrace that will cement their reunion, tantalizing John and the reader while she verbalizes her love for her "dear old goose." Though she points out that they are only playing at normative heterosexuality, she insists it is a game she intends to continue: "And when I speak of people being middle-aged, and steady, John, and pretend that we are a humdrum couple, going on in a jog-trot sort of way, it's only because I'm such a silly little thing, John, that I like, sometimes, to act a kind of Play with Baby, and all that: and make believe" (234). Dot, John, and the reader acknowledge the theatricality of this enactment of heterosexual marriage, yet their January–May marriage thrives. When Dot allows herself to be held, Dickens directly addresses the reader: "You never will derive so much delight from seeing a glorious little woman in the arms of a third party, as you would have felt if you had seen Dot run into the Carrier's embrace" (235). Dickens finally encourages readers to enjoy watching the marriage of father and daughter that they have heretofore been encouraged to imagine and to reject.

Dickens's central January–May romance does not present a definitive new verdict on the incest taboo. Several parallel January–May romances that serve as subplots within the story complicate the implications of John and Dot's marriage. The proposed marriage "on the last day of the first month in the year" (181) between the elderly Tackleton and young May Fielding signals Dickens's conscious manipulation of the "January–May" tradition and provides a foil for John and Dot's idealized incest. Bertha, the blind daughter of Caleb, initiates another January–May romance through her unrequited love for Tackleton (or at least for the inaccurate construction of Tackleton as a kind and gentle man that her father has instilled in her). Bertha's close emotional and domestic relationship with her father adds a fourth January–May/father-daughter relationship to the story, and worth mentioning, if only in passing, is the rumored love affair between May and Edward—who appears in an old man's disguise.

Inundated with January–May romances, *The Cricket on the Hearth* demonstrates Dickens's growing obsession with the incest narrative as an opportunity for reflecting on issues of gender and the power inequities in marriage. At first, the similarities between the marriage of John and Dot and the proposed marriage between Tackleton and May suggest that the latter could be another depiction of the January–May romance as idealized incest. Coincidentally, they plan to marry on the same date as John and Dot. Dot's real name, Mary, is conspicuously close to that of May, with whom she shares girlhood memories of school, and Tackleton is eager to befriend John and Dot, whom he deems "just such another couple. Just!" (181). Inviting John to the wedding, Tackleton explains with a nudge, "We're in the same boat, you know. . . . A little disparity, you know" (181). Attempting to align himself with John in some sort of older-husband cohort, Tackleton arranges to have May visit Dot in hopes that Dot's happiness in marriage will have a beneficial influence on his own young bride. Speaking to John, Tackleton reasons, "It's as much your interest as mine, you know, that the women should persuade each other that they're quiet and contented, and couldn't be better off" (182). But Tackleton's engagement to May never attains the status of idealized incest modeled by John and Dot.[26] A toy-maker, Tackleton ironically "despised all toys," and his profession alludes to the economic advantages linked to age. Children support him, but he consumes them; he "had been living on children all his life, and was their implacable enemy" (180). Tackleton's pursuit of May reeks of incest as violation, and, like Dickens's earlier treatments of January–May marriages, their story insists that the incest taboo is best maintained.

Despite her similarities to May, Dot does not see parallels in their relationships, declaring, "he's as old! As unlike her!" (175) about the other couple, even though, because of her inability to pinpoint the distinguishing difference, she leaves the similes and her thoughts unfinished. To Dot, Tackleton is exceedingly older than John, and she asks her husband to clarify how much older Tackleton is, but John evades a direct answer. If they are the same age, Tackleton is not John, and Dickens presents Tackleton as "a domestic Ogre" (180). Thus, instead of inculcating May with hopes of wedded bliss, to Tackleton's horror, Dot playfully exposes the irregularity of the January–May arrangement. At the gathering arranged by Tackleton, Dot directs the conversation:

> "Ah, May!" said Dot. "Dear, dear, what changes! To talk of those merry school-days, makes one young again."
> "Why, you an't particularly old, at any time; are you?" said Tackleton.
> "Look at my sober plodding husband there," returned Dot. "He adds twenty years to my age at least. Don't you, John?"
> "Forty," John replied.
> "How many *you*'ll add to May's, I am sure I don't know," said Dot, laughing. "But she can't be much less than a hundred years of age on her next birthday."
> "Ha ha!" laughed Tackleton. Hollow as a drum, that laugh though. And he looked as if he could have twisted Dot's neck, comfortably. (203–4)

Dot continues her cheeky critique of Tackleton by overriding his evident displeasure until she goes too far and is chided by her husband, but despite this check, Dot's message is successful. Dickens conveys Tackleton's lecherous desire for May as both distinctly different and perversely problematic.

The Tackleton-May subplot serves several objectives. It functions as the more stereotypical January–May relationship that Dickens has already presented through Arthur Gride and Quilp, and, as such, it captures readers' likely responses to the incestuous connotations of January–May marriages, luring negative attention away from the idealized couple of John and Dot. Evidencing the necessity of the incest taboo, their foiled romance encourages traditional gender identifications, which come to fruition when Edward, like his literary precursor Nicholas Nickleby, sweeps in to rescue and wed May moments before she plans to marry Tackleton. The abuse of class power in the proposed marriage also taints Tackleton's attempt to marry "a young wife . . . a beautiful young wife" (181) because of the economic advantages that he offers May and her mother. Here, the insinuation of the traffic in young women moves their relationship further from idealized incest. In these two contrasting couples, Dickens balances positive and negative portrayals of his incest narrative, but what complicates the reading of the incest narrative in *The Cricket on the Hearth* is the additional January–May "couple," Bertha and "Tackleton," who is really Tackleton's impoverished employee Caleb and her father. Loving both her father and Tackleton in a strangely bifurcated January–May theme, Bertha drives the incestuous implications of the January–May marriage home.

Bertha is blind and unable to see Tackleton for what he is, imagining him only as her father has constructed him; to Bertha, Tackleton is an honorable, compassionate, fatherly man worthy of her passionate devotion. Because of her father's protective deception, Bertha never envisions Tackleton as "cold, exacting, and uninterested" but rather as "an eccentric humourist who loved to have his jest with them, and who, while he was the Guardian Angel of their lives, disdained to hear one word of thankfulness" (189). Bertha pines for her "Guardian Angel" in secret longing, and, because of her consistent and unfounded delight when he visits, Tackleton believes her to be an idiot. Bertha's misguided fantasy leads her to desire "To be his patient companion in infirmity and age" (196), and she jealously, though submissively, tells May, "the knowledge that you are to be His wife has wrung my heart almost to breaking!" (208). Through the contrast between the real and imagined Tackleton, Dickens offers a biting analysis of paternal aggrandizement. Like the dashing and debonair persona Caleb forms for himself, the character that he has constructed for Tackleton is a lie, grown from the "enchanted" world that Caleb has built for Bertha from "the magic of devoted, deathless love" (188). Unwittingly, Caleb has conflated his own idealized persona with that of Tackleton, fashioning an invented father figure who, in truth, emotionally mirrors himself. When he realizes that he has raised his daughter to love a romanticized version of himself, he recoils at the horrific incestuous connotations, yet, knowing Bertha will not consummate her love with Tackleton or with himself, is dismayed that she will be left alone. He remorsefully asks, "have I deceived her from her cradle, but to break her heart at last!" (208).

Repeating the expressions of Bertha and Caleb, Tilly Slowboy, the nursemaid, relates in a drowsy, singsong lullaby the hope and the horror that surround the story's multiple depictions of the January–May marriage as incest: "Did the knowledge that it was to be its wifes, then, wring its hearts almost to breaking; and did its fathers deceive it from its cradles but to break its hearts at last!" (213). Coming at the climactic point in the story where Dot's infidelity is most suspect and May's marriage to Tackleton most likely, Tilly's use of the gender-neutral "its" extends the implications of her song from the baby to Dot, May, and Bertha—as well as to John, Tackleton, and Caleb. The song's mixed messages about incest, parental deception, and unfulfilled desire resonate within the text's multiple readings of incest. The knowledge that "it was to be its wifes" almost makes "its hearts" break seems to indicate incest as horror; however, since Tilly mimics Bertha's despairing line about her loss of Tackleton to May, the song participates in the perpetuation of incestuous desire. According to the song, hearts break because of incest *and* because of the incest taboo, and the text simultaneously encourages the reader to accept some January–May unions and to reject others.

Bertha's displaced desire for her father falls on Tackleton because of her father's deceit. Bertha takes Tackleton's hand affectionately and kisses it, caressing it within her hands and resting "her cheek against it tenderly" (193) before letting go. Bertha's blindness provides for this otherwise unlikely display as well as her verbal rhapsodies of "blind" devotion to what the text makes clear are troublesome January–May/father-daughter arrangements. Elisabeth Gitter correctly notes that Dickens uses blindness and other Oedipal echoes to negotiate "incestuous transgressions": "Her dead eyes cannot awaken guilt. . . . Both literally and figuratively the blind girl is the daughter who cannot see the sins of the father" (682–83). For most of the story, those around Bertha perpetuate her mistaken understanding of Tackleton, and Bertha clings to a vision of her father as handsome and powerful provider for their home. She has not seen "that Caleb's scanty hairs were turning greyer and more grey, before her sightless face" (189). With Caleb's "confession" near the end of the narrative, she learns that Tackleton is "a hard master" who is "ugly in his looks and in his nature," and she initially blames her father: "Why did you ever fill my heart so full, and then come in like Death, and tear away the objects of my love!" (228). Caleb is creator and destroyer of her romantic fantasy, and Bertha comes close to rejecting his true self as she rejects that of Tackleton.

Gitter's reading asserts that incestuous desire merits the father's "guilt," but Dickens quickly replaces Bertha's anger toward her father with her renewed love for him, punishing neither incestuous love nor premeditated deception as "sins of the fathers." Instead, he suggests that Caleb's actions are worthy of readers' pity—if not their approbation and consent—since the trickery was backed by good intentions. Dickens affirms that the real tragedy is not in the lie, but in the misguided efforts of the father. Dickens makes Bertha reflect on the years of scanty resources her father suffered to perpetuate her happy illusion of their economic well-being, and like the magical presence that "appeared behind her, pointing to her father" (228), she recognizes him for his selflessness as Dickens deftly reworks her imagined January–May romance into sentimentalized father-daughter love. Her father rises in her esteem, and when he admits his position as "an old man, worn with care and work," Bertha declares, "The greyer, and more worn, the dearer, father!" (230).

In her happiness, Bertha embraces her father, "caressing him with tears of exquisite affection" (230), and acknowledges the thinness of the ruse that distinguished the idealized Tackleton from her father and her fantasy-father from the real. Her newfound appreciation of her father smoothes paternal anxiety, and she lets it be known that there is no other man she "would love so dearly, and would cherish so devotedly" (230) as her father. While Bertha embodies the feminine loyalty and antimaterialism of popular domestic ideology, her love for her father implies more than is typical of a dutiful daughter because of its incestuous insinuations by way of the January–May romance. Indeed, the merging of father and lover in Caleb is essential to the story's happy ending, and the slippage between father and lover directly contributes to the recovery of the "bad" man Tackleton. Sudden awareness of his position in Bertha's deception makes Tackleton apologetic for his earlier abuses, and he rejoins the others with hat in hand, now happy to be an equal among his social inferiors, while the narrator gaily quips, "what had the Fairies been doing with him, to have effected such a change!" (239). While this revision of masculinity is too neat and quick to be realistic, it suggests the January–May marriage's dramatic potential to revise gendered power.

Dickens's later novels rework the basic January–May frameworks that he details in *The Cricket on the Hearth* to different ends. Successful January–May marriages appear alternately as conservative (*Little Dorrit*) and progressive (*David Copperfield*) models. The failure of January–May marriages works as both an emblem of sacrificial masculinity (*Bleak House*), and as a means for making masculinity less rigidly self-centered (*Hard Times*). As Dickens writes and rewrites these stories of intergenerational romance, he exploits the inconsistencies of the theme. David L. Cowles asserts that Dickens's "treatments of women probably engender more unintentional self-contradiction than any other topic" (80), and while I agree with Cowles's basic premise, I believe Dickens's contradictions extend beyond "women" to men, sexual relations, and indeed to gender identification itself. Dickens enjoys the pliable nature of the January–May theme, rhetorically adapting it as needed for his narrative objectives. In the remainder of this chapter, I will explain how Dickens expands the circumstances he forms in *The Cricket on the Hearth* in subsequent depictions of January–May marriage. By extending the sympathetic portrayals of older husbands he has fostered with John and Caleb, Dickens develops some additional January–May narratives as idealized incest. And by following the example set by Tackleton, in later works Dickens also presents incestuous desire as a force for resolving abuses of masculine power.

## Incest and the Rebirth of Masculinity in *Hard Times* and *Little Dorrit*

*The Cricket on the Hearth* reveals that Dickens conceived the January–May marriage as a scenario that could generate sympathy for his older men and also could offer a system for their improvement. John the Carrier and Caleb might be "good" fathers who deserve more pity than scorn, but what about those bad dads who, like Tackleton and his predecessors Gride and Quilp, abuse the powers associated with their age and gender? Two of his later novels that center on January–May marriages attempt to revise and restore problematic masculinity through their suggestions of incest. Though *Hard Times* and *Little Dorrit* differ in their strategies and their objectives, these novels organize a new and improved masculinity around the family romance.

Critics have largely ignored the implications of father-daughter incest that shadow Louisa Gradgrind's January–May marriage to Josiah Bounderby in *Hard Times* to focus on the "abnormal" brother-sister relationship between Louisa and her brother Tom. In 1964, Daniel P. Deneau directed attention to the bedroom scene in which Louisa, "barefoot, unclothed, [and] undistinguishable in darkness" (*Hard Times*, 144), attempts to learn the truth from Tom about the robbery. Deneau suggests that this scene is seductive, and later critics have furthered his claim. Richard Fabrizio points to the Louisa-Tom relationship to support his theory that "before Freud, Dickens demonstrated incest's mechanics in the capitalist system" (236). Russell Goldfarb pushes the novel's incestuous overtones into physical certainty; referring to the dynamics of the bedroom scene, he believes the details "show explicitly that Louisa is sexually involved with her brother" (128). These critics explain that Dickens enjoys constructing relationships that deny easy understanding, and I am less concerned with arguing the physical consummation of incestuous desire than with analyzing that desire's larger effects on gender and power. Implications of sibling incest between Louisa and Tom coalesce with suggestions of father-daughter incest in Louisa's relationships with her husband, Bounderby, and with her father, Thomas Gradgrind. The incestuous aspects of Louisa's January-May marriage critique both normative heterosexuality and traditional marriage as the novel reveals the interdependence of normative sexuality on "perverse" or "incestuous" tendencies. Although Louisa's marriage to Bounderby has the potential for reconciling the family romance into a socially acceptable format, this move toward stability fails because taints of "perversion" pervade the January–May marriage. Ultimately, the novel rejects marriage as a means for remedying sexual and gender trouble and, instead, proposes that the proliferation of incestuous desire contains its own restorative strategies. Thus, through Louisa's relationships with her brother and father, Dickens develops the incest theme as a method for transforming "bad" men into new, improved models of masculinity.

Dickens's depiction of incest in this novel is as full of incongruities as might be expected at this point of an analysis of his broader use of the theme. He hints seductively at the transgression of the incest taboo, and then he faithfully reinforces it. "Facts" do not help the characters negotiate the irrational or the perverse, and amid powerful desires and "hard times," they struggle to ascertain what is "right" and to refrain from doing what is "wrong." Louisa is unable to fulfill her love for her brother, her father, or, later, for her brother's friend James Harthouse. When she eventually leaves her husband to return to her father's home, she explains her yearning and her resistance: "With a hunger and thirst upon me, father, which have never been for a moment appeased; with an ardent impulse towards some region where rules, and figures, and definitions were not quite absolute; I have grown up, battling every inch of my way" (164). Rejecting her father's pragmatic, utilitarian teachings, Louisa's words denote her opposition to heteronormative, exogamic, and monogamous ideals of love and sexuality, even though neither Tom nor her father seems worthy of her fight. Both are manipulative individuals, largely lacking compassion for others and the ability to imagine beyond the systems of power in which they are enmeshed.

Displacement of the incest theme onto her intergenerational marriage to Bounderby does not prove liberating for Louisa either, but her marriage serves as a site for the domestication of sexual deviance, and, rather than working as a restorative tool in gender relations, further disrupts the stability of kinship structures within the novel. When Louisa's mother frets, "Whatever I am to call him, Mr. Gradgrind, when he is married to Louisa! I must call him something. It's impossible . . . to be constantly addressing him, and never giving him a name. . . . Am I to call my own son-in-law, Mister?" (80), she raises structuralist concerns over kinship and nomenclature.[27] Though Bounderby is not yet kin, his age has already placed him in a kindred parental position with Louisa's mother and father, and Mrs. Gradgrind's confusion demonstrates the effects of intergenerational marriage on family systems. Intentionally or unintentionally, Mrs. Sparsit has similar trouble in knowing what name to use for Louisa and calls Louisa "Miss Gradgrind" and even "Mrs. Gradgrind" instead of "Mrs. Bounderby." "Miss" and "Mrs." convey provocative identities for Louisa as her father's daughter and her father's wife, but Dickens offers another possibility in Mrs. Sparsit's half-hearted apology to Louisa: "she begged pardon, she meant to say, Miss Bounderby—she hoped to be excused, but she really could not get it right yet" (147). Whereas the other appellations suggest Mrs. Sparsit's unwillingness to think of Louisa as Bounderby's wife, "Miss Bounderby" underlines her propensity to think of Louisa as his daughter.

In Louisa's unhappy marriage to Bounderby, Dickens portrays what might have happened if Madeline Bray's father had not died and she had married Arthur Gride.[28] The reader can likewise envision how May's marriage to Tackleton might have concluded in a Dickensian world. "Old Bounderby," a friend of Louisa's father, is "seven or eight and forty" and Louisa "fifteen or sixteen" when the novel opens, and Mrs. Sparsit deems him "quite another father to Louisa" (38). Though Bounderby is not as old as Gride, and perhaps not as harsh as Tackleton, his courtship and marriage of Louisa are equally disturbing, and the relationship's overt associations with pedophilia weave sexual perversion into the fabric of conjugal stability. For example, when Bounderby enters the Gradgrind children's study to let them know that their father's anger over their visit to the circus was waning, he enters as an adult into the punished children's space. He plays the card of parental authority, soothing Louisa and her younger siblings with his promise that "It's all right now. . . . you won't do so any more. I'll answer for its being all over with [your] father," but then he shifts his role from that of parent to that of lover, negotiating payment for his allegiance to the children's cause: "Well, Louisa, that's worth a kiss, isn't it?" (20).

Bounderby's slippery movement from father figure to seducer coincides with his trespassing into the children's study, and his request to Louisa, customary enough in appearance, disturbs Louisa greatly. Louisa allows him to kiss her, "rais[ing] her cheek towards him, with her face turned away," but her effort to remove the memory left by his lips indicates her revulsion at his affection and signals a similar response from readers who are ready to sympathize with Louisa.[29] After Bounderby deems Louisa "Always my pet" and says good-bye to the children, "she stood on the same spot, rubbing the cheek he had kissed, with her handkerchief, until it was burning red. She was still doing this, five minutes afterwards" (20). When her brother Tom warns that she will "rub a hole in [her] face," she bitterly replies, "You may cut the piece out with your penknife if you like, Tom. I wouldn't cry!" (20). Louisa's response leaves little doubt that Dickens intends Bounderby's attraction to Louisa to be read as disturbing, and this scene clarifies the text's positions regarding "normal" and "deviant" behaviors that remain inextricably fused in the dominant culture. Louisa's abhorrence of Bounderby's fatherly physical affection conveys ingenuous understanding of "good touch" versus "bad touch," indicating that abuse of power can be sensed intuitively. Additionally, the imposition of courtship into this scene of discipline collapses divisions between the stabilizing heterosexuality that leads to marriage and the unorthodox sexuality that leads to child molestation. Generational privilege, heterosexual marriage, and familial loyalty appear as shabby veils that disguise sexual coercion, and Bounderby's "normal" request for a kiss and his "normal" proposal of marriage appear anything but.

Not only do these implications of pedophilia and incest taint Louisa's marriage to Bounderby, but the marriage's interconnectedness with Louisa's brother and father and their effectual prostitution of her body for their own ends further the sexual manipulation in this family romance. Louisa enters the January–May marriage because her brother and father wish it; ironically, her "unnatural" feelings for her family drive her into this superficially normative but intrinsically troublesome marriage. Louisa's love for her brother gives Tom the upper hand in their relationship, and he directs her to his benefit. When he considers Bounderby's job offer, Tom reasons that his employment will be all the easier because of Bounderby's desire for his sister: "You are his little pet, you are his favourite; he'll do anything for you," and he concludes that "I had better go where I can take with me some advantage of your influence" (44). Teasing Louisa with the thought of being close to him, Tom exploits Louisa's love to persuade her to accept Bounderby's proposal: "We might be so much oftener together—mightn't we? Always together, almost—mightn't we? It would do me a great deal of good if you were to make up your mind to I know what, Loo. It would be a splendid thing for me. It would be uncommonly jolly!" (74). When, in the garden, he describes his reliance on Louisa's financial help to Harthouse, Tom vents his guilt from pimping his sister's body by violently "biting the rose-buds . . . and tearing them away from his teeth with a hand that trembled like an infirm old man's" (134). Tom is almost in tears during this display, but he poses, "What *is* a fellow to do for money, and where *am* I to look for it, if not to my sister?" (134). Tom exercises his power to cajole Louisa, although he lacks the economic advantage traditionally associated with masculine privilege. Louisa's marriage to Bounderby and her commitment to doing the unspeakable "I know what" benefit her brother more than herself, and her incestuous bond with her brother promotes her January–May marriage.

Thomas Gradgrind, a "man of facts and calculations" (6), is keenly aware of the benefits of marrying his daughter to Bounderby, who is "a rich man: banker, merchant, manufacturer, and what not" (15), and while it is difficult to imagine such a pragmatic man influenced by forces of desire (his marriage seems void of emotion at best), the novel concludes that no one, not even Thomas Gradgrind, can subsist on facts alone. Writing about *Hard Times*, Anne Humphreys explains that "the father of Western father-daughter narratives frequently tries to negotiate his desire to keep the daughter by selecting the man she marries (not uncommonly she is given to his relative or friend), thus giving an additional turn to Eve Sedgwick's thesis of homosocial desire" (178). Whereas the prostituting of Louisa is an economic act, it is a sexual act as well, requiring that Louisa's father contemplate and control Louisa's sexuality. In marrying Louisa to his "bosom friend," Thomas Gradgrind participates in the sexual exchange, which holds his gratification as much as Bounderby's as its goal. At "fifteen or sixteen" Louisa realizes that her father is thinking about her sexually, pondering her sexual marketability, and planning on her effectual prostitution. She knows that her father is grooming her to be Bounderby's wife, and when her father speaks to her of Bounderby, she "st[eals] a look at him, remarkable for its intense and searching character" (14).[30]

Thomas Gradgrind's rationalizing of the "facts" of Louisa's marriage to Bounderby also necessitates his consideration of the compatibility of their ages as husband and wife, and since he is only "a year or two" older than Bounderby, his report on the facts of marriage displays his biased interest in imagining intergenerational romance. Stacking the evidence to his own advantage, he reasons that statistically, many marriages in England and Wales "are contracted between parties of very unequal ages, and that the elder of these contracting parties is, in rather more than three-fourths of these instances, the bridegroom" (77). Dickens meaningfully pairs this chapter, "Father and Daughter," with the next, "Husband and Wife." Marrying Louisa to Bounderby satisfies her father's social and economic needs, while gratifying his restrained interest in Louisa as a sexual entity.

To please her father and her brother, Louisa marries a man old enough to be her father, effectually substituting the almost-incestuous dynamics of the January–May marriage in lieu of the more overtly incestuous tensions within the Gradgrind family. Her family rewards her for following the well-traveled path to normative heterosexuality, praised by both father and brother, when she marries Bounderby. Her father blesses her as his "favourite child," and "detaining her in his embrace" and soliciting her kisses, he tells her how pleased he is at her "sound decision" (80). And despite Louisa's evident distress on her marriage day, Tom commends her self-sacrifice: "What a game girl you are, to be such a first-rate sister, Loo!" (85).

Thus far, the novel follows a classically Freudian trajectory: incestuous desires are tempered by the incest taboo to drive individuals into sexual orientation and normative heterosexual relationships. Such (self-)congratulations are premature, however, because Louisa's marriage to Bounderby does not complete the Freudian blueprint for sexual normalcy. Since Louisa's marriage is itself tainted with sexual improprieties, the taboo against incest fails to reinstate sexual stability and kinship order and only leads to more play with gender.

After his honeymoon, Bounderby seems more aware of the sexual tensions present in his January–May marriage than before, blusteringly acknowledging to his rival, "You observe, Mr. Harthouse, that my wife is my junior. I don't know what she saw in me to marry me, but she saw something in me, I suppose, or she wouldn't have married me" (99). Despite Bounderby's initial desire, the marriage languishes—likely as the result of both his sexual inadequacies (Mrs. Sparsit is fond of calling him a "Noodle") and Louisa's unwillingness ("she baffled all penetration") (99). The novel attributes much of this incompatibility to their ages—"the differences," Mrs. Sparsit points out, "being such" (142). The novel has already predicted that this marriage would falter. No one could be surprised after Louisa's repugnant wiping of her cheek that sexual relations in the marriage would be strained, if not forced, and this January–May marriage's "perverse" taints of pedophilia, incest, and prostitution hinder its success at reconstituting fragmented gender identities. Moreover, when Harthouse arrives in Coketown with his Byronic "what will be, will be" philosophy, he introduces even more sexual disorder into the plot rather than representing regulatory same-age, male-female, "natural" sexuality. With little regard for sexual propriety or social laws, Harthouse deems that he has "found it all to be very worthless" (100), and as Louisa's attraction for Harthouse grows, her compliance with expected feminine subservience lessens. Within the January–May triangle, her gender identity is even less stable than it is before her marriage, and Louisa is less prone to sacrificing herself for the men in her life. She addresses her husband "coldly," and "with a proud colour in her face that was a new change," challenges his authority over her. "What is the matter with you?" she demands of Bounderby, before giving up her attempt to understand him: "You are incomprehensible this morning. . . . Pray take no further trouble to explain yourself. I am not curious to know your meaning. What does it matter!" (148). After Louisa leaves her husband, she goes to her father, not only to seek the help that his masculinity affords, but also to challenge that very masculinity. Her father is confused by what he sees; Louisa is "so colorless, so dishevelled, so defiant and despairing, that he [is] afraid of her" (163). She laments her birth and criticizes the father who pushed her from incestuous desire into a flawed system of heteronormative sexuality: "What have you done, O father, what have you done, with the garden that should have bloomed once, in this great wilderness here!" (163).

Dickens does not suggest that Louisa, or anyone, can remain in a pre-Oedipal state of gender and sexual freedom. Though the "facts" of the incest taboo and normative heterosexuality do not explain everything, they do not disappear, and like other Victorian writers, Dickens does not allow for the realization of Louisa's extramarital desire. But in permitting Louisa to return home and in having Bounderby accept the loss of his wife, Dickens returns to the family romance as a site for remedying, at least partially, the confusion of familial and sexual relations in the novel.[31] Because Louisa's marriage to Bounderby fulfills the drive to exogamic marriage, Louisa and her father and brother can return to the state of incestuous longing that comes before gender and sexual orientation are determined, and Louisa's homecoming leads to a reconsideration of the traditionally masculine positions of her father and brother. The morning after Louisa's confrontation with her father, he questions his authority over her. Sitting by her bed, he explains that he has come to "mistrust" himself, for what he has done in the past, and for what he may do in the present and the future. Questioning whether he deserves her trust and whether he possesses "the right instinct," he prepares to speak on her behalf to Bounderby. He chastises himself for the path he has advocated for Louisa, concluding that it has fostered qualities in her that are "a little perverted" (181). Thomas Gradgrind acknowledges that the men in Louisa's life have accrued a "debt" to her from having taken from her more often than they have given, and he advocates that Bounderby, "so far her elder," accept responsibility for his part in the overall masculine abuse of Louisa: "we may all be more or less in the wrong" (183). Because of the incestuous dynamics of their family and the January–May marriage, Gradgrind rethinks his claim to masculine power, and Dickens suggests that alternatives exist to prescribed patterns of gender formation when Louisa promises, "Dear father, you have three young children left. They will be different, *I* will be different yet, with Heaven's help" (205). Although shaken, Thomas Gradgrind becomes "a wiser man, and a better man," and he replaces his maniacal insistence on "facts and figures" with "Faith, Hope and Charity" (205). Her brother also revises his masculine identity as the result of their "abnormal" relationship. Banished because of the robbery, Tom writes to Louisa on "paper blotted with tears, that her words had too soon come true, and that all the treasures in the world would be cheaply bartered for a sight of her dear face" (221). The brother who exploited his sister's "abnormal" love for him by prostituting her body reconsiders his abuse, and though his apology comes late, he makes her name his last word, dying "in penitence and love" (222) for Louisa.

While the novel's depiction of Bounderby recalls Dickens's early characterizations of intergenerational relationships as repulsively incestuous, the novel does not condemn incestuous desire, but rather argues that inexplicable, extramarital, and "deviant" yearnings can lead to improved gender relations. Normalizing social structures like marriage contribute to gender inequities, and in greatly altering the theme from its predecessors, the novel provocatively suggests that incest is most problematic in the sanitized form of the January–May marriage, yet demonstrates that incestuous desire is restorative when returned to play out in the family home—unfulfilled, yet always lingering.

* * * * *

Of *Little Dorrit*, Sadoff observes that "Amy and Clennam's marriage appears the perfect narcissistic paradise. The entire family genealogy (the space and time of engendering identity and difference) and the entire oedipal triangle (the structure of desire) collapse on this bride and groom" ("Storytelling," 242). As Sadoff suggests, incestuous relationships abound within this text, and multiple father-daughter romances form a plot in which the kinship roles of father-husband-son and daughter-wife-mother often converge. Amy or "Little" Dorrit is just that: she is small, petite to the extreme, diminutive, and childlike.[32] When Clennam first sees her, he believes she is a "girl," and on further scrutiny, he finds "she had all the manner and much of the appearance of a subdued child" (68), calculating that "she might have passed in the street for little more than half" (67) her actual age of twenty-two years. Appearing even younger than her "little" predecessor Nell, Little Dorrit blurs the filial and the maternal; she is alternately known as "Little Mother" within this domestic prison pastoral, and she claims that her two "little" names are "just the same" (183).[33] And though she is small, she dotes on her father and on Clennam with loving, motherly attention. When her father is troubled, she watches over him in bed, "at times kissing him with suspended breath, and calling him in a whisper by some endearing name" (249). Little Dorrit's ability to be "all" a woman can be to those near her has not escaped the notice of critics. Though Steven Wall claims in his introduction to the Penguin edition that Dickens's "stress on her innocence shouldn't be attributed to post-Freudian anxiety about attachment between daughters and fathers" (xxv), other critics are less willing to overlook the intimations of incest and pedophilia in her relationships with Clennam and her father. Brenda Ayres deems that "she is the perfect Dickensian daughter, devoted to the exclusion of all else to the care of her father. The daughter acts as a mother and a wife to her father; and a mother to his other children" (77). Ayres also sees in Little Dorrit "an Electra complex" and notes the text's reference to "a classical daughter once—perhaps—who ministered to her father in prison as her mother had ministered to her" (*Little Dorrit*, 247), comparing Little Dorrit to "the Euphrasia woman: the daughter who kept her father alive in prison through feeding him with her breasts" (77).[34] This image of the breastfeeding daughter captures many of the incestuous tensions implicit in Little Dorrit's nursing of her father, and later, when Clennam's financial fall places him in the former prison cell of her father, in her nursing of her future husband.[35] Avrom Fleishman agrees that "Amy is both child and mother to her lover, as she had been to her father" (585).

Appropriate to expectations of the domestic woman, Little Dorrit's actions are dutiful and maternal, but they are sexually stimulating as well. Ayres proposes that Little Dorrit, like Dickens's other "little" women, is one who "can sexually arouse, but sex with her cannot be consummated, so that the man is always in a state of arousal" (77). But this reading pushes Little Dorrit further into the sexually taboo than she really is. Though she may look eleven, she is legally of age and thereby legitimate material for both fantasy and fulfillment.[36] While there is no reason to think her unchaste, there is likewise no reason to think her devoid of sexual desire. One of the few Victorian heroines to propose to her husband, she marries Clennam, and there is no evidence that their relationship will be nonsexual or that, as Ayres asserts, "Arthur does not seem sexually responsive or sexually interested in Little Dorrit" (78). Indeed, the novel reveals that Little Dorrit is sexualized from an early age, and the text repeatedly eroticizes her for the reader. Her childhood admirer, John Chivery, "played with her in the yard" by pretending to lock her up, releasing her only in exchange for the payment of "real kisses" (228). Because of her poverty, Little Dorrit is always "lightly clad" (182) throughout the first half of the novel, and her lack of proper clothing exposes how "delicate and slender she is" (191). The shabbiness of her attire reveals her body to the reader and to other characters in tantalizing glimpses, a hole in her shoe allowing Clennam to touch a foot "like marble" (183). When she and Maggy are locked out of their prison home, Little Dorrit hazards physical and sexual violence on the dark streets of London: "They had shrunk past homeless people, lying coiled in nooks. They had run from drunkards. They had started from slinking men, whistling and signing to one another at bye corners, or running away at full speed" (190). That evening on the streets, Little Dorrit's childlike body saves her from the "knot of brawling or prowling figures in [her] path" (190), and identifies her as one who needs protection, like a child, from harm, but Dickens's attention to her physical vulnerability rests on a shared understanding of potential sexual violation.

As "little" mother-daughter-lover, Little Dorrit can use the privileges of any one of her roles to promote the interests of the others. As Clennam's "dear child" and "poor child" (182), she visits him in his lodgings at the unseemly hour of midnight, and "At no Mother's knee but her's [sic]" (848), Clennam receives her care when he is in prison.[37] Precisely because of her associations with daughterly and maternal devotion, Little Dorrit is afforded opportunities to touch, caress, and embrace without eliciting societal scorn. Soothing her father during one his attacks of self-pity, she "cling[s] to him with her arms," takes his arm and lovingly "trie[s] to put it around her neck." He eventually "suffer[s] her to embrace him, and take charge of him" and "let[s] his grey head rest against her cheek" (246). When

Clennam kisses her hand "fervently" in thankfulness for her care, she allows her hand to linger "where it was, it seemed to court being restrained," and later, "the hand he held, crept up a little nearer to his face" (849). Just as Little Dorrit's childish appearance protects her when she is locked outside of the Marshalsea, her ability to enter and exit the familial positions of mother, daughter, and wife allows her to advance relationships with her father and Clennam. Little Dorrit is thus "by far the best loved" of her father's three children, and she convinces Clennam to marry her even though he once discouragingly instructed that "So far removed, so different, and so much older, I am the better fitted for your friend and adviser" (404).

Little Dorrit's story proves that intergenerational romance can make one "the best loved," because its incestuous connotations address multiple kinship needs within one relationship. However, whereas *The Cricket on the Hearth* uses the successful January–May marriage as a tool for revising gender roles and redistributing male power, *Little Dorrit* manipulates the incest taboo to foster a return to conventional masculine and feminine identities. It is difficult to put a finger on the places in this narrative where the January–May marriage and its incestuous connotations begin to glue together the fractured remains of gender identities and normative sexuality that litter the novel. Granted, Little Dorrit's relationships with older men follow many of the plot conventions typical of gender subversion within the larger January–May tradition. Until the very end, the reader is taunted with the possibility that the couple will not unite, and the text emphasizes the fatherly role assumed by the January husband by stressing details such as Clennam's being twice Little Dorrit's age and by punctuating his addresses to her with "my child," "dear girl," and "dear child."[38] Moreover, like her predecessors Nell, Dot, and Annie Strong, Little Dorrit assumes typically masculine roles in her relationships with her father and with Clennam. But the novel lays bare the contradictions inherent to the incest theme. In *Little Dorrit*, masculinities prove so pathetically weak and femininities seem so disruptively emboldened that Dickens employs the January–May marriage between Little Dorrit and Clennam to restore gender and sexual conventions that have already been challenged.

Male figures of authority in *Little Dorrit* are problematic, perhaps more so than in any of Dickens's other January–May novels. In "Do It or Dorrit," Ruth Bernard Yeazell highlights the practical and sexual ineffectiveness of Clennam, and the other prominent men in the narrative are likewise useless, often causing more harm than good in the lives of those around them. Little Dorrit's father performs so many acts of feminine helplessness that Alison Milbank deems him a "'female' in his situation and dependence" (107). His assumption of the hyperpaternal position of "Father of the Marshalsea" is pitiable; while his gentlemanly manners and former life of privilege gain him additional respect within the prison, he is more parasite than patriarch, expecting and accepting monetary tributes from debtors who leave the prison and from those who visit. Little Dorrit's brother Tip seems full of masculine potential, but he lazes away his youth and wealth, requiring his sister's assistance in later life as he did when young. Mr. Merdle, businessman, politician, and father-in-law to Little Dorrit's sister Fanny, commits suicide when his financial plans crumble and he loses his wealth and the investments of all who trusted him. Not "man" enough to stand up to his uncle's plans for him to marry a woman he does not love, Clennam's father abandons the mother of his child and largely fails in love and in life. Henry Gowan successfully woos Pet but proves a lousy husband whose artistic vision, youthful charm, and financial well-being quickly deteriorate. Even the frightening villain Monsieur Rigaud is absurdly ineffectual. His scheme to blackmail Clennam's mother fails, and he dies in the ruins of her home. While Dickens presents unimpressive men in his other works, there never are so many as in *Little Dorrit*, and when the central male figure is flawed, as with David Copperfield, Oliver Twist, or Pip, it can often be attributed to the character's youth and the larger narrative development of the *bildungsroman*. Clennam and the other male figures in *Little Dorrit* do not enjoy these pretexts for their shortcomings. They fail to convey heroic masculinity on multiple levels—financially, emotionally, morally, and sexually.

Excepting Little Dorrit, who ably affects female submissiveness while performing masculine acts, most women in the novel likewise fall short of conveying appealing images of femininity. Little Dorrit's sister Fanny is a bad daughter: selfish, hard, and "rather flaunting" (255). Completely defying expectations of maternal sentiment, Mrs. Clennam is "beyond the reach of all changing emotions," and "with her cold grey eyes and her cold grey hair" (50), she dominates Clennam and, while he was alive, Clennam's father, who flees to China to escape her control. Flora Finching irritates and annoys; although she is kind, she is unable to fulfill feminine gender expectations because, though the same age as Clennam, the middle-aged woman visually and behaviorally destroys his social and sexual fantasies of the feminine ideal.[39] Hopefully anticipating the reunion with his former lover, Clennam is crushed when he finally meets the woman who "always tall, had grown to be very broad, too," and "Clennam's eyes no sooner fell upon the object of his old passion, than it shivered and broke to pieces" (164). Clennam's rejection of Flora leads directly to his pursuit of Pet Meagles, who, like Little Dorrit, is half his age, but who, unlike Little Dorrit, mistakenly prefers the company of a pretentious misogynist "barely thirty" (218). And Miss Wade, an unsympathetic caricature of Victorian lesbians, demonstrates Dickens's ideas of what could go wrong with women when they reject all conventional gender identities. She lurks throughout the narrative and threatens to attract and brainwash dissatisfied women like Tattycoram to her seditious agenda.[40] Overall, the women in *Little Dorrit* are too insensitive to be considered daughterly, too domineering to be motherly, too old and too young to be wifely, even too queer to be womanly.[41] Considering this crisis of gender that Dickens presents, it is unsurprising that he adapts the January–May marriage as a restorative agent in gender identity so that the legitimacy and stability of their marriage buries the disruptive effects of their implied incest.

Noteworthy differences exist between the relationship of Little Dorrit and Clennam and Dickens's other successful January–May marriages. Before the happy ending, this novel dwells on Little Dorrit's unrequited love for Clennam while he mourns his failure to court Pet, but the more typical pattern in *The Cricket on the Hearth* and *David Copperfield* involves the older husbands' concerns that their younger wives no longer love them. *Little Dorrit* extends John Chivery as a potential rival for a love triangle, but this youthful lover is no real threat, and John even advances Little Dorrit's interest in Clennam, since he is so frustratingly oblivious to her desire. Additionally, in this novel consumed with financial gains and losses, economic power is more evenly distributed within the January–May marriage; indeed, financial equality seems necessary to its culmination, since Clennam will not marry Little Dorrit when he believes he stands to profit by his marriage. Only after she reveals that "I have nothing in the world" (849) can she propose, "O my dearest and best, are you quite sure that you will not share my fortune with me now?" (850). Ironically, the news of Little Dorrit's poverty is wonderful for Clennam and for the reader, and Dickens does not have to narrate Clennam's response to her proposal, because now that they are financial equals, his answer is evident. And even though Dickens emphasizes the generation gap that separates Clennam and Little Dorrit throughout the novel, enjoying the mingling of roles in this family romance, he backpedals in the final chapter to normalize their intergenerational match. Whereas Clennam earlier explains to Little Dorrit that "I counted up my years, and considered what I am, and looked back, and looked forward, and found that I should soon be grey. I found that I had climbed the hill, and passed the level ground upon the top, and was descending quickly" (404), Clennam is revised in the final chapter as "the happy child" and recast in a youthful position in relation to his friends Mr. Meagles and Daniel Doyce. Only in his fifties, Meagles now appears as a "jolly father" to Clennam and calls him "my boy" (854). Dickens crafts Doyce as a "paternal character," releasing Clennam from his atonement in prison with the reward of a position in Doyce's business and supporting Clennam like a father during his wedding. Although the text has earlier emphasized the difference between his age and that of Pet and Little Dorrit, the final image of Clennam is that of a young man. Dickens attempts to squelch the gender trouble that runs rampant earlier in the novel by glossing over the age difference and incestuous allusions in preparation for the return of normative heterosexuality, but the effectiveness of his erasure at such a late point in the narrative is questionable.

\* \* \* \* \*

Dickens's varied use of the incest theme within the January–May marriage is fascinating, and although many other nineteenth-century authors invoke the familial and sexual tensions initiated by the age differences of the marriage partners, no other writer manipulates this small leap in logic to such a degree and in so many separate texts. A pattern emerges across his novels that suggests a move from simplistic characterizations of the January–May marriage as horrific incest to a much more complex use of the theme, though Dickens never settles into a formulaic pronouncement. Precisely because January–May marriages brought to readers' minds thoughts of nonstandard, improper sexual relations, they enjoyed a prominent place in Dickens's works, and they merit scholarly attention for what they reveal about the multiple possibilities the theme afforded.

CHAPTER 3

VISUALIZING POWER

AGE, EMBODIMENT, AND AESTHETICS

"The tragedy of old age is not that one is old, but that one is young," asserts Lord Henry Wotton in Oscar Wilde's *The Picture of Dorian Gray* (178). Though this 1890 novel treats January–May romances only tangentially, its emphasis on aging, art, and gender leads us into this chapter on the aesthetic dimensions of January–May marriages, since Dorian's portrait captures the essence of contemporary fears about masculinity and aging. Growing visually hideous over time, the portrait produces its effect only in conjunction with Dorian's unvarying youthful beauty, and, as Lord Henry's quote suggests, it is loss of power to another that drives the tragedy of the binary of youth and age. Dorian concurs: "Your picture has taught me that. . . . Youth is the only thing worth having. When I find that I am growing old, I shall kill myself," cries Dorian. "I am jealous of everything whose beauty does not die. I am jealous of the portrait you have painted of me. Why should it keep what I must lose?" (26). By selling his soul, Dorian wards off the old age that is magically reflected in his portrait. Because it is so dangerous, the image of idealized masculine beauty eroding over time remains, like aberrant sexualities, in the closet— simultaneously hidden from view but, through the novel's discourse, on display for public scrutiny. But as Dorian comes to realize, social aesthetics linking beauty and power to youth inevitably curtail masculine authority by giving it an expiration date.

Nonetheless, the privileging of youthful masculine beauty directs the actions of the novel's three main male characters: Dorian, Lord Henry, and the artist Basil Hallward. The older men instruct Dorian to value his youth, above all other means, as power. Discussing Dorian's exposure to the sun, Lord Henry stresses why Dorian should protect his looks:

> "Because you have the most marvellous youth, and youth is the one thing worth having."
> "I don't feel that, Lord Henry."
> "No, you don't feel it now. Some day, when you are old and wrinkled and ugly, when thought has seared your forehead with its lines, and passion branded your lips with its hideous fires, you will feel it, and you will feel it terribly. Now, wherever you go, you charm the world. Will it always be so?" (22)

Lord Henry considers youth as both a fleeting possession and a visible marker of power, attesting that aging and the "decline" of life were of real concern to Victorian men who felt challenged by the aesthetics of youth. Though Lord Henry's comments oversimplify the physical process and social reception of aging, they establish youth and old age as binaries—much like masculinity and femininity—that correlate directly to real power, and, more important, they suggest men's duplicity, however unwitting, in a system that eventually removes them from power. As Jonathan Crary explains in *Techniques of the Observer*, the development of visual technologies like the camera obscura and photography had led to an increasingly visual culture invested in the exchange and valuation of aesthetic signs (12–14). As part of the growing print culture, images regulated cultural ideals, equating physical traits like those associated with youth or muscularity with social power. The January–May marriage theme offered a convenient opportunity for visualizing the embodiment of gendered power, since the triangular romantic structure contrasted aging masculinity with feminine and masculine youth, creating three distinct specimens of age and gender for social perusal. Every January–May text from *Sense and Sensibility* to *Jude the Obscure* lingers over detailed descriptions of the physical bodies of the older husbands, younger wives, and young suitors and encourages readers to visualize aesthetic differences as the characters vie for authority and control within the narratives.

Theorizing about the material bodies of fictional creations might seem a contradiction in terms, but literature and art present important venues for discussions of corporeality and its relation to gender because they draw attention to the discursive processes that lead to gender identification. Bodiless, characters become corporeal through the written word and painted line, and they give insight into the society that creates and consumes them. Thus, like other visual markers of gender identity, age operates on literary flesh and blood to create signs—wrinkles, gray hair, a different gait—that translate into degrees of power. Viewers have learned, however misguidedly, to correlate signs of age that are written on the surface of the body (and by age I mean not just "old" age, but "youth," "middle" age, or any age) to interior conditions such as vitality, knowledge, and health, which render an individual powerful in society. Literary January–May marriages operate aesthetically through cultural assumptions, often reinforcing ageist and sexist stereotypes of the body while providing a means for a critique of gender.

Visual dimensions of the age and gender nexus draw attention to the role of the body in identity formation, but rethinking the body's relationship to power does not signify a simplistic return to equating gender with innate physical difference. What is needed is a new awareness of corporeality and of male, as well as female, embodiment that acknowledges the significance of cultural assumptions about the aesthetics of aging.

Age, while of the body, resists positive determinations of gender identity as constructed through "fixed" markers such as a penis, a vagina, or breasts because age is transitory in nature, constantly rewriting one's contract with gender and power. Sexed bodies are also aged bodies, and the temporal and social processes that contribute to aging also formulate gender identities. Yet age proves to be a more individualized and more negotiable trait than gender. Even when one examines one's age at a specific time, that age is only meaningful in relation to the ages of the others with whom that individual shares power. Like conventional male-female binaries, old age and youth often suggest the privileging of one over the other, although, as I have suggested, these power divisions are unsettled. Reading age as a component of gender emphasizes the precariousness of power because a body changes over time, and aging thus challenges gender as a stable entity.

Age and gender are spectacles produced and perceived in specific social contexts. Many older women, including Austen's Lady Catherine de Bourgh in *Pride and Prejudice* (1813) and Dickens's Miss Havisham in *Great Expectations* (1861), control the men in their lives. Although the effects of women's aging in nineteenth-century literature deserves more attention, this chapter focuses on the aging male figure and views him in contrast with his youthful rivals for power.[1] While images of January–May marriages beg analysis of the visual construction and consumption of young male and female bodies, it is their attention to the aging male body that distinguishes them from staid visual codes that automatically link maleness to authority. Because men enjoyed privileged positions over women in their same class, the visible effects of aging on men and the accompanying loss of male authority are of special importance to those interested in either the subversion or affirmation of gendered power.

The January–May marriage theme does not suggest that women must be young to be beautiful or to exert power in society, or, conversely, that aging implies only a decline in social power for older men. While the theme's parodic dimension unabashedly draws on centuries of ageist and sexist stereotypes, including myths of impotency, senility, and heterosexuality, the January–May theme encourages the reader to reimagine the forces at work in ageism and sexism. In one sense, women of all ages benefit from the aesthetic drama of the January–May marriage, while men universally suffer. Images conjured by the January–May theme give convenient opportunities to attack male privilege when both the older male and younger male figures find themselves in compromised positions because of the effects of aging. The young wife's claim to power corresponds to her age, but because the relationship uncovers a weakness all men face, her triumph extends to women in general, who, as participating witnesses to the January–May spectacle, use it to mock masculine bastions of authority. In another sense, aesthetic images of older husbands and younger wives could critique specific advances that women claimed during the nineteenth century and lament the dishonor of a fallen patriarch. Younger wives could appear as callous, mercenary individuals whose feminist beliefs and dangerous sexualities undermine idealized marriage unions. Furthermore, inscribing the singular figure of the older husband with the blame for women's brazen assumption of their rights potentially frees other men from responsibility in women's oppression and rebellion, effectively reaffirming all other forms of masculine clout except that of the January husband who was foolish enough to wed a May bride.

Nineteenth-century depictions of January–May marriages often simultaneously urge both viewers' empathetic pity and anxiety for the older husband's fallen status and silent satisfaction at the wife's *coup*. Relishing the ambivalent responses prompted by the topic, William Quiller Orchardson centered several of his narrative paintings on the power inequities of the January–May marriage, which his work stages in three distinct phases: the beginning, middle, and end of the romance. *The First Cloud* (1887) portrays an initial dispute between an older husband and younger wife, *Mariage de Convenance* (1883) captures a similar couple in the midst of their troubled marriage, and *Mariage de Convenance—After!* (1886) displays the older husband alone, presumably left by his wife for another man. All three paintings depict the dramatic tension between youth and age as a visual argument, and they suggest that assumptions about age can trouble, if not reverse, traditional gender roles. Since Orchardson was almost fifty when he painted *Mariage de Convenance*, one might assume that the works sympathize with the plight of the rejected husband, disparaging the mercenary wife for neglecting her marriage vows. But the paintings call attention to the body of the older husband and challenge notions of the authority of men's gaze by emphasizing male abjection and by recognizing women's active participation in the visual spectacle.

Although artistic depictions of January–May marriages were common earlier in the nineteenth century, paintings by Orchardson and Edmund Blair Leighton from the 1870s and '80s represent the climax of the image's popularity in visual art and suggest a direct correlation between the aesthetic image and contemporary worries about the decline of male power through the law. Neither the Married Women's Property Act of 1870 nor the Matrimonial Causes Act of 1878 provided a married woman with equal legal recourse to her property, earnings, or right to exit a marriage, but both marked progressive reforms in favor of women and opened doors for later legislation such as the Summary Jurisdiction Act of 1895, which was more lenient on adulterous wives and supportive of women's ability to leave abusive husbands prior to filing for legal separation. The aesthetic images of January–May marriages provide a rich medium for investigating such challenges to masculine legal privilege; it is important that these narrative paintings be interpreted in their historical contexts.

In his 1899 study *British Contemporary Artists*, Cosmo Monkhouse applauds the dramatic effect of Orchardson's *The First Cloud* (Figure 3.1), which he suggests could "furnish the germ of a three-volume novel" (183). Monkhouse's comments collapse divisions between art, literature, and life, suggesting that Orchardson's January–May paintings capture the "tragedy" of an "old story," a narrative that "it is feared will go on repeating itself till love and money cease to be" (183). Though Monkhouse takes care to differentiate Orchardson's artistic agenda from the more outright didacticism of Hogarth's earlier *Marriage à la Mode*, he nevertheless reads the figures of aging husband and younger wife as commentary on a social "tragedy," and deems Orchardson a "man of good sense and right feeling" in his portrayal of events. For Monkhouse, *The First Cloud* is a conservative critique of the growing independence of the "new" woman and her challenges to male power. Still, reading the image as critical of the effects of feminine liberty on traditional marriage misses the overwhelming anxiety over the loss of male power that the canvas displays. Connecting the painting more directly with growing concerns over women's ability to sue for divorce, Joseph Kestner, in his *Masculinities in Victorian Painting*, asserts that "Orchardson did indeed experience anxieties about the function of males in the novel climate of advancing divorce legislation" and observes that "the masculine paradigm within marriage was exploding under the press of new judicial formulations which males could not ignore" (169). Here, the older husband becomes the embodiment of and scapegoat for challenged male authority. The painting is subversive in its melodramatic rendering of a scenario that captured public interest because of contemporary divorce legislation and the Matrimonial Causes Acts of the 1880s.

The play of the gaze between husband, wife, and viewer demonstrates the January–May marriage's peculiar ability to draw attention to the aging male body as a weak figure. While the husband directs his attention to his wife, she elects not to recognize or return his gaze, and

**Figure 3.1** *The First Cloud* by William Quiller Orchardson. © Tate, London 2007.

**Figure 3.2** *Mariage de Convenance* by William Quiller Orchardson. Glasgow City Council (Museums).

looking beyond the image's frame, she negates her husband's power, as well as the viewer's, by directing her eyes elsewhere and turning her back to inquiring eyes. If she remains a part of the drama, she clarifies that she is on her way out—exiting the theatrical display through the painting's red, stagelike curtains—and headed toward a relationship with a younger man. Although the husband's gaze remains on the wife, he appears a shunned and ineffectual being who is deprived of agency, and instead of brandishing subjective authority, he becomes the visual object as the viewer's eyes return to him. With his chin down, shoulders stooped, and head extended, the frustrated husband conveys a submissive model of masculinity, and his hands, shoved into his pockets, represent his inability to exert control over the marriage.

Judged in 1884 by the *Art Journal* to be "a very fine picture—a sermon—and a dismal tragedy" (210), Orchardson's *Mariage de Convenance* (Figure 3.2) tenders a similar paradigmatic image of the spectacular bodies of husband and wife. As in *The First Cloud*, while the husband imploringly stares at his younger wife and attempts to bring her thoughts back to their dinner and to their marriage, she resists his advances and limits her participation within both the dramatic imagery and the marriage. Far removed from domestic bliss, the placement of the husband and wife allows viewers to envision the tension and boredom of marital breakdown, and to experience vicariously the excitement of a dysfunctional relationship while reinforcing their own aesthetic assumptions about age, economics, sexuality, compatibility, and gendered power. The painting makes sense to its audience, who apply the gendered economy of the day to the painting's title.

Physical markers of age carry the visual argument. The wife's hourglass figure contrasts with the pouting immaturity her posture conveys, and both features make her the prototypical Victorian woman-child. Sulkily, she displays her discontent, little concerned with affecting customary courtesy or dutiful submission. Her husband's image conveys the rest of the story: though dignified and wealthy, her husband is distinctly older—old enough that, excepting the painting's title, the image could represent a different family scene in which a father gives unwelcome advice to a wayward daughter.[2] His gray, balding head connects him to the middle-aged servant beside him and suggests that his age makes him a second-class citizen. More subtle signs of aging further imply that the couple's age difference leads to their unhappiness and the husband's disempowered position. Although not heavyset, the husband has a thick torso, and his posture, slouching forward instead of back, suggests he is middle-aged. Moreover, the sagging jowls, sunken eyes, and bushy brows of the husband (all painted with fewer fine details than the wife's features) carefully construct *his* age, rather than the wife's, as the root of the marital problem.

The painting intends a degree of sympathy for the older husband. He extends himself and finds himself rejected. Thus, the older husband is feminized not only by his sensitive deference to his wife's dour mood, but also because he evokes the viewer's pity. The *Art Journal* critic says, "At the one end of the richly-appointed table sits the young wife—ambitious, disappointed, bored, sullen, unutterably miserable. At the other end of the table sits the husband—old, blasé, roué, bored too, and the more pitiable in that he has exhausted all his feelings, and has only boredom left" (210). This interpretation of the painting correctly depicts the abject state of the husband and wife, and in deeming the husband "the more pitiable" denotes that, however miserable the younger wife is, she has not "exhausted all [her] feelings." Pity for the husband stems from an assumption of his loss of wife and power and from the inference that she has more options than he. While the servant fills the husband's glass, the painting urges the viewer to commiserate with the husband who turns to wine for comfort.

Yet amid the pity, the painting displays a degree of contempt for conventional masculine authority and delights in its undoing. The *Art Journal* critic's depiction of the older husband as a "roué" indicates that viewers were aware of the husband's complicity in his own demise. If the younger wife and the power she wields are painful to her husband, they can be read as due punishment for his rakish lifestyle while a young man and for his continued participation in systems of male privilege. Orchardson develops this disruptive potential even more clearly in his painting *Mariage de Convenance—After!* The sensational title underscores public interest in witnessing the spectacle of masculinity defeated.

In *After!* the table is set for one, and the decanter of wine is prominently displayed as evidence of the husband's persistent need to drown his sorrows (Figure 3.3). Abandoned by his wife, he slumps alone before the fire in an attitude of helpless despair. Though he wears evening attire, he looks disheveled: his shirt protrudes from his vest, as if he has given up on appearances. Either because years have passed since the scene at the table or because the marital tensions have drained him, his face looks noticeably older than in *Mariage de Convenance*. His eyes now have drooping bags, and his chin doubles on his chest. Yet frozen in youthful beauty, his wife looks down on him in judgment from her portrait, condemning the objectification of women by her spouse and society and redirecting attention to the theatrical display of despondency and loss by the male body. In this image, the gaze is even more clearly focused on the husband than in the other paintings in the series. Moreover, while the figure of the deserted older husband solicits sympathy, his destitute state appears suitable retribution for his sexual deviance as a *roué* and as a January husband. Kestner explains, "it is clear that his promiscuous past life, recognized by reviewers, has now been punished by the wife who abandons him" (168). The public regard given to the painting suggests the popular desire to view the anticipated conclusion to January–May marriage. Nominated as the picture of the season in 1886 by the *Portfolio* and the *Illustrated London News, After!* fulfilled staid social expectations about age differences in marriage while projecting social fears (and hopes) of a masculinity that has been disciplined and punished.

Other artists express the visual argument that aging disrupts conventional understandings of gender and power in January–May marriages. Edmund Blair Leighton's *Till Death Us Do Part* (1878) depicts an older man and younger woman walking down a church aisle (Figure 3.4). Their movement away from the altar indicates that the man is her husband and not her father, as viewers might otherwise conclude, and the bride's sad expression casts their vows in a somber light. Though the groom is slender and upright, his rigid posture and snowy white hair emphasize his advanced years. While

**Figure 3.3** *Mariage de Convenance—After!* by William Quiller Orchardson. © Aberdeen City Council, Aberdeen Art Gallery & Museums Collections.

he stoically gazes ahead, onlookers in the pews appear more mournful than celebratory. On the left, a same-aged former lover tries to catch the bride's eye as she passes, fulfilling the triangular structure and sexual tension that viewers have come to expect in January–May marriages. These bodies correspond with the painting's title: the final promise in traditional vows. Even though the melancholy atmosphere renders "till death us do part" a sentenced punishment, the signifiers of age—implying death will soon release the wife from her vow—are optimistic.

The painting offers multiple visual perspectives. Behind the young man stand a young boy and girl. Representing the power inequalities of same-age relationships, the boy pulls the girl, who looks rather uncomfortable, to him as he whispers teasingly in her ear. The other viewers' reactions vary. In the background, middle-aged men whisper to one another as they nod at the bride and groom with knowing smiles, while in the foreground, women of various ages contemplate what such unions mean concerning gender roles and traditional allotments of power. An older woman with a widow's cap solemnly reflects on the social privilege that affords the older husband—perhaps the same age as she—such an opportunity in his late life, and young women ponder intergenerational marriage as a potentially advantageous alliance. The painting's original title, *LSD*, which refers to pounds, shillings and pence or "£, s, d," might have brought these financial considerations to the fore. However, by renaming the painting, Blair Leighton refocuses the message of the painting, making sexual economies secondary to physical bodies. Attention converges on

**Figure 3.4** *Till Death Do Us Part* by Edmund Blair Leighton. John Schaeffer Collection, Australia.

the figure of the older husband, and evaluation of his body becomes crucial to interpreting the painting; if the groom's body suggests he has one foot in the grave, the bride will not have long to wait. If the groom's body appears vigorous, then the painting's title becomes more ominous.

Literary visualizations of January–May couples are often openly hostile to the figure of the husband. Employing humor, descriptions of aging lovers accentuate the ludicrous posturing of these men as they try to affect youth. For example, when the sixty-five-year-old General Tracy courts twenty-one-year-old Isabella Somerive in Charlotte Smith's *The Old Manor House*, his body forms the comic basis for Smith's critique of his marriage proposal. Smith encourages readers to consider the effects of the "progress of years" on his body, "a progress indeed which he took the utmost pains to conceal" (146). Smith explains that "he was very long at his toilet every day, to which no person, not even his valet-de-chambre, was admitted" (146). That General Tracy pays close attention to his body indicates that readers should too, and although his beauty secrets are just that, Smith urges readers to be imaginative as they ponder his aged body. She lists "Olympian dew, cold cream, and Spanish wool" as a few of the treatments he uses to combat wrinkles, and "several contrivances, of his own invention" to shape his body beneath his clothes "to make them fit with advantage to his person" (146). This war hero and symbol of masculine economic power looks silly when Smith fashions him in the role of a vain coquette, and Isabella, pragmatic but resentful regarding the possibility of their marriage, takes every opportunity to ridicule his body.

Isabella sees Tracy as "ridiculous," and his body becomes an object of private and public derision. Among the women of her family, she laughs about "her old beau" and calculates "the trouble she knew his toilet cost him"; even her sensible mother "oftener smiled" (165) at Isabella's sharp remarks than reproved them. Isabella amuses them with a story about her experience riding with Tracy, when she deliberately turns her horse into the wind and canters to disturb Tracy's false hair: "these ill behaved curls deserted, and were flying, like two small birds tied by the leg, half a yard behind him; and if he had been commander of a town suddenly blown up by the enemy, he could not have looked more amazed and dismayed, than he did when I called out to him—General! your curls are flying away!" (165–66). This image of Tracy's body devastates his power—as if his town had been "suddenly blown up by the enemy." Tracy tries to recover from the embarrassment and attribute his hair loss to a recent fever rather than to age, but Isabella retains control over the exchange and even exaggerates the aesthetic image for her audience. Warning Tracy that he might catch cold without his false hair, she suggests that he wrap his handkerchief around his head for warmth. He refuses, but the damage is done. His body is comical, not commanding, and the women enjoy the opportunity to deflate male power.

But Isabella stresses that the aged male body incites only disdain when it affects youth and courts young women. To her sister's and mother's polite objections that age is not "a proper subject of ridicule," Isabella responds, "Well, if this worthy man will flirt with and make love to girls young enough to be his grand-daughters, I must laugh, if it *be* wrong" (167). Notably, Tracy's body is not funny by itself, but only in conjunction with his January–May romance; it is not funny because it is old, but rather because it attempts to be young. As Isabella reasons, "how is it possible to help laughing at a man who fancies that, at sixty, he can pass of six-and-twenty?" (167). Isabella doesn't find her father ridiculous, and she asserts, "I think [General Tracy] would be a thousand times more agreeable, if he could be persuaded to appear as my father and other men do, of the same age.—Instead of putting on toupees and curls, which it requires so much art and time to make fit snug and look natural, how preferable would a good comfortable wig be to his poor old head!" (165). But General Tracy will not act his age because he wants to chase young women, and January–May dynamics prompt these comical representations, transforming the aged body into an object of humiliation.

Though most January–May texts conjure visual images of aged bodies to support their manipulations of gendered power, there is an increased interest in spectacular manifestations of the January–May marriage during the Victorian period. In *Middlemarch*, the older husband comes under aesthetic scrutiny. *Middlemarch* emphasizes him as visual object, crafting through specific discourse an image of the aging male body as unattractive—a metaphor for the blight of male domination. Though the spectacle relies on ageist stereotypes about beauty and cultural fears of aging, this critique of the January husband proves effective, offending even those individuals seeking to preserve male privilege, who like Dorian Gray witness their own physical and social demise in the distortedly mirrored image.

## "Like a death's head skinned over": Looking and Laughing at Casaubon

In *Middlemarch*, Eliot delights in the display of the January husband's body and paints a distinct portrait of Casaubon's body for the public gaze.³ Despite the legal and social systems that Casaubon enlists to exercise power over Dorothea, his privileged status within a patriarchal society diminishes when age is understood as a component in the complex machinery of gender and power. Specifically, Casaubon's position as older husband weakens his hold on gendered authority, and the visual effects of such disruption to normative modes of power stretch further than his "dead hand" can reach.

The focus on Casaubon begins with the introduction of his character at the dinner party in Book I, and the first description of his physical appearance binds him to a specific work of art, a portrait of John Locke.⁴ Dorothea admires this semblance. The narrator discloses, "His manners, she thought, were very dignified; the set of his iron-grey hair and his deep eye-sockets made him resemble the portrait of Locke. He had the spare form and the pale complexion which became a student; as different as possible from the blooming Englishman of the red-whiskered type represented by Sir James Chettam" (11). The comparison to Locke continues after the dinner, when Celia and Dorothea retire to the drawing room and are able to talk freely about the appearance of their new guest. Celia begins the appraisal:

> "How very ugly Mr Casaubon is!"
> "Celia! He is one of the most distinguished-looking men I ever saw. He is remarkably like the portrait of Locke. He has the same deep eye-sockets."
> "Had Locke those two white moles with hairs on them?"
> "Oh, I daresay! when people of a certain sort looked at him," said Dorothea, walking away a little. (13)

As Dorothea's distancing move suggests, Celia's view of Casaubon represents more than the perspective of "people of a certain sort"; her perceptions as observer are representative of larger Middlemarch society, with a nod to a Swiftian world where the moles and hairs of others are conspicuous. This conversation makes two important points: first, it clarifies the normative view of Casaubon that the reader is to expect from society at large, and, second, it distinguishes Dorothea's aesthetic and sexual preferences as quite dissimilar to that norm.⁵

Critics have thus far overlooked the subversive qualities that Casaubon's association with the portrait of Locke introduces. Hugh Witemeyer, in *George Eliot and the Visual Arts*, reads the analogy as a mistaken idealization on the part of the youthful Dorothea. He writes, "Idealizing portraiture provides no coherent vision in this novel of incomplete insights. . . . just as Mr. Casaubon more obviously eludes . . . Dorothea's comparison of him with 'the portrait of Locke'" (87). While Witemeyer's assessment of Dorothea's critical misjudgment is justified, it neglects to read the portrait of Locke through eyes other than Dorothea's—such as those of the narrator, Celia, the other members of Middlemarch, or the reader. Moreover, though Dorothea and those in the county who consider Casaubon "a man of profound learning" idealize his intellectual prowess, his physical resemblance to Locke never appears as ideal to anyone but Dorothea. The dynamics of heterosexual relations open possibilities for a valid critique of masculinity, and it is the visualization of Casaubon as a lover, not a scholar, that changes his access to power and authority.

Aesthetic objections to Casaubon therefore increase when his role changes from that of country scholar to bridegroom; in effect, the characters hold his age and appearance up against those of Dorothea, and Casaubon is found wanting. Some characters offer cautions against Dorothea's decision that appear kind and reasonable. On the marriage offer, her uncle advises, "Well, but Casaubon, now. There is no hurry—I mean for you. It's true, every year will tell upon him. He is over five-and-forty, you know. I should say a good seven-and-twenty years older than you. To be sure,—if you like learning and standing, and that sort of thing, we can't have everything. . . . Still he is not young" (26). But others barely conceal their alarm and revulsion. Celia feels "disgust" at the thought of her sister marrying Casaubon and "a sort of shame mingled with a sense of the ludicrous" (31). Chettam, as the early rival for Dorothea's affection, reacts even more strongly. He too is appalled at the news of her engagement, and the novel reveals that "Perhaps his face had never before gathered so much concentrated disgust as when he turned to Mrs Cadwallader and repeated, 'Casaubon?'" (37). He continues, "Good God! It is horrible! He is no better than a mummy!" and Mrs. Cadwallader affirms that Casaubon is a "great bladder for dried peas to rattle in!" (37). Chettam furthers his hyperbolic objections, asking, "What business has an old bachelor like that to marry? He has one foot in the grave," to which Mrs. Cadwallader promptly retorts, "He means to draw it out again, I suppose" (37).

The effects of aging on the male body weaken his status within society and within the marriage. His engagement to Dorothea prompts the Middlemarch community to scrutinize his every attribute, and he becomes the target of malignant, though often humorous, gossip. Mrs. Cadwallader and Lady Chettam have a good laugh over his physical appearance in the following exchange:

> "*He* does not want drying."
> "Who, my dear?" said Lady Chettam, a charming woman, not so quick as to nullify the pleasure of explanation.
> "The bridegroom—Casaubon. He has certainly been drying up faster since the engagement: the flame of passion, I suppose." (58)

Mrs. Cadwallader goes on to contrast Casaubon with a more idealized image of manhood, Lady Chettam's son Sir James: "Really, by the side of Sir James, he looks like a death's head skinned over for the occasion" (58). The pleasure the women garner from their conversation is intrinsically seditious and is aimed not simply at Casaubon the man, but at a larger system of power, displaying what Eileen Gillooly defines as "feminine humor" in her study *Smile of Discontent*. Feminine humor, Gillooly claims, has "a combative component as well, aimed not at the Other but at the Law—the authority of the 'situation'" (24). The women's mockery of Casaubon's physicality points to a weakness among men in general, and their attack is coded by conventions of sexual ability and gender identity.

Mrs. Cadwallader's sarcastic reference to Casaubon's "flame of passion" highlights the sexual tension and gender subversions that erupt within the marriage. On various levels, verbal attacks that play on the sexual imagery of Dorothea and Casaubon disrupt the nineteenth-century order of masculine domination and feminine submission. Casaubon's age marginalizes his body, and the sexual union between his aging body and Dorothea's youthful flesh connotes sexual deviancy to Middlemarch society. Chettam struggles to distance his own desire for Dorothea after her acceptance of Casaubon, intimating that her sexual "perversity" could taint his own normative sexuality: "Sir James said to himself that he had completely resigned her, since with the perversity of a Desdemona she had not affected [*sic*] a proposed match that was clearly suitable and according to nature" (*Middlemarch*, 43). Chettam casts Dorothea's choice of husband and lover as an Othello, and Chettam's determination that such sexuality is not "according to nature" aligns her marriage with nineteenth-century fears of miscegenation, incest, and pedophilia. Additionally, Casaubon appears as one who cannot control or satisfy the sexual appetite of his partner. Openly critiquing monogamous marriage, Mrs. Cadwallader suggests, "Casaubon has got a trout-stream, and does not care about fishing in it himself: could there be a better fellow?" (45). Coming a few pages before the introduction of young Will Ladislaw, this remark establishes the likelihood that, if Casaubon doesn't visit his "trout-stream," someone else will, and the additional threats of Dorothea's youthful, feminine sexuality and a young male rival further Casaubon's already disempowered position. His jealousy and sexual anxiety initiate the controversial codicil to his will that shames not just Dorothea but, perhaps more pointedly, himself, and he writes his own legacy as that of the threatened patriarch who must invoke legal and economic means to enforce a loyalty that he alone could not inspire.

The introduction of Will further contrasts Casaubon's aging body with that of Will. As the Brookes tour Lowick, Celia reports with delight that she has seen "some one quite young coming up one of the walks," adding that "I only saw his back. But he was quite young" (49). The male body, even the fully clothed back of the male body, becomes an image immediately coded by an age association—not only by Celia, but also by Mr. Brooke, the narrator, and even Casaubon, as "young" and "youthful" appear over twelve times in less than three pages surrounding Will's introduction. He is "young Ladislaw," a "youngster," and a "young relative," as Eliot emphasizes, almost to the point of incredibility, his difference from Casaubon in age and appearance.[6] Near the end of the description, Casaubon suggests that they return to the house, "lest the young ladies should be tired of standing" and Will's youthful associations extend to Dorothea and Celia, categorizing the three as young people and distinctly grouping Casaubon and Mr. Brooke with Mr. Tucker (the just-departed curate) who is "just as old and musty-looking as [Celia] would have expected Casaubon's curate to be" (49). Will, who has been in a subservient position to his cousin because of Casaubon's claim on the family fortunes, is suddenly empowered by his awareness of the age difference between Casaubon and his bride and by his own age-based advantage. "The notion of his grave cousin as the lover of that girl" tickles Will's "sense of the ludicrous," and he delights (even without the pun on "grave" by the narrator) in the new weakness he sees in one who has hitherto oppressed him. The narrator relates, "When their backs were turned, young Ladislaw sat down to go on with his sketching, and as he did so his face broke into an expression of amusement which increased as he went on drawing, till at last he threw back his head and laughed out loud" (51). So that readers can continue to like Will, and to distinguish him from the gossiping Middlemarchers, the narrator clarifies that his laughter "had no mixture of sneering and self-exaltation" but was "the pure enjoyment of comicality" (51). Will simply witnesses the entertaining spectacle of his older cousin playing the fool.

Casaubon conducts himself foolishly indeed. He has married with the idea that in taking a young wife, he selects a mate whom he can raise to be his obedient helpmate and fertile producer of male heirs. But despite Casaubon's poor judgment, the narrator attempts to give him an equal opportunity to express his feelings about the relationship, stating:

> I protest against all our interest, all our effort at understanding being given to the young skins that look blooming in spite of trouble; for these too will get faded, and will know the older and more eating griefs which we are helping to neglect. In spite of the blinking eyes and white moles objectionable to Celia, and the want of muscular curve which was morally painful to Sir James, Mr Casaubon had an intense consciousness within him, and was spiritually a-hungered like the rest of us. He had done nothing exceptional in marrying—nothing but what society sanctions, and considers an occasion for wreaths and bouquets. (175)

On the narrator's advice, Casaubon's pain should be read compassionately, but to read it honestly, it is nevertheless pain that results from a shifting of traditional male privilege to the "young skins" that remain distinct from him. Furthermore, though it is pain, it is the pain that emerges from a gendered society—it is, after all a societal problem, as he has done "nothing but what society sanctions"—struggling with power, for Casaubon's choice to enter a marriage with a great age difference is a premeditated attempt to retain a position of masculine dominance and control. The narrator explains, "It had occurred to him that he must not any longer defer his intention of matrimony, and he had reflected that in taking a wife, a man of good position should expect and carefully choose a blooming young lady—the younger the better, because more educable and submissive" (175). But his plan for maintaining power backfires, and because of the age discrepancy in the marriage, Casaubon does not find what he had expected: "Mr Casaubon had thought of annexing happiness with a lovely young bride; but even before marriage, as we have seen, he found himself under a new depression in the consciousness that the new bliss was not blissful to him" (177). Casaubon finds himself in a weakened position, both intellectually and physically, and his anxiety increases as his young wife threatens his understanding of his gender identity. Dorothea's enthusiasm for Casaubon to complete his enormous *Key to all Mythologies* fosters more unease than encouragement in her husband. Her very presence amplifies his apprehensions about his abilities, and he finds that "this cruel outward accuser was there in the shape of a wife—nay, of a young bride, who instead of observing his pen-scratches and amplitude of paper with the uncritical awe of an elegant-minded canary bird, seemed to present herself as a spy watching everything with a malign power of inference" (128). Reversing the gender roles that the audience would have expected from John Stuart Mill's *Subjection of Women* (1869), he finds marriage "more of a subjection than he had been able to imagine"(129).[7] Once Dorothea has access to the current, or "young," scholarship that displaces Casaubon's outdated theories, he senses another challenge to his authority, so he attempts to solicit her promise to complete the *Key* after his death according to his judgment and not her own. This effort to bend her intellectual will to his suggests Casaubon's intimidation at Dorothea's growing prowess as a scholar herself, and the novel makes the superiority of Dorothea's abilities clear: "in spite of her small instruction, her judgment in this matter was truer than his: for she looked with unbiased comparison and healthy sense at probabilities on which he had risked all his egoism" (297).

Yet Dorothea's youth troubles Casaubon physically even more than it does intellectually. Unlike some other literary January husbands, Casaubon does not seem driven by sexual desire for Dorothea. Though Dorothea aspires to "pour forth her girlish and womanly feeling" on Casaubon, he remains cold and unreceptive. Like "every sweet woman," Dorothea childishly longs to "[shower] kisses on the hard pate of her bald doll, creating a happy soul within that woodenness from the wealth of her own love" (127). But emotionally and physically unresponsive, like a bald, wooden doll, Casaubon resists her advances, and Mrs. Cadwallader's prediction comes true, as he has no wish to fish in his "trout-stream." The metaphor of the doll implies that it is Casaubon who is infantilized by the January–May marriage, not Dorothea. Though older, he is physically immature, even babyish, compared with his wife, and because of his infancy, he is unable to procreate. Although he had at one time thought that marriage would bestow on him the "family pleasures" that would allow him to "leave behind that copy of himself which seemed so urgently required of a man—to the sonneteers of the sixteenth century," the novel explains that "Times had altered since then, and no sonneteer had insisted on Mr Casaubon's leaving a copy of himself" (175–76). Dorothea's honeymoon fantasies remain unfulfilled; she had yearned "to have kissed Mr Casaubon's coat-sleeve, or to have caressed his shoe-latchet, if he would have made any other sign of acceptance than pronouncing her, with his unfailing propriety, to be of a most affectionate and truly feminine nature, indicating at the same time by politely reaching a chair for her that he regarded these manifestations as rather crude and startling" (127). Casaubon's lack of sexual interest in Dorothea evolves into uneasy awareness of his own sexual inabilities and into fears of Dorothea's sexual desire for another man. His anxieties lead to numerous attempts to exclude Will from their immediate contact, and Casaubon appears more than capable of imagining the sexual possibilities that he does not physically enact. Will's unwelcome appearance at Lowick "brought Mr Casaubon's power of suspicious construction into exasperated activity," and "Suspicion and jealousy of Will Ladislaw's intentions, suspicion and jealousy of Dorothea's impressions, were constantly at their weaving work" (261).

At this point, it is tempting to read Casaubon's reluctance to submit to the more conventional romance between Dorothea and Will as an unconscious stance against the powers of patriarchy and privileged masculinity. When Casaubon finds himself subjected as a marginalized, oppressed example of a subordinate masculinity, he rebels against the figure of Will, who embodies traditional virility. Certainly, when the novel depicts Dorothea's body with Casaubon's, her figure is much more subversive than when paired with Will's. For example, when the novel links Dorothea's and Will's youthful bodies to art, they continue to portray a conventional nineteenth-century hierarchy of masculine control and feminine submission. In "'A Microscope Directed on a Water-Drop': Chapter 19," Juliet McMaster unravels the novel's depictions of Dorothea and Will in the Vatican museum by aligning their characters with the museum's sculptures the *Ariadne* and the *Apollo Belvedere*. Both of these pieces portray bodies that support conventional readings of masculinity and femininity, making essential the physical according to socially constructed gendered norms. The *Ariadne* captures the sleeping mythological figure at Naxos, still unaware that she has been abandoned by Theseus and yet to be rescued from her despair by the god Dionysus, who eventually marries her. This disempowered image of woman contrasts with the virile masculinity of Will as the *Apollo Belvedere*. As McMaster observes, Dorothea/Ariadne will eventually be saved from her loneliness by her own young god: "Will, generally identified with a classical young male deity" (113). The young bodies of Dorothea and Will play out the traditional, even classical, myth of female passivity and male agency, and, as we see at the end of the novel, the marriage between these partners of similar ages does conform to conventions of male and female roles within society and marriage. However, deeming her marriage to Casaubon "the most horrible of virgin-sacrifices," Will casts Casaubon as monster and their union as comparable to the legend of the virgin and the dragon, saving the role of St. George for himself: "And Casaubon had done a wrong to Dorothea in marrying her. A man was bound to know himself better than that, and if he chose to grow grey crunching bones in a cavern, he had no business to be luring a girl into his companionship" (225). But the novel questions whether same-age marriage can save anything. Describing Dorothea's second marriage, Eliot urges readers to lament the limited possibilities available for married women in the nineteenth century: "Many who knew her, thought it a pity that so substantive and rare a creature should have been absorbed into the life of another, and be only known in a certain circle as a wife and mother. But no one stated exactly what else that was in her power she ought rather to have done" (513).

The novel presents a vastly different power relationship between Dorothea and Casaubon. Certainly far from ideal to either Dorothea or Casaubon, or equal in any sense of the word, the distribution of power is nevertheless multidirectional. In a vicious cycle, Casaubon's aging body and the anxieties that it produces feed on one another, and he finds himself in the position he had hoped to make for Dorothea—as a feminized, subservient child bride. Just as his body fosters concern about his claim to gendered power, his concerns exacerbate his weakened condition. In Chapter 29, a heated discussion with Dorothea over a letter from Will initiates the heart trouble that foreshadows Casaubon's oncoming death. When Casaubon offensively instructs Dorothea to refrain from having Will visit Lowick, Dorothea responds with passionate strength at treatment she finds "stupidly undiscerning and odiously unjust." She retaliates against his rule, even though Casaubon still considers her to be "too young to be on the formidable level of wifehood": "With her first words, uttered in a tone that shook him, she startled Mr Casaubon into looking at her, and meeting the flash of her eyes" (178). Casaubon tries to restore her to a feminized position, but she refuses, and in an uneasy silence, they take up their work. As Casaubon tries to write, his body betrays his inward instability, and "his hand trembled so much that the words seemed to be written in an unknown character" (178). Conversely, despite her anger, Dorothea remains strong: "She began to work at once, and her hand did not tremble; on the contrary . . . she felt that she was forming her letters beautifully, and it seemed that she saw the construction of the Latin she was copying, and which she was beginning to understand, more clearly than usual" (178–79). In this crisis of gender roles, Casaubon experiences "bodily distress." Dorothea helps a feminized Casaubon to the couch as if he were a swooning heroine. On recovering, Casaubon is all too aware of the disempowered position his body continues to occupy, and he resents Mr. Brooke's suggestion that he take up a hobby like making toys while recuperating. "In short you recommend me to anticipate the arrival of my second childhood," he retorts "with some bitterness" (180). As Casaubon struggles against the ebbing of his masculine powers, he finds himself unhappily associated with femininity and childishness as a direct result of his age.

Casaubon's illness attracts even more eyes to his physical body, which, now under the care of the physician Lydgate, becomes increasingly pathologized.[8] Lydgate explains to Dorothea that her husband's life expectancy is "difficult to pronounce" and that he "may possibly live for fifteen years or more, without much worse health than he has had hitherto" (182). Dorothea, with a polite reference to physical relations, clarifies, "You mean if we are very careful," and Lydgate warns against "excessive application" and also against "mental agitation of all kinds," stressing that "Anxiety of any kind would be precisely the most unfavourable condition for him" (182). Unfortunately, anxiety about bodies remains ever present in their January–May marriage, and Casaubon's efforts to maintain any semblance of masculine authority further weaken his health. Medical discourse about his body alienates his body parts and objectifies his organs. Consulting with Lydgate privately, Casaubon discovers that he suffers from "fatty degeneration of the heart" (263) and must face the realization that he is further losing control of the body that is responsible for his loss of control. Even more frightening to Casaubon than his own demise is the pity that Dorothea conveys. The narrator reminds the reader to "Consider that his mind was a mind which shrank from pity" (265), yet it is difficult not to pity Casaubon in his new powerless position.

Ultimately, Casaubon's body fails him, and he is finally objectified as "the dead hand" of Book V, reduced to a body fragment that is frozen like sculpture as it rests on the stone table. This individual body resonates within the social body, and the death of Casaubon expresses both the temporality of the body and the transitory nature of gendered power. The January–May marriage between Casaubon and Dorothea need not be tragic, as some characters would suggest.

Though Dorothea is certainly not free from systems of masculine power (which even her romantic marriage to Will reinforces), she finds power first as a young wife and then as a young widow.

\* \* \* \* \*

The aesthetics of aging highlight that gender is not an unalterable agent of authority, and literary descriptions of January–May marriage partners and artistic representations of intergenerational couples allow the reader to visualize age as an essential component in gender formation. When authors prolong the development of their January–May narratives with detailed renderings of the bodies of the groom and bride, they connect their works to a broader nineteenth-century visual culture and employ shared assumptions about aesthetically "ill-matched" couples. Like *Middlemarch*, many nineteenth-century texts use the January–May image rebelliously against gender norms, and the older husband's body becomes a source of subversive humor as well as a symbol of male power isolated and contained. However, Dorian Gray's privileging of youth over aging ultimately leads to his demise, and efforts to replace gender inequities with an age-based hierarchy only shift the focal points of power. *Dorian Gray* also points to limitations of associating outer bodies with inner realities; Dorian may be outwardly beautiful, but he is inwardly corrupt. His body attests to the collective error of relying on visual perceptions to evaluate power and worth, and January–May bodies that represent happily married couples likewise challenge the validity of using aesthetics as narrative signposts.

Some January–May texts thus reverse the *Dorian Gray* formula. Instead of reading the exterior appearances of husband and wife as aesthetic foreshadowing of the failure of their marriage, these January–May texts delight in refusing to accept an aesthetic norm. Dickens's *David Copperfield* runs counter to readers' expectations because of its teasing nonfulfillment of standard January–May tropes and because of its incestuous subtext, but it also breaks from visual conventions, discordantly holding aging male and younger female bodies in comparison, and then guiding aesthetic judgment by declaring that the unlikely combination works. Similarly, Brontë critiques a tradition of pairing beautiful, same-aged bodies in the central romance of *Jane Eyre*. While she is young, Jane is not beautiful in the same way that most popular heroines in nineteenth-century fiction are, and Rochester is neither young nor handsome. By the end of the novel, idealized images of husband and wife are even more unsettled when Rochester appears blind and injured. Rochester's aging and disfigured body borders on the monstrous, but Brontë confronts aesthetic standards by depicting the older husband as both desiring and desirable and by encouraging the reader to reconsider predictable interpretations of the January–May image. Readers might enjoy the opportunity to mock the aging male body, but intergenerational relationships that resist aesthetic conventions demand that readers reconsider their qualifications as visual interpreters.

January–May aesthetics are in many ways predictable, but some January–May texts defy the tradition and encourage new ways of seeing intergenerational romance. Even texts that remain invested in the objectification and containment of the male body find alternative channels for their visual depictions. But there remains a pattern in the January–May tradition that relies on aesthetic conventions to create a more specific image of the aging husband as monster. January–May texts that exaggerate the physical characteristics of the older spouse, driving him hyperbolically even further into the visually horrific, encourage readings of the January–May marriage as Gothic nightmare. To this spectacle, I turn next.

# Chapter 4

## The Horror of Aging

### The January–May Marriage as Gothic Nightmare

When Sue Bridehead's older husband, Richard Phillotson, accidentally enters her bedroom instead of his own and begins to undress in Thomas Hardy's *Jude the Obscure*, Sue wakes, cries, and promptly jumps out of her second floor bedroom window. Running outside to her aid, Richard finds that she has not "broken her neck," and though she is dazed by her fall onto the gravel, she accounts for her drastic actions: "'I was asleep, I think!' she began, her pale face still turned away from him. 'And something frightened me—a terrible dream—I thought I saw you—'" (181). Sue breaks off because waking does not resolve her nightmare, yet Phillotson is a dubious monster. Hardy takes care to stress that Sue's dramatic flight was unnecessary; at least on this occasion, it was not sexual desire but rather Phillotson's scholarly "preoccupation" in thinking of "Roman antiquities" that led him to Sue's room. He is understandably "horrified" by Sue's action, which she commits "before he had thought that she meant to do more than get air" (180), and he injures himself on the banister in his haste to help her. Nonetheless, the idea of marital relations with Phillotson inspires a Gothic horror so terrific that it causes a young bride to leap out a window. And although Phillotson is distressed that he has inadvertently caused her panic, he finds he cannot separate her horror from himself. Like the monster in Shelley's *Frankenstein*, he arouses fear and disgust, and he finds that "the significance of all this sickened him of himself and of everything" (181).

*Jude the Obscure* is infused with a Gothic horror, expressed most obviously in the novel's somewhat sensational story of child murder and suicide and in the more tedious awfulness of the protagonist's frustrated life.[1] Without sinister monks, supernatural forces, or mysterious passageways, Hardy "realistically" positions the Gothic within intergenerational marriage by drawing on widespread public antipathies that mingle fears of aging, sex, and death.

Not all January–May texts emphasize the Gothic aspects of these marriages, but ominous sexual scenarios between older men and younger women were integral to the Gothic tradition from its beginnings in the eighteenth century, and it is easy to see how these two popular nineteenth-century forms could overlap. Much of the terror in Horace Walpole's *The Castle of Otranto* (1764) arises from the sexual threat posed by Manfred to Isabella, who has intended to marry Manfred's son. Similarly, in Elizabeth Helme's *The History of Louisa, the Lovely Orphan; or, The Cottage on the Moor* (1787), the title character almost falls into the lecherous clutches of her much-older guardian. Intimidating older men loom darkly over beautiful young women in Ann Radcliffe's *The Romance of the Forest* (1791) and in her *The Mysteries of Udolpho* (1794), and part of the Gothic thrill lies in the exposure of these beautiful heroines to the demands of older men. January–May elements were added to Radcliffe's *A Sicilian Romance* (1790) when Henry Siddons adapted it for the London stage in 1794; in the play, the January figure keeps his same-aged first wife confined to a cave while he pursues the much-younger heroine. Predatory older men become such a stock component of Gothic fiction that Austen mocks the trope in her parody *Northanger Abbey* (1818) through Catherine Morland's belief that General Tilney has murdered or imprisoned his same-aged wife.

Beyond these sinister and threatening older men, other commonalties exist between these two literary traditions. Like the January–May marriage, the Gothic uses its peculiar position on the margins of respectability to comment on power relations in the nineteenth century, and the two traditions share ambivalent agendas regarding gender as well as several narrative strategies that advance their objectives. Gothic tales could be morally instructive and supportive of traditional gender and sexual codes, or they could be radically subversive; as Fred Botting says of Gothic fiction: "Some moral endings are little more than perfunctory tokens, thin excuses for salacious excesses"

(8). Both traditions rely on excessive situations to further their plots; the age difference between partners in January–May marriages amplifies accepted traits of masculinity and of femininity, taking experience and innocence, wealth and poverty, and aggression and submission to new extremes. As well, both traditions opportunely engage emotions of fear and desire. I see in these Gothic January–May texts a common interest in historical anachronism, a trait Robert Mighall deems essential to the Gothic narrative, which "at its emergence and in its development through the nineteenth and twentieth centuries, testifies to a concern with the historical past, and adopts a number of rhetorical and textual strategies to locate the past and represent its perceived iniquities, terrors, and survivals" (xiv).[2] These works did not need to include ancient castles or historic relics because the historical anachronism was present in the January–May couple itself.

Gothic dimensions of the January–May marriage emphasize the complexities of relations within conventional heterosexual relationships. In one sense, the older husband figures as the stereotypical monster by abusing power to elicit fear from his wife, who is supposedly less powerful because of her youth and gender. Although these narratives play into conventions of masculine domination and feminine submission, they demonstrate a desire to censure and to curtail such monstrous exploitations of power. Thus, Gothic versions of the January–May theme require that readers pay attention to the weaknesses of the older husbands and the systems of gender identification that contribute to their power. Readers focus on the means to end inequities: sunlight, the Cross, holy water, a stake through the heart—whatever will redistribute power. Moreover, some texts highlight the weaknesses of "monsters" like Phillotson to such an extent that their claims to power become entirely questionable. I will return to *Jude the Obscure* later in this chapter as I use it with Bram Stoker's *Dracula* and several other "vampire" texts to illustrate the Gothic dynamics of the January–May marriage theme and their implications regarding gender and power, but I first want to establish a historical and theoretical framework that accounts for Sue's jump from her bedroom window.

## Growing Old in the Nineteenth Century

I began the previous chapter with a discussion of Wilde's *The Picture of Dorian Gray* and its expression of *fin-de-siècle* anxieties about the aesthetics of aging, but I do not claim that aging was always presented by writers and artists in such dismal terms. Robert Browning's opening stanza from "Rabbi Ben Ezra" (1864) optimistically promises,

> Grow old along with me!
> The best is yet to be,
> The last of life, for which the first was made:
> Our times are in His hand
> Who saith "A whole I planned,
> Youth shows but half; trust God: see all nor be afraid!" (1–6)

This pronouncement of the validity of aging is bound to a faith in God, and similar positive depictions of old age across class lines can be found elsewhere in nineteenth-century literature. Wordsworth's "Simon Lee" (1798) and "Resolution and Independence" (1802) display a reverence for aging working-class masculinity, as does Eliot's *Silas Marner* (1861). Encouraging images of aging appear throughout the century, though largely overshadowed by darker, more troublesome views on "the last of life." Rabbi Ben Ezra's advice "nor be afraid" presumes that a fear of aging already plagues his listeners, and he is correct. I want to stress that I am not suggesting that people in the nineteenth century were, *en masse*, afraid of the elderly or openly advocating attacks on aging.[3] As Rabbi Ben Ezra demonstrates, worries about aging often translated into renewed praise for the later stages of life. But debates over the 1834 Poor Law Amendment Act reveal that feelings about aging were ambivalent, encompassing a wide range of humanistic and economic issues. Pat Thane explains that "there were conflicting attitudes to the role of the workhouse in the lives of the aged poor, between those who believed . . . that it should be a grim deterrent designed to force younger people to save for old age, and others who saw it as a haven where the helpless, friendless, aged could . . . 'enjoy their indulgences'" (*Old Age in English History*, 166). Whether Poor Law reform was viewed as protection or punishment for Britain's elderly poor, reforms of public policy drew attention to the "helpless" condition of many aged, and fueled fears about potential burdens that an aging population could place on individual family members or on the nation. These fears conjured their own monsters—an increasing medicalization of the aged body as diseased and a growing association of aberrant sexualities with aging—and led to a rising literary interest in the January–May marriage as a Gothic narrative.

While fears of aging can be found before and after the nineteenth century, certain historical factors intensified concerns over old age during this period. Social historians now distance themselves from previous theories that reductively called preindustrial society a "golden age" of communal appreciation and familial inclusion of elderly people, but the effects of industrialism nevertheless deeply altered public perceptions of aging.[4] Although statistics do not support the idea that things were better for older people before industrialization, literature from the period insists that agrarian systems of extended families diminished problems associated with aging. For example, Wordsworth's "Michael" (1800) tells the story of an older couple whose only son does not provide for his parents in their later years. The son leaves his parents and their rural life for the "dissolute city," and they all suffer the consequences. Similarly, Dickens's work in the 1850s for workhouse reform emphasizes the plight of the elderly in an industrial city, painting the urban Gothic with a keen eye on the elderly:

> Aged people were there, in every variety. Mumbling, blear-eyed, spectacled, stupid, deaf, lame; vacantly winking in the gleams of sun that now and then crept in through the open doors, from the paved yard; shading their listening ears or blinking eyes with their withered hands; poring over their books, leering at nothing, going to sleep, crouching and drooping in corners. There were weird old women, all skeleton within, all bonnet and cloak without, continually wiping their eyes with dirty dusters of pocket-handkerchiefs; and there were ugly old crones, both male and female, with a ghastly kind of contentment upon them which was not at all comforting to see. ("A Walk in a Workhouse," 88)

Dickens connects this frightening picture to the urban elderly's inability to return to "the far-off foreign land called Home" (91) and its rural network of familial comforts. Print culture spread the idea that industrialism had changed the position of older people within the family and within society. Even if, as historians now claim, there were no "golden age," nineteenth-century citizens who read the literature of the day would have believed not only that one existed, but more pointedly, that they were no longer in it. Extended family structures that were thought to have provided for the elderly were perceived as broken. Now, older people were alone—one could even say astray—and this characterization fueled public fear *for* and *of* them.

Burgeoning cities like London, Manchester, and Liverpool brought increasing numbers of older people together, forming a collective presence that was more visible and, consequently, in greater need of social regulation. Older people often appeared as powerless figures, but alternately, they wielded power garnered by their age, experience, and financial capital, and they could place demands on the young people around them. Teresa Mangum explains that it was not only fear of masses of poor older people financially encumbering the younger generations that inspired social alarm, but that worries about wealthy older people living too long and denying young people the enjoyment of their inheritances also emerged in the literature of the period: "one recurring character type hints that older people who held on too tightly to property or to power were more unnerving than those who became burdens" (101).[5] While the average lifespan did not increase, a decline in birth rates led to a disproportionate number of older people during the Victorian period, which further contributed to the intimidating notion that there were more elderly people than before (101). Mangum links anxieties about aging to Malthusian theories of overpopulation made popular by the *Essay on the Principle of Population* (1798) as well as to a "growing Victorian concern over what was falsely perceived to be an increasing 'aged' population in an era obsessed with youth, energy, activity, and progress" (98).

Fears about aging abound in the literature and art. Byron's "On This Day I Complete My Thirty-Sixth Year" (1824) attempts to rouse the poet from succumbing to "the worm, the canker and the grief," but its failure is evident. The answer to Byron's question, "If thou regret'st thy youth, why *live?*," is not an invitation to a peaceful and contented later life but a call for immediate and violent death:

> The Land of honourable Death
> Is here—up to the Field! And give
> Away thy Breath! (34–36)

Aging is dreadful to other Romantic poets, who show it to be a time of certain decline. Both Keats's *Hyperion* (1819) and *The Fall of Hyperion* (1819) present the shift in power from the "old" Titans to the new Olympians as heartrending, though written into our Western mythology. In *Hyperion* Keats crafts Saturn as "old," (89) "gray-hair'd," (4) with "faded eyes," (90) "palsied tongue," (94) and "wrinkling brow" (100)—linking old age with the necessary, albeit painful, loss of his throne. Fear of aging helps to explain the Romantic preference for those who die young. Literature and life idealized Chatterton, Lucy, Adonais, and others who remain forever young through early death.

Victorian writers envisioned other appalling scenarios regarding old age. Tennyson's "Tithonus" (1859) recounts the legend of the son of Laomedon who received immortality from the gods so that he could marry Aurora, goddess of the dawn, but did not receive eternal youth. In an interesting twist on the January–May theme, Tithonus ages while Aurora stays the same, and she rejects him:

Coldly thy rosy shadows bathe me, cold
Are all thy lights, and cold my wrinkled feet
Upon thy glimmering thresholds. (66–68)

Additionally, Browning's portrayal of aging in "Andrea Del Sarto" (1855) is much darker than in his "Rabbi Ben Ezra." While the title character claims that "I am grown peaceful as old age tonight. / I regret little, I would change still less" (244–45), the poem emphasizes the artist's missteps in life—not the least of which is his marriage to the young and beautiful Lucrezia, who leaves him at the end of the poem to be with her "cousin." Tithonus and Andrea Del Sarto present pathetic and frightening—and subversive—images of a disempowered and aging masculinity.

New strategies for classifying the populace by age reveal a telling desire to manage older people so that their liabilities can be minimized and benefits can be maximized for the larger social good. In "When Does 'Old Age' Begin?: The Evolution of the English Definition," Janet Roebuck points out that the 1834 Poor Law Amendment Act that established workhouses in response to widespread poverty fostered a need for clarification regarding the designation of old age. Initially, what was meant by terms like "the elderly" and "old age" was ambiguous, and the elderly were merely a subset of those who were unable to provide for themselves. But by 1836, Poor Law Commissioners designated that the "impotent poor" in the workhouse over the age of sixty should be allowed small portions of butter, tea, and sugar in their dietary provisions, and Roebuck concludes that "the fact that those over sixty were allowed a better diet quickly created a general impression that the 'aged and infirm' were people over sixty" (419). Roebuck finds that the British public continued debates to clarify classifications of the elderly, which culminated again in the 1880s and '90s regarding governmental pensions for older people. Without established definitions outlining the onset of old age, a unified public-assistance program for the elderly would be difficult; however, practical reasons for defining old age obscure a more desperate wish to standardize and to police aging within society.

This type of regulation initiated by larger social fears of aging resulted in an increased pathologizing of the aged body as abnormal, deviant, and diseased. Regarding the medicalization of old age, Mangum cites the work of scientists like Jean-Martin Charcot, who stressed the scientific exploration of the aging body rather than the treatment of older people. Texts like Sir Anthony Carlisle's *An Essay on the Disorders of Old Age* (1817) and Charcot's *Clinical Lectures on the Diseases of Old Age* (1867) contributed to a proliferation of new medical discourses surrounding aging, as did a larger societal hope that the effects of aging could be held at bay, if not totally overcome.[6] As the century progressed, skin tissue, body organs, and cells were examined with enhanced microscopic technology to discern how each was altered by the processes of aging, and large charity hospitals serving the aging poor conveniently provided a large pool of aged bodies as objects for scientific inquiry (Mangum, 105). Aged bodies were readily available for widespread scrutiny. The Anatomy Act of 1832 provided that the bodies of those who died in workhouses and hospitals unable to pay the costs of their burials, many of whom were elderly, would be donated to scientific research and curbed the illegal practice of robbing graves for medical dissection (Joseph and Tucker, 117). Scientists probed the causes of wrinkles, gray hair, impotence, and senility in their explanations of aging, suggesting that if these "abnormal" conditions could be quantified, then the horrors of aging could be mitigated and contained.[7]

But research failed to assuage public fears of aging and eventually contributed to the staging of old age as a Gothic horror show. Clinical approaches to aging that moved old age from being a natural part of the life cycle to being a repository for various diseases did little to control the aging process or the aging population. However, these scientific studies did bolster public opinion that something was wrong with the aged body. Aged bodies became diseased bodies, and diseased bodies easily slipped into being sexually deviant bodies. This trajectory is most evident in the antimasturbation literature that proliferated during the nineteenth century and in the spermatorrhea panic of the second half of the century, when major medical journals like *The Lancet* took up the theory that sperm was an important vital fluid for the body, and its loss was severely detrimental.[8] Fears of aging and death were compounded when conflated with fears of aberrant sexuality, and old age emerged as a disease that could be brought on not by sexual contact with another, as with syphilis or gonorrhea, but by sexual "abuse" of oneself.

In *Solitary Sex*, Thomas Laqueur traces increased interest in masturbation to the early eighteenth-century text *Onania* and to cultural consumerism and its associated pleasures of excess, acquisition, and gratification. Ostensibly a treatise against "self-pollution," *Onania* was viewed as "a freestanding work of soft-core pornography" by the end of the eighteenth century, though its contribution to social attacks on masturbation had already been achieved (Laqueur, 25). *Onania* inspired the Swiss physician Samuel Auguste David Tissot's *Onanism;*

*or, A Study of the Physical Maladies Produced by Masturbation* (1760), which Laqueur describes as "an instant literary sensation" that fed and shaped nineteenth-century curiosities surrounding masturbation. Although Laqueur does not explicitly connect the public investment in (anti)masturbation literature to fears of aging, his conjecture that "masturbation was an expression of anxiety about a new political economic order writ on the body" (280) highlights a connection between material culture and concerns of the body. Because of their tacit associations with pedophilia and incest, January–May marriages were already linked in the public imagination with nonstandard sexualities, and masturbation opportunely converges aging and sexual deviancy into one social "vice," as premature aging is promoted as a definitive symptom of the unrepentant masturbator.

A French antimasturbation pamphlet from the 1840s, *Le Livre Sans Titre*, calls attention to the correlation between sexual deviancy and aging through word and image, eroticizing the male body even as it invites readers' disgust.[9] The book describes the "Successive States of a Masturbator" and supports its warning with sixteen colored engravings. The narrative begins with a drawing of a handsome, "healthy" young man who is "the hope of his mother" (Figure 4.1). After masturbation, he begins to age quickly: "He corrupted himself! . . . soon he carries the punishment of his sin, premature aging . . . his back curves." In a subsequent image, his "teeth are damaged and fall out." Soon, "his beautiful hair falls off like in old age" and "his head is prematurely bald" (Figure 4.2). Unable to stop abusing himself, he declines quickly into old age and death: "His body becomes all stiff" and "his members stop functioning." Finally, an old man before his time, he dies in horrible pain at seventeen.

Sexually deviant behavior initiates a rapid tour of expected visual signifiers of the aging process: curvature of the spine, loss of teeth, male-pattern balding, wrinkles, and stiff joints.[10] Aging is the "punishment of his sin" and, as such, is inextricable from his unnatural sex acts. Moreover, the images of his aging body are captivating, and they are meant to frighten. The strangely erotic display of the aging male body, bare-chested to reveal his withered and frail physique, excites and horrifies as it (con)fuses the effects of masturbation and physical decline. The text constructs the aging male body as monstrous, but because the body we see is not really old—only seventeen—it emphasizes the consanguinity between the young and old, the "normal" and the "deviant." Youth is permeated with the effects of aging, and the effects of aging are tainted with sexual perversity.[11]

*Il etait jeune, beau: il fesait l'espoir de sa mère....*

**Figure 4.1** "Juene" by Anon. *Le Livre Sans Titre* © British Library Board. All Rights Reserved 12316.eee.11.

A similar conflation of aging and sexual deviancy runs parallel with nineteenth-century fears of masturbation through the literature about the January–May marriage, which provided—like antimasturbatory tracts—a unified site for attacking and enjoying the monstrous powers of aging, death, and aberrant sexuality. As I discussed in Chapter 1, January–May marriages were problematically sexual because they toyed with social taboos against pedophilia, incest, and infidelity. And

# The Horror of Aging 123

*Ses cheveux, si beaux, tombent comme dans la vieillesse; sa tête se dépouille avant l'âge....*

**Figure 4.2** "Tombent" by Anon. *Le Livre Sans Titre* © British Library Board. All Rights Reserved 12316.eee.11.

because this theme played on ageist stereotypes that implied these marriages were orchestrated to appease the male partner's sexual desire, which usually appears as independent, if not entirely at odds with the female's desire, January–May sex acts were, in a sense, already masturbatory practices that left only one partner satisfied.[12] Though texts that take on the January–May theme often titillated audiences with the threat of intergenerational sex only to avert the horror at the last moment, the terrible suggestion of deviant sexualities initiated by the age difference corrupts "normal" marital sexual practices. Thinking about intergenerational sex required that readers confront the terrors of aging and sexuality within the normalizing framework of traditional heterosexual marriage and thus allowed for both the spread and control of subversive sexualities.

Gothic elements of literary January–May marriages complicate how critics should approach these uniquely gendered power structures. Centering on the sexual pursuit of beautiful young women, these relationships play into misogynist fantasies of male domination, but the literature also focuses attention on abusive male behavior, making masculinity appear villainous by collapsing it with other dangerous identifiers like old age and perverse sexualities. In January–May texts, older husbands often exert intellectual, physical, psychological, economic, and even supernatural powers over their younger wives, but when their wives snub their sexual threats, their power to inspire fear actually decreases the powers of their gender. Like Phillotson, who discovers that being objectified as a monstrous figure in his marriage "sickened him of himself and of everything," older husbands find masculine privileges do not guarantee sexual or romantic success. These Gothic January–May marriages encourage an ageist demonizing of the older husband as a sexual monstrosity, but the critique of gender inequities must look beyond textual elements that drive a figurative stake through the heart of aging masculinity. These monstrous older men do wield some power, even if they are shown to abuse it, and even when they are deprived of power, they elicit pity for their hideous condition.

Additionally, these texts implicate the readers in gender inequities and in sexually deviant behaviors. In *Embodying the Monster: Encounters with the Vulnerable Self*, Margrit Shildrick theorizes that "although the very word 'monster' is a common term of abuse, implying a denial of any likeness between self and other such that a barrier is put in place between the two, the very force of rejection of such otherness cannot but suggest a level of disturbing familiarity, even similarity. The monster is not just abhorrent, it is also enticing, a figure that calls to us, that invites recognition" (5). January–May texts reveal a cultural tendency to proscribe the horrors of deviant sexuality to the aging male figure because he already embodies expectations of both the possession and the loss of gendered power, but they depend on moments when age transgresses the boundaries of the older husband's body and threatens to penetrate the young bodies around him—most poignantly through sexual intercourse. Like the way age infects the body of the young masturbator, an aged body similarly threatens to contaminate a young body as the married couple unites as "one flesh." Thus, while these texts attempt to classify and regulate the monstrous body as distinct and isolated, these segregating strategies always fail. They point to the instability of categories such as the normal and the deviant, and they emphasize where their boundaries are permeable.

Thus, the January–May marriage encapsulates the historical anachronism that Mighall deems essential to the Gothic, and the consummation of these marriages threatens the viability of any clear divisions between past and present. Moreover, the power struggle represented by these Gothic marriages is laden with conflicting social desires. Nineteenth-century antipathies toward aging and deviant sexualities compete with a cultural compulsion to confirm the sanctity of marriage, which, as I have pointed out in earlier chapters, was marked socially, religiously, and legally by a man's conjugal rights to his wife's body. I want to return here to the Gothic drama of *Jude the Obscure* as a case study of how these various objectives operate within the January–May marriage theme.

## "And now the ultimate horror has come": Sex, Marriage, and the Monster in *Jude the Obscure*

Phillotson's marriage to Sue inspires its own nightmares that arise from the century's larger Gothic interest in intergenerational sex. Before Sue jumps out the window, Hardy provides several hints that her marriage with Phillotson will be problematic, and he explicitly links their troubles to their age difference and to sex. Sue and Phillotson are eighteen years apart—hardly the largest age difference in this study—but the text emphasizes the gap between them to such an extent that it seems much larger. When Phillotson first enters his relationship with Sue as her employer and teacher, he finds it absurd that "a respectable, elderly woman should be present at these lessons when the teacher and the taught were of different sexes," since he is "old enough to be the girl's father" (86). The reason for such precautions soon becomes apparent, and Phillotson overcomes his fatherly inclinations to make romantic advances on Sue. When Sue and Phillotson exit the vicarage as "two figures under one umbrella," the image of their bodies in close proximity is intended to shock, and Jude and the reader watch with trepidation as Phillotson twice puts his arm around Sue's waist—rejected at first but then accepted. The horror of intergenerational sexual relations overwhelms Jude, who voices the expected ageist condemnation of what he has witnessed: "O, he's too old for her—too old!" (89).[13] When Jude questions Sue about Phillotson, she rejects the idea that she would consider the affections of "an old man like him" (107), though, when pressed, admits a few lines later that she has agreed to marry Phillotson in two years. Jude and Sue repeatedly try to accept the idea of a sexual relationship between old and young bodies, but their efforts always fail. This cyclic reconsideration of the possibility of sex between Sue and Phillotson provides a convenient means for perpetuating the sexually perverse. The characters explore intergenerational sex, decide it is horrible, and explore it again, *ad infinitum*. Jude seems perversely committed to playing devil's advocate to his own expressed opinion, rationalizing that "many a happy marriage had been made in such conditions of age" and that "he's not so very old," but spitefully reflects again on Phillotson's age prior to the wedding ceremony and reaffirms that Phillotson is old enough to be Sue's father (89, 107, 137). Sue argues with Jude that their case is atypical: "He's as good to me as a man can be, and gives me perfect liberty—which elderly husbands don't do in general. . . . If you think I'm not happy because he's too old for me, you are wrong" (152). But shortly thereafter, she admits that she "ought not to have married" (153). While the text first presents Phillotson as a "spare and thoughtful personage of five-and-forty" (83), it later casts him as unattractive and anachronistic, explaining that "the schoolmaster's was an unhealthy-looking, old-fashioned face, rendered more old-fashioned by his style of shaving" (129), and Aunt Drusilla, an old woman herself, declares her loathing of Sue's husband openly: "I don't want to wownd your feelings, but—there be certain men here and there that no woman of any niceness can stomach" (153).[14] Ultimately, Sue acknowledges "a physical objection" (167) to her husband, and although she attributes her disgust to her own "wickedness" (168), the novel has so firmly linked Phillotson's body with social prejudices against the aged that Sue's avowal that she feels "a repugnance on my part, for a reason I cannot disclose" (169) needs no explanation because it is already justified by a cultural horror of—and longing for—intergenerational sex. When Sue confesses to Jude that "What tortures me so much is the necessity of being responsive to this man whenever he wishes" (169), she titillates Jude and the reader with an image of her compulsive participation in repulsive sexual acts.

Hostility toward Phillotson's aging body and the privilege it represents results in much of the blame for the marriage being directed toward him. Not only does Phillotson appear to be depriving young

Jude of the normative sexual relationship he desires with Sue, but Phillotson also marries Sue through an abuse of his age- and gender-based power. Sue implies Phillotson was unethical to marry outside of his age group, pointedly asking, "Do you think, Jude, that a man ought to marry a woman his own age, or one younger than himself—eighteen years—as I am than he?" (169). Hardy critiques the legal rights a husband maintained over his wife's body on various occasions, soliciting sympathy for Sue when she confides to Jude that "it is a torture for me to—live with him as a husband" (169), undermining the faulty assumption that law or religion can guarantee desire when Phillotson unscrupulously declares to Sue that she is "committing a sin in not liking me" (177). Most of the power seems in Phillotson's grasp as Sue begs to be released from her wifely duties. She urges her husband as she would a master: "But cannot you have pity on me? I beg you to; I implore you to be merciful!" (179). The novel asserts that as a middle-aged man, Phillotson should have known better than to have wed a young woman and that he exploits his position of gender and age authority to get what he wants. In this sense, Phillotson is the monster of the plot who must be overcome for abuses of power to be stopped.

Sue's efforts to escape from sexual relations with her aging husband move the narrative further into Gothic conventions. Without telling Phillotson of her plans, Sue leaves their marital bed and creates a "nest" for herself in the back of their closet. Her provisions for her security are odd, and moreover, they are ineffective: she ties the door to the closet with a piece of string because it has no lock, and Phillotson easily breaks the string and opens the door. The scene is awkward and even a bit ridiculous, though infused with Gothic horror. When the door opens, Sue "[springs] out of her lair, great-eyed and trembling," and upbraids him for intruding: "You ought not to have pulled open the door!" (176). She laments a universe that is "horrid and cruel," and returns to sleep in the closet, which Phillotson discovers the next day is full of spider webs. He begins to surmise his position as monstrous husband, remarking darkly: "What must a woman's aversion be when it is stronger than her fear of spiders!" (176). Sue's horror of her husband culminates in the bedroom scene that begins this chapter: a scene in which the horror of her husband's naked body is so overwhelming that Sue jumps out her window.

But if Phillotson is a monster—more terrible than spiders—he is not all powerful, nor is he alone. His display of force in the closet scene is minimal at best, as he destroys a piece of string rather than ropes and chains. On discovering Sue in the closet, he calls *her* behavior "monstrous," and though this is certainly an act of psychological manipulation, it points to his own powerlessness and pain within his marriage. Phillotson rejects his role as monster, concluding that he should divorce Sue even though it goes against the "doctrines [he] was brought up in" (183). He sees what his age, his gender, and his January–May marriage have created for him, and chooses to withdraw: "Now when a woman jumps out of a window without caring whether she breaks her neck or no, she's not to be mistaken; and this being the case I have come to a conclusion: that it is wrong to so torture a fellow-creature any longer; and I won't be the inhuman wretch to do it, cost what it may!" (183). He relinquishes Sue to Jude, and even Sue must admit, "He's a good fellow, isn't he!" (191).[15] When Phillotson reenters the narrative years later, he is an object for pity more than terror. He is an "elderly man" with a "slovenl[y]" appearance who has lost his reputation and employment because of his scandalous divorce—an isolated and disempowered man "who was his own housekeeper, purveyor, confidant, and friend" (250).

Intergenerational sex with Phillotson is a method of self-flagellation for Sue and an opportunity for more sexual terror for the reader. Sue returns to Phillotson and asks that he take her back. Phillotson, naturally forgiving and likely lonely, "did more than he had meant to do" and kisses Sue on the cheek. Sue's reaction is strong and immediate: "Sue imperceptibly shrank away, her flesh quivering under the touch of his lips" (288). Hardy's descriptions of Sue's quivering flesh and Phillotson's "renascent" desire are meant to send shivers, and fantasies, through the reader, but the possibility of reading intergenerational sex as an abuse of male power is complicated. Phillotson is hurt by Sue's lingering "aversion" to him, and agrees to their remarriage only if Sue is certain. Moreover, even though he desires Sue sexually, he sees their remarriage primarily as an opportunity to improve his standing in the community, and he flatly tells Sue he will not demand his conjugal rights, promising, "I shan't expect to intrude upon your personal privacy any more than I did before" (293). Sue "brightens" at this clarification but later, when struggling over her feelings for Jude, decides she must consummate her remarriage to Phillotson as penance. Sue "begs" to be admitted into her husband's separate bedroom, and it is a nightmarish seduction that she conducts. He repeatedly protests that he does not want her "against [her] impulses," but Sue persists and eventually convinces him as he reflects on her "thin and fragile form" beneath her nightgown. He advances and Sue retreats in disgust until "Placing the candlestick on the chest of drawers he led her through the doorway, and lifting her bodily, kissed her. A quick look of aversion passed over her face, but clenching her teeth she uttered no cry" (316). When Jude learns of Sue's resumption of sexual relations with Phillotson, Jude cries, "And now the ultimate horror has come" (317).[16]

While *Jude the Obscure* plays on ageist stereotypes of sex between older men and younger women to effect this Gothic conclusion, the novel also connects much of the "horror" to social and religious doctrines surrounding marriage and divorce rather than attributing the abuse of power solely to aging masculinity. Sue is bound by conventions of matrimony and by realities of law despite her aspirations toward a "New Woman" ideal. She returns to Phillotson because she sees herself the victim of a divine persecution for her subversion of gender and marital norms in divorcing Phillotson and living with Jude; in her mind, the death of her children is a "judgment—the right slaying the wrong" (277). But if the social, religious, and legal customs that bind individuals in marriage are corrupt, then the January–May marriage becomes an easy means of highlighting broader issues in marriage. Although the January–May marriage is not entirely at fault, it contributes to the horror conveniently and in a well-established pattern. In *Jude*, crossing generational boundaries is problematic, and the January–May marriage's associations with sexual deviance lead to premature aging or death for everyone in the triangle. When Arabella visits Jude before his death, she calls him "old man" (295), and Mrs. Edlin describes Sue as "Years and years older than when you saw her last" at the close of the novel (324). Expected horrors that surround fears of the aging male body penetrating youth drive the plot, and it is impossible to read *Jude* thoroughly without considering its participation in the January–May marriage theme.

*Jude the Obscure* demonstrates how the January–May theme conceals Gothic elements, but perhaps more important, how the January–May marriage was already embedded in traditional Gothic forms. As I explained earlier, fear of older men and the contradictory economic and sexual powers and weaknesses they embodied were integral parts of Gothic tales from the eighteenth century. But an examination of the vampire motif as a dominant Gothic theme confirms how crucial age is to the Gothic's negotiation of gender and power. Throughout the nineteenth century, from Polidori's vampire, to Varney, to Dracula, the vampire motif allows for a January–May marriage that is consummated by blood rather than by religion and the state. Ageist fears rally against the gluttonous penetration of youth by one, in these cases, who is *hundreds* of years her senior, and these vampire stories provide a controlled medium for exaggerating, perpetuating, and regulating the horrors of aging, of power inequities, and of nontraditional sexual practices.

## VAMPIRES AND THE JANUARY–MAY MARRIAGE

After reading dozens of nineteenth-century January–May texts, I began to notice a number of similarities between narratives of intergenerational marriages and those of vampires. On the surface, these two themes seem to have little in common. However, they share several characteristics, and each displays an intertextual understanding of the expectations and conventions of the other tradition. Both themes work in excesses, in anachronisms, in sexual improprieties, and in triangular romances. Both themes respond to nineteenth-century fears of aging and the points through which aging can breach the boundaries of youth. I do not contend that all texts that take up the theme of the January–May marriage draw on the popularity of the vampire legend in nineteenth-century fiction. Comparing older husbands with bloodsucking monsters would certainly seem to undermine the objectives of texts wanting to reaffirm the paternal role of husbands, but texts that strive to project older husbands as villains have much to gain by drawing on connections between intergenerational relationships and the paranormal thirst for young blood. Arthur Gride in *Nicholas Nickleby*, for example, touches on the vampiric when he calls Madeline a "delicate morsel" (710) and fantasizes about devouring her. Vampires can be sympathetic figures, but the tradition also benefits from the rise of ageist fears that I have detailed and from the contrasting feelings of loathing and pity that accompany those fears. The nineteenth-century vampire legend likewise capitalizes, quite clearly, on the January–May marriage tradition in literature, and some vampire texts participate in the tradition to such an extent that they merit readings as January–May texts.

Several critics, most notably Carol Senf, James Twitchell, and Nina Auerbach, have described the evolution of the vampire figure throughout history and literature. Auerbach stresses the difference between different vampire characters and their correlation to different social and political movements, asserting that "there is no such creature as 'The Vampire'; there are only vampires" (5), but I find in nineteenth-century vampire narratives a remarkably similar interest in casting these monsters as aged creatures who strive to defy death through drinking blood. Vampires may vary, as do their motivations, weaknesses, and techniques, but they can be identified in the nineteenth century by their depictions as "old" as much as by their desire for blood.[17] Vampires need not be associated with old age; Twitchell explains that in folklore, vampires were dead bodies made to rise and attack because their souls were trapped in their bodies by the devil (7–10). It stands to reason that the deathlessness of vampires would lead to "old" vampires, even though, in earlier literature, old age is not an integral characteristic of the vampire. But early nineteenth-century literary and artistic depictions of vampires are clearly interested in how age works within the vampire motif.

Ageist fears are evident in Henry Fuseli's *The Nightmare* (1781), which Twitchell describes as a protovampiric image (24). The demonic figure's face is markedly wrinkled, and though his masculine body is largely shielded by darkness and his crouched position, his eye-catching grimace reflects an aged and toothless mouth (Figure 4.3). Associations between the demonic figure and old age increase as Fuseli's painting resonates within nineteenth-century culture. Twitchell explains how Fuseli's *Nightmare* spawns a number of

**Figure 4.3** *The Nightmare* by Henry Fuseli, 1781. Founders Society Purchase with funds from Mr. and Mrs. Bert L. Smokler and Mr. and Mrs. Lawrence A. Fleishman. Photograph © 2005 The Detroit Institute of Arts.

imitative images, including the 1830 illustration "Cauchemar" for a novel by Michel Raymond. In "Cauchemar," the male figure who sits on the female victim is even more clearly cast as aged than in Fuseli's *Nightmare*; his thin arms grasp at the unconscious woman's breast, and his wrinkled face leers lecherously down on her sprawled figure (Figure 4.4). Twitchell uses these illustrations to support his argument regarding the "sharpening of the vampire image . . . within the first fifty years of the nineteenth century" (29), but I want to further his claim by pointing to increasing interest in cultivating a horrific image of aging—specifically, a sexualized image that juxtaposes an

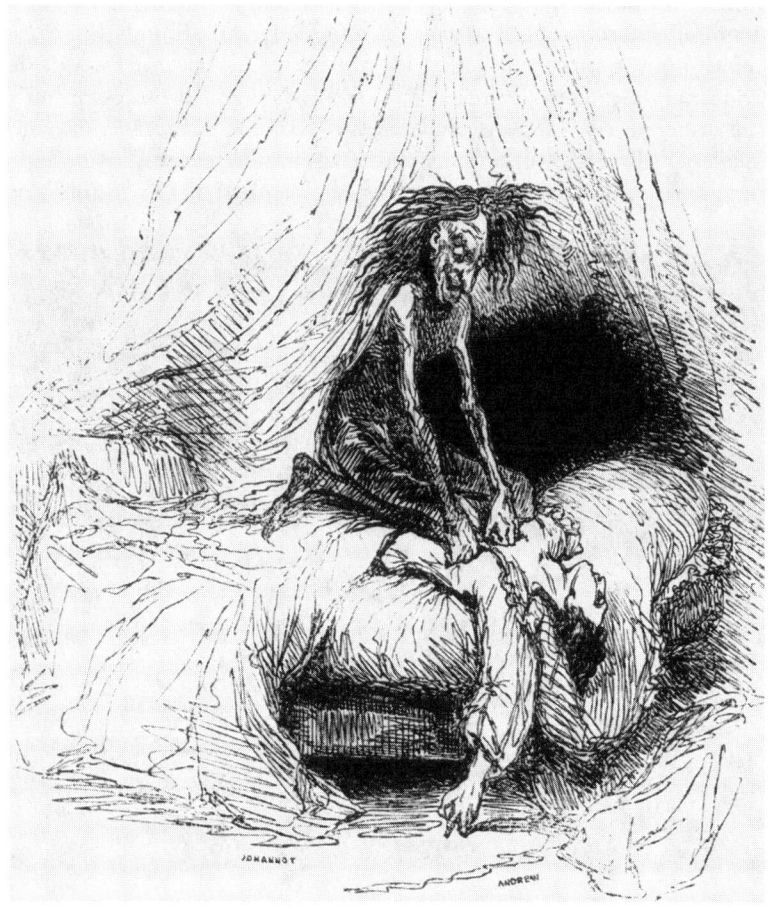

**Figure 4.4** "Cauchemar" by Anon. Book Illustration after Tony Johannot for a novel by Michel Raymond. University of Oxford, History of Art Department.

older male body with a younger female body. The "nightmare" that the Gothic vampire produces is distinctly erotic, as many critics like Eve Sedgwick and Judith Halberstam have already noted, but it is also distinctly coded by age, as one generation stands poised to penetrate the other either by tooth or phallus.

John Polidori's *The Vampyre* (1819) is one of the first substantial treatments of the vampire theme in British literature, and it reveals the growth of interest in teaming January–May dynamics with the monstrous. Beyond the nineteenth-century cultural impetus toward youth, Polidori privately fostered his own jealous admiration of an "older" and more powerful man, Byron, who became a model for Lord Ruthven, the vampire of his story.[18] Lord Ruthven is simultaneously attractive and repulsive; his "dead grey eye" and "the deadly hue of his face" contrast with the "beautiful" (3) form and outline of his body. Painting Byron with one foot in the grave gave Polidori more than a method for publicly ridiculing his nemesis from a safe distance; it established a correlation between the demonic and the necrophilic in vampire lore, and it lent to the emerging vampire tradition a slew of ageist associations that had already developed over centuries through the January–May theme.

Byron furnished much of the material for *The Vampyre* during the famous 1816 storytelling contest that led to Mary Shelley's *Frankenstein*, and Polidori's *The Vampyre* was first attributed to Byron. In June of 1816, Byron wrote a fragment of a novel very similar to Polidori's *The Vampyre*. In Byron's tale, the narrator's friend, the slightly older Darvell, suffers from a mysterious ailment. Though "in early life more than usually robust," Darvell "had been for some time gradually giving way, without the intervention of any apparent disease: he had neither cough nor hectic, yet he became daily more enfeebled . . . he was evidently wasting away" ("Augustus Darvell," 248). Darvell's inexplicable physical demise is remarkably similar to the premature decline of the young man depicted in *Le Livre Sans Titre*. Unfortunately, Byron leaves off his story before Darvell can rise as a vampiric masturbator.

Byron's brief reference to vampire lore in *The Giaour* (1813) does not dictate that the vampire be old or that the victim be young:

> But first, on earth as Vampire sent,
> Thy corse shall from its tomb be rent;
> Then ghastly haunt thy native place,
> And suck the blood of all thy race,
> There from thy daughter, sister, wife,
> At midnight drain the stream of life. (755–60)

In later lines, Byron lingers over the death of the Giaour's youngest child, but his inclusion of the victims "sister" and "wife," presumably similar in age to the Giaour, does not suggest a necessary age difference between the vampire and his victims. Thus, Byron adheres to the Greek belief that vampires devoured those closest to them as their first victims. But Polidori makes intergenerational coupling a vital part of the myth. Aubrey's love interest, the Greek maiden Ianthe, whom Polidori depicts as "an uneducated Greek girl," full of "innocence" and even "infantile" (10), becomes one of the vampire's victims, but not before she relates to Aubrey the legend of the vampire with distinct reference to the monster's age. As evidence of her story, she pointedly refers to specific "old men, who had at last detected one [a vampire] living among themselves" (9). To "prolong his existence for the ensuing months" (9), Ruthven seduces and replenishes himself with Ianthe and then with other young women. After Ianthe, he takes an "innocent, though thoughtless girl" (8) as his victim in Rome before focusing his attentions on Aubrey's eighteen-year-old sister.

Polidori heightens the nightmarish implications of the story by emphasizing age difference and by making Ruthven's advances toward Miss Aubrey more matrimonial than amorous in design, and these revisions are important. By the time he meets Miss Aubrey, Ruthven has already "ruined" several women, but has not yet found it necessary to attach himself in marriage to satisfy his desires. Ruthven's proposal of marriage ups the ante of horror by locating sexual perversion within the sanctity of marriage. Moreover, the conclusion situates the decision to allow a January–May marriage—and, in this case, the sexual perversion and death that accompany it—within a morally relative society. Miss Aubrey's January–May marriage to Ruthven is consummated because social and moral codes permit and require it: the marriage is wrong, but the alternatives are more wrong. Aubrey has promised not to reveal the vampiric identity of Ruthven until one year has passed since Ruthven's supposed death, and, because of this oath, Aubrey feels that he is unable to provide the evidence that will stop his beloved sister from marrying a vampire. When Aubrey considers breaking his oath to save his sister, Ruthven uses another social code against him. Warning Aubrey that his sister will be "dishonoured" if their engagement is broken, Ruthven insinuates that he has already had sexual relations with her. Aubrey is quick to believe Ruthven's assertion that "Women are frail" (22), and, to preserve his sister's honor, he fails to give the information that could save her. Polidori clearly intends his readers to writhe at the double bind Aubrey faces, and he frames the conclusion so that the January–May marriage and its horrors are the only moral solutions to the dilemma. Aubrey and the reader are forced by principle to consider the intergenerational "bride and bridegroom" on their honeymoon and to reflect on a union initially demanded by society and ultimately "solemnized" (23) by religion and the state.

Unsurprisingly, this January–May marriage proves destructive on multiple levels, and although *The Vampyre* critiques a system in which masculinity and age exploit power, these imbalances remain unchecked at the story's close, when Ruthven vanishes. The story may demonize old men, but in the end they are victorious, defeating young women and men. Aubrey's sister marries Ruthven, and symbolically penetrated by the vampire, Aubrey breaks a blood vessel in his frustrated, helpless condition and dies. *The Vampyre* therefore equivocates in the implications of its plot. When masculinity triumphs, it is bound with sexual perversity and aging, and the presumptive hero of the story dies an ineffectual and feminized death. The homoeroticism of Aubrey's figurative penetration by Ruthven, the depiction of marriage as an imperfect arrangement in an immoral world, and the criticism directed at abuse of masculine power also work subversively in the text. But the conclusion insinuates that abuses of gendered power will continue and captures the contrary incentives of the January–May marriage theme.

Although Polidori has been criticized as a fawning plagiarist of Byron, he moves the vampire legend beyond Byron's conception. Polidori's emphasis on age dynamics in the vampire narrative takes advantage of a synthesis of the aged and the monstrous that had already been festering in Gothic narratives and thereby influences the future of the vampire legend in nineteenth-century literature as an outlet for negotiating anxieties about gender and power through age.

In her preface to Devendra Varma's edition of *Varney the Vampyre*, Margaret Carter deems that "the fatal Lord Ruthven is the ancestor not only of Sir Francis Varney and Count Dracula, but of all the vampires who have since crept through the pages of English fiction" (xxxi). *Varney the Vampyre*, originally published serially as a penny dreadful in 1845, then issued in novel form in 1847, and Stoker's *Dracula* (1897) employ many of Polidori's details—the practice of biting victims on the neck, the power of moonlight, the vampire's superhuman strength—but what I find most interesting is that they incorporate and manipulate images of intergenerational sex. These mid- and late-nineteenth-century texts explain how vampires became increasingly associated with old age in literature and in the public imagination, and

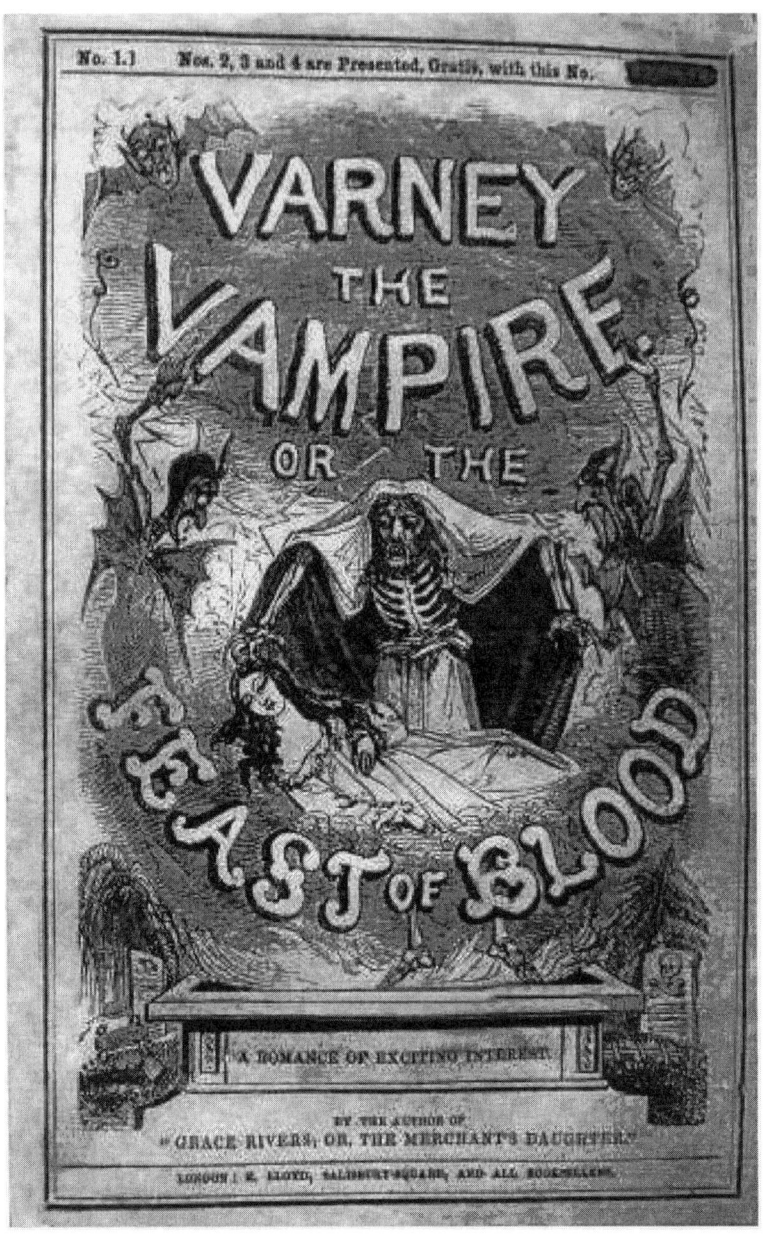

**Figure 4.5** *Varney.* Cover Art by Anon. Courtesy of Michael Holmes Collection.

how the January–May marriage theme works in conjunction with the Gothic tradition. *Varney the Vampyre* provides illustrations throughout the serial's publication to encourage shared visions of an old, even skeletal, vampire forcing himself on the body of a young woman, and the success of the serial cannot be separated from its participation in the nineteenth-century obsession with older man and younger woman relationships.[19] The cover snares readers' attention with the central image of the shrouded, deathlike figure hovering menacingly over the sleeping figure of a young woman, and if the novel's subtitle, *A Feast of Blood*, or its promise to be "A Romance of Exciting Interest" failed to entice buyers to relinquish their pennies, the threat posed by an aged male looming over a defenseless female body was sure to draw a riveted audience (Figure 4.5). The bodies float over a bedlike crypt, and goblins and tombstones flank the image. Sex and death are inseparable, and the illustrations of Varney ravishing young women work with the text to conjure images that invite readers to condemn perverse sexualities while fostering mildly pornographic scenes of sexual aggression toward women.[20]

In one of the most extreme versions of a January–May relationship imaginable, Varney is a very old lover. Dating him through an old family portrait, characters in the novel guess Varney's age to be about 150, and the initial scene of his violation of Flora in Chapter 1 stresses the signifiers of aging on his body. As she crouches in bed paralyzed by fear, she hears his "long nails, that appear as if the growth of many years untouched" scratching on the windowpane before "a long gaunt hand, which seems utterly destitute of flesh" (3) creeps into her bedroom. Soon, "a hissing sound comes from the throat of the hideous being, and he raises his long, gaunt arms—the lips move" (4). Flora tries to move away, but Varney drags her by her hair back to the bed, where he runs his "glassy, horrible eyes" over her "beautifully rounded limbs" with "hideous satisfaction" (4) before he bites her neck. The opening illustration for Chapter 1 shows Flora sprawled upside down across her bed with her leg cocked. Varney conveniently manages to grasp her breast while en route to her neck, keeping one hand and leg poised toward the window for a quick getaway from the scene of his crime while his victim struggles ineffectively (Figure 4.6).[21]

This image of vampiric rape proposes that old age is both the agent and the result of sexual sin, and because vampirism is infectious, once

Figure 4.6  *Varney*. Art from Chapter 1 by Anon. © British Library Board. All Rights Reserved C.193.a.26.

bitten, Flora faces the prospect of becoming a vampire and suffering its age-associated curses. Indeed, focusing outside of the text to examine the effects of Varney on the reading public, one can see the correlation between the fear of perversion and the fear of aging through such an illustration; because of the misinformation promoted by antimasturbation literature, an image of an "old" vampire groping a young woman could provide cheap masturbatory material for a young person who fears that premature aging could be the likely result of the solitary vice. Although the image of Varney ravishing Flora urges that standards of normalcy like youth and sexual propriety need to be protected, it also promulgates desire and thereby destroys the possibility of security. Chapter 1 ends with this image of Flora's body about to be penetrated by Varney's, and the horror that this narrative has taken as its theme inspires fear and awe.

Certainly, through such scenes *Varney* participates in an earlier nineteenth-century movement, which Diane Long Hoeveler identifies in *Gothic Feminism* as the "gendering [of] victimization" (51), but what is happening in this image and in this novel moves beyond a fixation on the violence against women that is undoubtedly present in the text. Varney's signs of aging intensify the perverse but also signal a parallel social investment in violence against the aging male body. Even in his daylight identity as Sir Francis, Varney finds his aged body marginalized by Flora's brother Henry and her lover Charles, who both represent standard masculinity and normative sexuality, and Varney's place outside of masculine conventions and the public demand for his death feminize him as he emerges as a potential victim. If Varney is at first the "hunter," he becomes the "hunted" as young male characters in the novel and the readers' collective resentment unite to seek his destruction, and the plot thrives on moments that envision the penetration of his aged body. For example, an angry mob storms Varney's house, driving a stake through a dead male body that they assume to be one of Varney's victims along the way. The image of the stake in this dead body captures the mob's sexual desire to violate Varney, even though the text carefully constructs the mob as ignorant, riotous, and even "maniacal" (216).

*Varney* eventually solicits readers' sympathy for Varney's persecution, and the conflicting tendencies to demonize and victimize the vampire parallel similar propensities to ridicule and sympathize with older husbands in nineteenth-century literature. *Varney* cultivates contradictory urges to kill and to save its protagonist throughout the novel. Again and again, the plot leads to scenes in which Varney is trapped by the representatives of civilization that surround him, only to delight readers with his narrow escapes. These tantalizing episodes in which the monster is almost captured and disempowered are unbelievably fantastic, though the supernatural elements of the Gothic and readers' ambivalent feelings about Varney encourage a willing suspension of disbelief that permits such elusiveness. In one scene, townspeople surround Varney and are ready to annihilate him, but he charms them with his "gentlemanly and collected behavior" (228) before he gets away. Even the main characters opposed to Varney begin to sympathize with his position at certain points. Immediately after a physical struggle between himself and Varney, Henry awaits the mob's search for the vampire with "a strange mixture of feeling" (191). While Henry recognizes that the "destruction of Sir Francis Varney" would be for the greater good, he recoils "with horror from seeing even such a creature as Varney sacrificed at the shrine of popular resentment, and murdered by an infuriated populace" (191). Henry's "generous nature" senses the power inequities that characterize this unified attack on a single representative of aging masculinity, and against his reason, he cries, "I do hope, after all, the vampyre will get the better of them. It's like a whole flotilla attacking one vessel" (191).

Sympathy for Varney becomes so central to the story that the text toys with the idea of advocating the marriage between the young heroine Flora and the aged vampire, and *Varney* suggests that a January–May love can free the vampire from his curse. This move has provocative implications, since it implies that legitimizing the sexually "perverse," as the text presents Varney's relationship with Flora, is a method for coping with sexual deviancies. If marriage contains sexually deviant behavior, perhaps it can also control it. Varney expresses his disgust at the "hateful" condition that forces him "in a paroxysm of wild insanity" to need "the gushing fountain of another's veins" (157). He begs Flora to accept his proposal, because "if we can find one human heart to love us, we are free" (156). Flora refuses Varney's "horrible proposition," but she realizes that her inability to love him will likely lead to a chain of destruction as Varney remains "doomed yet, perhaps, for many a cycle of years, to spread misery and desolation around me" (157). While Varney is initially angry that Flora refuses, he quickly accepts her rejection and even instructs her how to escape from him. Thus, Flora's denial of Varney's salvation and his resigned acceptance of his plight increase pity for his cursed condition. Moreover, as Varney continues his pursuit of a young woman's "true love," the text raises questions of moral relativism when the sexual marketplace shades his January–May engagements with more mercenary bloodsucking. Subsequent volumes show Varney on the verge of marriage to several young women whose families are conveniently focused on his financial worth rather than his undead body. Varney's ulterior motives for intergenerational marriage appear benign, even meritorious, compared with those who orchestrate marriages for monetary gain, and readers vacillate between desire and disgust for these potential intergenerational unions.

By evoking readers' sympathy for the sexually deviant, *Varney* presses the vampire legend even closer to the theme of the January–May marriage. Varney escapes those who want to kill and control his aging body by committing suicide—jumping dramatically into Mount Vesuvius in a final act of defiance over his physical body and his cursed desire for young women. By the end of the novel, readers are as much sorry as relieved to see him go, a sentiment that Bette B. Roberts endorses in her essay "*Varney, the Vampire*, or, Rather, *Varney*, the Victim." She describes Varney as a character "whose name inspires more a smile than a shiver" (1).

Although Bram Stoker's *Dracula* is unquestionably darker and more threatening than *Varney*, the late-nineteenth-century vampire encompasses the same ambivalent feelings about the sexual deviancy of January–May relationships. What Dracula wants to do to young women is awful, but the text nevertheless encourages some degree of commiseration for the aging male body even as it urges its destruction.

Stoker's *Dracula* more than any of its predecessors emphasizes the appearance of the vampire as an elderly man. When Jonathan Harker details in his journal his first glimpse of Count Dracula as the door to the castle swings open, the sketch he provides uses age as a method of recalling a visual stereotype, and what will later be a sexual signifier. He writes, "Within, stood a tall old man, clean-shaven save for a long white moustache, and clad in black from head to foot, without a single speck of colour about him anywhere" (21). Although Dracula appears much younger when he later arrives in London, the reader is encouraged to think of him as an old man from his introduction, and Stoker emphasizes Dracula's advanced years throughout the initial depiction of his character so that his aged body becomes a vital component of his character. Harker explains that the "old man motioned me in" (22), and later qualifies his description of the ruddy color of Dracula's lips with the phrase "in a man of his years" (23–24). What follows Harker's entrance to the castle is a detailed analysis of the aging—as the Undead, or Almost Dead—male body. Though Dracula's grip is powerful, it is "as cold as ice—more like the hand of a dead than living man" (22). His eyebrows are "very massive," with "bushy hair that seemed to curl in its own profusion" (23). And Harker can't help but record that Dracula's "breath was rank," so revolting that "a horrible feeling of nausea came over me, which, do what I would, I could not conceal" (24). Harker has secured an "old and big" estate for Dracula to inhabit in England, but the anachronism of Carfax's setting diminishes in importance compared to the anachronism of Dracula himself, who readily admits to Harker, "I seek not gaiety nor mirth, not the bright voluptuousness of much sunshine and sparkling waters which please the young and gay. I am no longer young" (29). Dracula's insinuation that he is a benign and resigned elderly man is, of course, false. While he does not seek the same things as the young, he seeks the young themselves, and his need for intergenerational commingling and the power that he derives from it drive the terror of the plot.

When Dracula repeatedly refers to Harker as "my dear young friend" and "my good young friend" (37–38), he stresses the worth of the youthful body he plans to possess and enjoy.[22] The reason Dracula needs young blood remains unclear in the text, and throughout nineteenth-century vampire lore, the unstated bias toward young blood seems so explicit that it requires no explanation. Apparently, young blood is the secret to restoring youth as well as prolonging life because youth is associated with power throughout the text. The "weird sisters" find that Harker is "young and strong," and consequently reflect age-based stereotypes of sexual potency in speculating that "there are kisses for us all" (42). When Lucy requires a blood transfusion to save her life, Arthur volunteers to donate his blood, not because he is her fiancé, but because he is "younger and stronger" (113). During the transfusion, the value of young blood is reaffirmed. Van Helsing remarks with surprise that Arthur "is so young and strong and of blood so pure that we need not defibrinate it" (114).

Young blood supplies an indefinable something that vampires need, and when Harker first discovers that Dracula's successful exploits make him younger, the anachronism of youth and age culminates within the vampire's body. Investigating Dracula's "great box," Harker finds a body that defies age categorization: "There lay the Count, but looking as if his youth had been half renewed, for the white hair and moustache were changed to dark iron-grey; the cheeks were fuller, and the white skin seemed ruby-red underneath" (53). Dracula is younger, and as such, more powerful; however, the real horror of the novel is that this unnatural power of youth is assumed by an "old man" through his sexual deviancy.

Though earlier vampire texts stressed the necessity of blood to prolong life, and Le Fanu's "Carmilla" (1872) reveals how vampirism can make a woman who is 150 years old look attractive and young, *Dracula* stresses youth as a visual barometer of sexual deviance. Rejecting the myth of bodily decline through sexual perversion that antimasturbation texts like *Le Livre Sans Titre* tout, *Dracula* counterintuitively suggests that if sexual perversity can lead to premature aging and death, then more sexual perversity might be the solution to securing another chance at youth. When in pursuit of Dracula in London, Harker hears a carter's description of Dracula as "a old feller, with a white moustache," and Harker is "thrilled" (231) that Dracula has apparently not found a recent victim. Yet moments when Harker sees Dracula with his white hair turned "iron-grey" promote the troubling idea that a false youth can disguise true age. Indeed, it is the shock of the transformation from an elderly man appearing to be young, the implication that he has revived himself by blood, and the deceptiveness of such false appearances that terrify Harker when he first sees him in London: "I believe it is the Count, but he has grown young. My God, if this be so! Oh, my God! my God!" (155). Dracula's appearance is indicative of his unnatural acts, and although he is a much more sinister figure than Varney, his ability to bend age, and later, gender norms, by pointing to the theatrical nature of appearances is so subversive that it is terrifying.

Age penetrates youth not only through the aged body of Dracula but also through the text's treatment of his peculiar January–May "marriage" to Mina Harker when the sharing of blood makes them representative of the "one flesh" associated with a married couple. Already, *Dracula* flouts orthodox notions of marriage. Lucy's often-cited suggestion: "Why can't they let a girl marry three men, or as many as want her, and save all this trouble?" (60) has provided material for a number of gender critiques of the novel, and Robert Tracy identifies the polygamous union that Dracula shares with Mina: "If Lucy has five husbands, and Dracula five wives, Mina has six husbands, the five crusaders and Dracula" (46).[23] Mina takes a blood oath when Dracula drinks her blood, and she reciprocates the act by drinking blood from his chest; according to Tracy, Mina is very much Dracula's "wife." This January–May union, made while Harker sleeps beside them on the bed, overrides the same-age marriage Mina has with Harker until Dracula's death. Corruption and sexual perversion overshadow the sanctity of marriage, and Mina laments that she is "Unclean, unclean!" and can "touch [Harker] or kiss him no more" (248).[24]

This January–May union troubles gender and age identities on multiple levels, and it becomes the central component in a larger vie for power. Intergenerational sex becomes a strategic method of power that the old (Dracula) can exercise over the young (Harker). In this sense, the young wife is the sexual prize in a male-male intergenerational competition. Dracula articulates this perspective, tying his struggle specifically to his age: "My revenge is just begun! I spread it over centuries, and time is on my side. Your girls that you love are mine already; and through them you and others shall be mine—my creatures, to do my bidding and to be my jackals when I want to feed" (267). The "girls" are the point of entry into the power realm of the young, but the January–May marriage provides a means to further homoerotic desires. In *Dracula*, the homosociality of the relationship between the older and younger men in the January–May triangle is more explicit than in most examples in the tradition. When he saves Harker from the weird sisters' attempts to kiss him, Dracula unabashedly identifies Harker as an object of his sexual desire, saying "in a soft whisper" that "I too can love" (43).[25] Consequently, the January–May marriage seems a convenient method to bring old and young male bodies together as though the ultimate objective of the heterosexual January–May union is to effect a homosexual end: "through them you and others shall be mine" (267). Dracula's intergenerational penetration of Mina, and conversely, her intergenerational penetration of him, also initiate a potential for sympathy, even empathy, with the sexually perverse. Dracula deems Mina "flesh of my flesh; blood of my blood, kin of my kin" (252), and as his wife, she shares his thoughts and experiences—a method for important moments of reconciliation with the aging male body, as well as the means for its destruction.

Because Mina now shares Dracula's understanding of nontraditional sexualities, she pities him, and she pleads the case of her older husband to those who seek his destruction. She reasons that the "poor soul who has wrought all this misery is the saddest case of all. Just think what will be his joy when he too is destroyed in his worser part that his better part may have spiritual immortality" (269). She urges Jonathan that the group "must be pitiful to him too, though it may not hold your hands from his destruction" (269). Since youth and age are so confused through the vampire's anachronism, in this January–May triangle, Harker even assumes the jealous position of a threatened older husband. Mina reminds the reader of the premature "poor white hairs" that serve as "evidence of what [Harker] has suffered," and when Harker damns Dracula's soul, Mina recoils with "fear and horror" (269) that Harker's wrath would be so severe on her and her lover. Although Mina is an "outcast from God" because of her unclean state, she nonetheless appeals to Christian forgiveness and redemption for herself as well as Dracula. She begs, "Oh, hush! oh, hush! in the name of the good God. . . . I have been thinking all this long, long day of it—that . . . perhaps . . . some day . . . I too may need such pity; and that some other like you—and with equal cause for anger—may deny it to me!" (269). Mina's moral superiority identifies her as the classic Victorian heroine, but her affinity with Dracula by way of sexual transgressions shifts perspectives of gender and age. Her plea demands sympathy with the aging body of Dracula, just as Harker's aging body solicits compassion, and Mina's wifely request exonerates Dracula by granting him the possibility of a spiritual salvation. Because she has been infiltrated by and has infiltrated the aging male body, her interests are now vested with Dracula's.

The disintegration of Dracula's body at the end of the novel caters to cultural fears of aging and death, but instead of restoring youth and age, masculinity and femininity, to conventional boundaries, the disappearance of his body encourages further confusion of age and gender identities. Mina watches her same-aged husband plunge a knife into the "deadly pale" throat of her January husband while another young man thrusts a knife into his heart, but these vengeful penetrations of age by youth do not lead to stability. Apart from the homoerotic implications of such acts that I alluded to earlier, Nina Auerbach and David J. Skal note that Dracula's "supposed" death is "riddled with ambiguity" (325) rather than resolution, and Stoker purposefully left the conclusion open by removing a paragraph in which Dracula's castle explodes in answer to his death. Dracula's "dissolution" instead of his death leaves gender and age categories unfixed. Mina describes a look of "triumph" in his eyes before the knives enter his body, and judges that in this moment of intergenerational, transgendered penetration, there is a kind of "peace" (325).

Thus, while *Dracula* participates in a larger nineteenth-century horror of the aging male body and intergenerational and deviant sexualities, the novel resists static formulations and instead draws attention to bodies that fracture such divisions. The birth of Mina's child that concludes the novel is Dracula's as well as Harker's; the child's body contains the blood of all three parental bodies, and—through the novel's sexual history of transfusions and suckings—the blood of other parents who are male and female, young and old as well.[26] The veneer of security that *Dracula* leaves at its conclusion is all too thin, and perhaps this is where the real horror of the novel lies. Beneath the nineteenth-century hostility toward aging runs a concurrent sympathy with the aged fostered by those who, like Mina, see the interests of the old and the young as intertwined. Vampire lore and January–May marriages express both animosity and longing toward intergenerational union.

# Chapter 5

## Sexual Economies and the January–May Marriage

### Money Matters:
### Valuing Youth/Valuing Age

A study of January–May marriages must consider the sexual economies contributing to the control and exchange of power in the marriage market. Since the age of Chaucer, literature has fulfilled tacitly understood social expectations of the exchange of youth for material wealth. Even in contemporary society where women have made enormous strides in professional fields, depictions of January–May romances frequently hinge on an economic framework and depict beautiful young women, like Anna Nicole Smith, marrying rich old men. Operating by way of a parodic rendering of the American family, the film comedy *Addams Family Values* (1993), for example, has Debbie the governess (known to police as the "black widow" because she has married and buried several husbands) wed the primordial Uncle Fester, and her gold digging is clear to all, even children in the audience, who recognize a familiar social exchange of youth and sex for money. The sexual economies of these marriages remain commonly accepted today, but nineteenth-century social conditions made these marriages even more conspicuous. In *The Culture of Love*, Stephen Kern writes, "Compared with twentieth-century women, young Victorian women had fewer educational and professional opportunities and were therefore more susceptible to parental or social pressures to marry older men for the money and security that they could not provide for themselves" (384). Responding to these conditions,

January–May marriages comment on a historical social dynamic and recognize an extensive male economic privilege. Money corresponds with masculinity, but age complicates that gender division by emphasizing other values in the sexual market. If it is money and not masculinity that matters in the nineteenth century, then men's hold on power is tenuous at best. Power passes easily from young to old, old to young, men to women.

In the nineteenth century not all marriages, nor even all January–May marriages, were made for the wife's economic convenience, although the general literary emphasis on the financial aspects of January–May relationships indicates an underlying desire for such a pat and controllable explanation of intergenerational romance. But material interests alone cannot capture the motives for a broad trend in marriage. If money resides at the base of each and every January–May marriage, there is no need to confront hidden agendas of incest, aesthetics, or horror. Such a reductive reading denies the complexities of January–May marriages. Though women were largely unequal participants in the nineteenth-century economy, they were not always financially disadvantaged. Reversing the theme's gender and financial norms in Wilkie Collins's *The Woman in White*, Sir Percival Glyde marries Laura Fairlie, who is twenty-four years younger, not for her youth and beauty, but for her money, and his surprisingly nonsexual incentive increases the sensational peculiarity and criminal motivations surrounding his marriage. In other novels, money appears to be of little concern in the selection of husbands. Eliot's Dorothea Brooke, Trollope's Eleanor Bold, and Austen's Emma Woodhouse represent young wives who marry older men for love, a freedom of choice their own financial independence allows.

Before I turn to January–May love in the final chapter, I explore here the exchange of youth for money that answers readers' expectations regarding these relationships. Yes, women marry old men for money. Some authors suggest this motive is acceptable; others balk at the corruption. Unfortunately, regardless of position, assumptions about this market have become so familiar that they are taken for granted and hence misunderstood. Because the traffic in young women has been so prevalent in Western society and its literature, readers must first defamiliarize January–May texts from a male-dominated sexual economy to theorize about their commentaries on money, age, and gender. Gayle Rubin describes the traditional exchange of women as a system in which "women are the gifts . . . it is men who are the exchange partners" (542), and while she illuminates how economic, psychological, and kinship systems support this male-controlled market, the emphasis on age in January–May texts reveals how these interrelated systems also contribute to a traffic in men. Although some texts do present the January–May exchange as a bad bargain for women, which relegates them to powerless and objectified positions, other works emphasize masculinity, or the lack thereof, as the commodity that can be bought and sold. And when women like Jane Eyre or Lady Audley settle their own engagements to older men, they challenge a masculine economy in which fathers or father figures orchestrate family connections, and thus young brides emerge as active negotiators who control their own sexual assets in the marriage contract. Rather than serving as evidence of a hegemonic system of women's oppression, January–May marriages estimate men's precarious worth in a nineteenth-century economy in the full bloom of industrial capitalism and its alienations. In this new economy, age increasingly reappraises notions of value, class, and gender. Most important, mercenary January–May marriages maintain that money trumps masculinity in power—a jaded claim, but a pragmatic and ultimately subversive one. Second, in emphasizing economic considerations, these relationships correlate marriage with work—in effect, marriage with prostitution. Both conclusions undermine marriage as an untainted foundation of society and masculinity as an automatic means to power.

The economic climate of the nineteenth century legitimized marriages between older men and younger women as a necessary component of financial security and social mobility. As economic expansion raised the expectations of many in the middle class and increased living expenses, more and more men waited until later in life to marry.[1] Austen's Emma tells Harriet that Robert Martin, who is twenty-four, must wait at least six more years to garner the financial capital to be a respectable husband: "that is as early as most men can afford to marry, who are not born to an independence. Mr. Martin, I imagine, has his fortune entirely to make—cannot be at all beforehand with the world" (30). Pushing Harriet toward the prospect of Mr. Elton, Emma presents a bourgeois family model for the upwardly mobile like Harriet to emulate, part of a larger political pattern of transcribing middle-class values on the working class that Nancy Armstrong traces in the nineteenth-century novel (19–26). Although sporadic recording of men and women's ages at marriage during the nineteenth century prevents an accurate summary of real-life January-May marriages, J. A. Banks claims that the average age for middle- and upper-class men between 1840 and 1870 was just under thirty years (48), and N. F. R. Crafts explains that men were often expected to be three to seven years older than their wives (21–25). Pat Jalland finds that upper-middle-class women were often significantly younger than their husbands, and that a twenty-five-year difference was not uncommon between spouses (79–84). Indeed, in nineteenth-century literature interclass and intergenerational relationships thrive in this booming middle class, and one may draw parallels between the growth of the middle class and the prevalence of literary age-disparate marriages.[2] In literature and life, many older middle-class men found that they could afford the luxury of a young working-class bride if she could expect to find her class position significantly raised, and records of breach-of-promise suits indicate that many middle-class men married much-younger women in their domestic employment.[3]

Nineteenth-century literary treatments of the January–May theme depict the marriage partners within a distinctly gendered economy. Limited options for education and employment and inequities grounded in property law forced women, especially middle-class women and those striving to be middle-class, to regard marriage to well-to-do men as the key to their financial security. Of this trend, Michael McKeon observes that among the middle class the "decrease of female employment in the latter half of the eighteenth century is closely correlated with a rise in fertility, whose principal causes are a fall in the age of women at first marriage and a rise in the number of women who married" (299). Unsurprisingly, in novels like Braddon's *Lady Audley's Secret* and J. Sheridan Le Fanu's *The Wyvern Mystery* (1869), the wife enters the plot in a lower social station than her future husband, often as a governess or dependent ward, and gains fortune and status through her marriage to an older man. This structure, however predictable, dictates that the commodities of age and money can be interchanged and exchanged, and society thus encourages the negotiation of gendered power.

Men of all ages found themselves under increasing pressure to bring a sense of financial security to relationships in the midst of higher standards of living, but instead of unifying masculinity with a "natural" responsibility to provide and protect, the emphasis on affluence further fragmented the idea of masculinity as a marker of an empowered identity. In an increasingly material culture, society esteemed power affiliated with wealth and rank over power linked to a masculine physical body. While the economic system kept riches mostly in male hands, images of older men marrying younger women conveyed the message that it was not manliness that afforded power. Older, often effeminized men repeatedly challenged and triumphed over their younger, more masculine rivals in January–May texts and revealed the disconnect of power from the body. Manliness loses viability when compared to the power of money, and the inherent transferability of wealth reinforces the elusive nature of the phallus; that is, January–May marriages prove that power is not intrinsic to maleness when financial power finds its way into the hands of young women. In a culture fascinated with rags-to-riches stories like *Great Expectations*, the dual realization that embodied masculinity could be supplanted by disembodied fortune and that fortune was a genderless vehicle for power alternately presents a threatening or liberating take on gender, depending on one's personal investment in maintaining male privilege.

In John Everett Millais's drawing *Married for Rank* (1853), financial clout is stronger than traditional male power (Figure 5.1). Though the drawing appears to be a conservative critique of feminine influence, in highlighting the January–May marriage as a source of social insecurity, it attests to the disruptive effects of age and class on gendered identities. Capturing the couple, apparently recently wed, joining a social gathering, the sketch relies on cultural assumptions about age for its meaning. If the husband were depicted as young rather than elderly, the insinuation that the wife has "married for rank" would be lost. The drawing operates from a mutual understanding engendered by their age difference and the shared logic—however biased against the elderly—between artist and viewer that there are no qualities present in the husband other than his social position that could possibly attract such a woman. The rest of the image completes the already implicit interpretation. In contrast with the other men in the image, the older husband conveys few markers of physical masculinity. His stature, stooped through age, is more diminutive than that of the other men in the room, and his wife towers above him as he deferentially nods to his host. The drawing suggests that while he extends his arm to lead his wife into the room, he is not supporting but rather being supported by his wife. While the host whispers his congratulations to the husband, the wife haughtily poses in her glory. With raised chin, she ignores the numerous sets of male eyes directed toward her and allows a young gentleman to scrutinize the ring, presumably large, on her finger. It is important to note how the wife's successful exchange of youth for affluence marginalizes the established representatives of masculinity to the peripheries of the scene. Beneath the drawing's bitterly misogynistic message that women craftily plot advantageous marriages resides the unsettling idea that masculinity does not guarantee access to power or to what one desires. Instead,

**Figure 5.1** *Married for Rank* by John Everett Millais. Courtesy of Nicolette Wernick.

masculinity appears as a disenfranchised presence, dislocated by both the older husband's effeminacy and the wife's assumption of control. Even the title, *Married for Rank*, hints at the limitations of masculine advantages. Though the wife seems to be objectified by the male gazes surrounding her and the sexual economy that encourages an exchange of oneself for financial and social gain, she does not remain in an object position. The title stresses her agency in the marriage decision; she has elected to marry for rank, and it is her subjectivity that resonates in the image, since viewers are never encouraged to consider the husband's perspective with a title like *Married for Beauty*, or, more crassly, *Married for Sex*. Even a romantic revision of the image entitled *Married for Love* would decrease the subjectivity of the wife; while she inhabits a pragmatic position in *Married for Rank*, an image of the younger wife marrying an older man for love might suggest she has been swept off her feet, passively submitting to her emotions despite the numerous reasons against such a marriage. In Millais's drawing, the wife occupies the central position, and the lines of her dress and stretched arms work in conjunction with the light coloring of her costume to illuminate her from the darker, less important figures around her. If Millais intends the drawing to delimit femininity to an object of male exchange, he loses control of his mission and instead reveals a mounting anxiety about the role of female choice in marriage.

Similar patterns of insecurity surrounding the prerogatives of women surface in Charles Darwin's theories of natural selection.[4] Darwin would graft middle-class ideals of masculinity and femininity onto his theories of evolution, often contradicting himself to create a system, in which males selected their female mates, that would agree with biological evidence to the contrary. Although Darwin concludes that in the animal kingdom female selection encourages the propagation of the strongest, most attractive males, he finds this system of female agency conflicts with a human mating system in which, he believed, females were naturally passive and inferior. He reasons that among the European aristocracy, male selection of the most attractive females over successive generations has resulted in the physical superiority of the aristocracy as a whole, yet he finds little scientific evidence to support this shift from female agency in animals to male agency in humans.[5]

Although the problematic logic supporting masculine authority reveals its inherent weaknesses, Darwin's theories and Millais's drawing both attempt to convey the notion that men control the mating process and women are bought and sold for their beauty. While the selection of wives—and in the case of January–May marriages, young wives—plays an important part in the nineteenth-century sex market, prospective wives and husbands move in and out of subject and object positions within the exchange. In a society that esteems financial stability over physical prowess, a rich older husband could serve as a better mate for a woman than a penniless young lover, however gallant. The older husband's usefulness as economic provider becomes a commodity on par with the wife's aesthetic, sexual, and reproductive qualities. Granted, these kinds of marriages do not maneuver in a society in which women and men are equally empowered; women in the nineteenth century faced a multifaceted orchestration of male power. But within the male-dominated system, these marriages show where weaknesses in masculinity and gender identities reside. Rather than depicting a unidirectional traffic in women, some literary January–May marriages present a ruthless pecuniary system, far removed from an ideal of marriage solely for love, but a system that engages in the traffic of both genders nonetheless.

Several of the basic dynamics of the economies of age and money develop in Jane Austen's *Sense and Sensibility* (1811), which relates the story of the Dashwood women, who find themselves in financial straits after Mr. Dashwood's death.[6] Because Marianne faces such dismal prospects at securing her own financial security (as do all the women in the Dashwood family), the novel suggests that she must marry as well as she can. She initially hopes to marry for love, not for money, and Austen baits the reader and Marianne with the young, romantic figure of Willoughby. But her sister Elinor explains why Marianne's first love would have given her little security: "Had you married, you must have been always poor. His expensiveness is acknowledged even by himself, and his whole conduct declares that self-denial is a word hardly understood by him. His demands and your inexperience together on a small, very small income, must have brought on distresses which would not be the *less* grievous to you, from having been entirely unknown and unthought of before" (350). Despite Willoughby's numerous masculine traits, including his untamable and often inappropriate behavior, his financial instability removes him from a position of real power in the economy. The marriage of Marianne at seventeen to Colonel Brandon, who is "on the wrong side of five and thirty" (34) is, however, "an excellent match" (36) in the eyes of the affectionate busybody Mrs. Jennings, and by the end of the novel, even to Marianne herself.[7] As Elinor instructs Marianne, the novel similarly inculcates the reader to appreciate a practical approach to matrimony; on rational reflection, irrational love pales in comparison to the economic necessities of life. Much of the novel aims to prove that sense about financial realities should prevail over sensibility, affinities, or sexual desire in women's selection of marriage partners, because marriage remains one of the few means middle-class women have to control their economic futures.[8]

The excellence of the marriage prospect between Marianne and Colonel Brandon centers on the equivalency of the exchange, which must gauge the values of wealth, desire, and age. Mrs. Jennings's proclamation as matchmaker about the prospective contract makes more sense in its full context: "It would be an excellent match, for *he* was rich and *she* was handsome" (36). Yet, from the first proposition of the marriage, the age difference threatens to undermine the trade of wealth for beauty. When Marianne first understands what is being suggested, "she hardly knew whether most to laugh at its absurdity, or censure its impertinence, for she considered it as an unfeeling reflection on the colonel's advanced years, and on his forlorn condition as an old bachelor" (37). As a romantic, Marianne values her own youth and beauty far more than the age and wealth of Colonel Brandon, and she scorns him for being so "exceedingly ancient" (37). Even Elinor, the more practical of the sisters, views the age difference as a detriment, theorizing that "Perhaps . . . thirty-five and seventeen had better not have any thing to do with matrimony together" (37).

Despite Elinor's initial reaction, the story of Marianne and Colonel Brandon encourages the sisters and the novel's readers to question what stands as fair exchange in marriage. The novel foregrounds the contract of marriage as one that is open to discussion, especially on the terms of age-based desirability and money. In response to Marianne's abrupt dismissal of Colonel Brandon due to his age, Elinor proposes that a smaller age difference would even the scales and acknowledges that it is no more Colonel Brandon's age than Marianne's that poses a problem to their union. She concludes that theoretically it would be fine for him to marry a twenty-seven-year-old woman—supposedly less desirable than her younger counterpart and therefore more fitting in exchange for Brandon's advanced years. Like her sister, Marianne realizes that the terms of marriage are negotiable, but it is precisely the fiscal component of marriage that she detests. Displaying little sympathy for the imaginary twenty-seven-year-old or Colonel Brandon, Marianne clarifies that her reflection on, and rejection of, a marriage market that traffics in women *and* men informs her romantic preference for love and desire over pecuniary matters. Regarding the hypothetical marriage of the twenty-seven-year-old and Brandon, Marianne reasons, "if her home be uncomfortable, or her fortune small, I can suppose that she might bring herself to submit to the offices of a nurse, for the sake of the provision and security of a wife. . . . It would be a compact of convenience, and the world would be satisfied. In my eyes it would be no marriage at all, but that would be nothing. To me it would seem only a commercial exchange, in which each wished to be benefited at the expense of the other" (38). But as the plot unfolds, Marianne learns that even idealized romances must face economic realities. Because of his own straitened circumstances, Willoughby mirrors Marianne's feminized economic position, and despite his love for Marianne, marries Miss Grey for her fifty thousand pounds and casts himself as a kept husband. Marianne learns that money is a force behind marriage for both men and women—in the words of Mrs. Jennings, "when there is plenty of money on one side, and next to none on the other, Lord bless you!" (194).

Some critics characterize "the old bachelor" Colonel Brandon, with his rheumatism and flannel waistcoats, as due punishment for Marianne's youthful romantic inclinations.[9] While the novel suggests that Marianne has grown into a more realistic outlook on marriage, it never gives evidence that she suffers from her acceptance of Brandon's proposal. At the novel's conclusion, Austen reveals that Marianne grows to love the man "whom, two years before, she had considered too old to be married" (378) as much as she loved Willoughby. Moreover, instead of languishing from her rejection by Willoughby or struggling to make ends meet with her mother, Marianne finds herself "the mistress of a family, and the patroness of a village" (379). By first choosing financial stability, Marianne finds that a steady love follows, and Austen offers this rational ideal to her readers as a way to have the best of both love and money; however, it is clear that economic security is of primary concern and love but a bonus to the real contract. Thus, Austen's declaration that "Marianne Dashwood was born to an extraordinary fate" (378) must be read ironically. Marianne's fate, Austen asserts, is realized by all women who come to understand the mercenary dynamics of marriage. Retaining Marianne's initial objection to the "commercial exchange," Austen nonetheless shows how women can make the exchange to their advantage.

## Governesses, Wives, and Prostitutes: Marriage and Women's Work

The question posed by Eliza Lynn Linton in her 1868 article "What Is Woman's Work?" is central in the literature of the century; it connects gender to a larger social interest in understanding how gender and class roles could be defined, attained, and maintained. The rapid growth of industrialism in the eighteenth and nineteenth centuries encouraged a shift in labor markets, and, as I discuss in Chapter 1, the presence of women in factories and mines blurred traditional gender divisions.[10] Class boundaries likewise became less clear. Although some works like Matthew Arnold's *Culture and Anarchy* (1882) presented a social order neatly divided into the "populace," "barbarians," and "philistines," much of the literature from Austen to Stoker depicts permeable social groups that elude tidy classifications. Many nineteenth-century January–May texts tell of young women dangerously perched between middle-class respectability and working-class disgrace, but because society discouraged middle-class women from carving their success within the new economy, options for social betterment were limited to fantasies of inheritances from rich distant relatives or the more tangible reality of social climbing through marriage. Much of women's work depended, it seemed, on the success or failure of finding a good—that is, financially well-to-do—husband. Nineteenth-century literature captures the possibilities for social improvement by way of the romance narrative, and rags-to-riches stories through fortunate marriages inspired the dreams of many readers, while tales of treacherous interlopers into the middle class cultivated fears of social mobility. This larger theme continues in literary depictions of January–May marriages, where categories of women's work conspicuously mingle to create uncomfortable associations. As individuals exchange youth for money, governesses become wives, and wives appear as prostitutes—threatening the validity of marriage as an institution and the gender stability that marriage upholds.

Linton's question "What is woman's work?" withholds several related but unspoken queries, including "What is the middle class?" and "What is a woman/man?" Markers of class, gender, and labor became increasingly (con)fused, and women's work evolved into a class issue, as those aspiring to middle-class respectability began to see feminine idleness as a necessary display of financial security. Although nineteenth-century literature frequently portrays middle-class women as busy, their occupations are superfluous to their own households' domestic economies; they embroider, they minister to the poor, and they model feminine grace, but they do not work to contribute to their financial support or to the support of their families. McKeon observes, "At the higher social levels, the differential process of class formation led women (and men) who aspired to a proto-'bourgeois' gentility to value idleness in women. In such households, women's work was increasingly oriented toward female accomplishments, while cheap wage labor did what was once the inside work of wives" (299). These strictures on women's work served multiple purposes. They distinguished middle-class families from the working poor and aligned the middle class with upper-class idleness. They preserved a system of male economic privilege. And they merged beliefs about labor, class, and gender to help assuage escalating insecurities about sexual difference.

As the century progressed, increasing numbers of women objected to restrictions on women's financial independence. Florence Nightingale harshly criticizes the relegation of middle-class women to a life of leisure in *Cassandra* (1852) and asks angrily, "why is it more ridiculous for a man than for a woman to do worsted work and drive out every day in the carriage? Why should we laugh if we were to see a parcel of men sitting round a drawing-room table in the morning, and think it all right if they were women?" (123). Summarizing the social conditions that invalidated work for most women, Nightingale writes, "Widowhood, ill-health, or want of bread, these three explanations or excuses are supposed to justify a woman in taking up an occupation. In some cases, no doubt, an indomitable force of character will suffice without any of these three, but such are rare" (124). If women were unfortunate enough to lose their husbands, suffer from sickness, or find themselves destitute, they could work, but these conditions carried their own social stigmas, and consequently distanced women from middle-class respectability. Only a small percentage of middle-class women managed to merge their careers and class affiliations with success.

Limited educational opportunities for women and a legal system protecting men's control of finances fortified the social dishonor linked to women's work and ensured that middle-class women would have limited control of their economic well-being.[11] John Killham describes a paradoxical education system for women, in which they were trained to be active entertainers on the marriage market—singing, playing, drawing—only to find that as wives they were expected to assume positions of graceful idleness. Even in the late 1880s, women like Edith Simcox publicly debated the right of women to equal education and the right to seek employment outside the home. In "The Capacity of Women," Simcox describes the blighted education of "poor Miss Fairfax" and, foreshadowing Virginia Woolf's story of Judith Shakespeare in *A Room of One's Own*, details how girls are "choked off into contented obscurity in each case at an earlier stage of their intellectual development than would be the case with a boy of corresponding character" (592). Social expectations and restrictions thus led many middle-class women to believe that marriage was the key to their financial security, but this solution trapped women in an ironic double bind, since, for much of the nineteenth century, property law relegated a wife's possessions and earnings to her husband upon marriage. Few middle-class families could afford the costly legal measures required to designate a wife as a *feme sole*, and, under the system of coverture, women had no recourse through law to their material wealth. Effectually, for most of the century there was little sense in married women working to ensure their financial security, since they had no legal right to their earnings.[12]

Poor women could work because they had to, but were ideally restricted to a domestic realm of household chores and unpaid labor, and from a middle-class perspective, even poverty or "want of bread" proved to be insufficient reason for women to enter the public workforce, since female labor jeopardized stable constructions of the home as well as masculine and feminine identities. In "Nearing the Rapids," Linton, a vocal opponent of women's employment and increased women's rights, declares, "The more women are employed where men used to be the sole wage-earners, the fewer marriages there will be, and the yet more and more number of women will be left unprovided for. Women work for less than men, and undercut wages all round. Their employment necessitates the exodus of the stronger sex; and so the vicious circle goes, ever increasing in evil consequences to society" (383). For Linton, women's work alienated men and threatened marriage and society. Mary Poovey explains how working-class women's participation in the labor force formed a persistent point of anxiety for middle-class Victorians and their understandings of gender: "the increasing numbers of women entering the labor force and the threat they potentially posed to male employment was most often submerged in arguments about social stability, a natural division of labor, and the welfare of marriage as an institution" (*Uneven Developments*, 153). Because work was bound to deeply held notions of gender and class, a degree of gender bending was inherent to all women's work, and a series of legislative acts throughout the century consequently "protected" working-class women from working outside the home. Rough and physical labor was particularly dangerous to then-current notions of gendered realms, and reformers often attempted to keep women from participating in employment that emphasized the body or exposed them to aspects of life detached from the domestic realm. Labor unions forced women, who usually worked for lower wages, out of workplaces, and the regulation of women's vocations operated through several layers of society.

Through Parliament, the 1842 Mines Regulation Act restricted women's employment in underground mines, and both the Factory Act of 1850 and the Health of Women Act of 1874 limited the number of hours women could work in factories. While all of these measures appeared to hold the interests of women as their central concern, they imposed middle-class gender limitations on working-class women and reinforced the divisions of labor that kept women from financial independence. Furthermore, they operated through a unified tenet: working women were dangerous to existing gender identities, while idle married women preserved them.

Like the argument of Millais's drawing and Darwin's theories of gender differentiation, the binary dividing working women and married women contained the tools for its own dismantling, and the very system designed to maintain gender identities led to their further unraveling. If women's work challenged the gender identities of the middle class, then little could be done to ensure gender stability unless social and financial reforms could keep women from employment altogether or unless impermeable divisions could be erected between the classes. But neither of these solutions could be implemented. Some women did work, and when middle-class families fell into embarrassed circumstances or when working-class individuals found ways to break into the middle class, class and gender strictures on work became nebulous. Additionally, many middle-class women who did not marry early had to support themselves until they found husbands, or if they never married, to support themselves for the rest of their lives. Although the middle class would have preferred clear boundaries around the terms "working-class women" and "middle-class women," economic realities fostered a third category of "working middle-class women." Weakening these boundaries further, the idea of marriage as the most legitimate alternative to work paradoxically developed a troublesome equivalency between marriage and work. Two of the most disconcerting types of women's work for nineteenth-century society—being a governess and being a prostitute—offer direct correlations to being a wife.

The instruction of children was an ambiguous area of employment for women, and it provided work for women both on their way up and on their way down the social ladder. For a middle-class woman, being a governess signaled a loss in caste. Before her marriage, *Emma*'s Jane Fairfax woefully envisions that she will become a governess, and Anne Brontë's Agnes Grey stoically models the path chosen by countless unmarried middle-class women. Yet for a working-class woman, being a governess was a step up in society.

Traditionally, the aristocracy employed the unmarried daughters of the gentry in these positions, but by the 1840s, the rise of the middle class created new jobs for governesses, and many working-class women who could secure places in wealthy families viewed being a governess as an opportunity to interact with their social superiors.[13] Whether the governess was middle or working class, she challenged strictures on work. Governesses proved to be upsetting on yet another front. While the nature of governesses' work relegated women to the home and seemingly distanced them from the male economy, their paid labor made them disturbing models of femininity in middle-class homes. Mary Poovey asserts, "Because the governess was like the middle-class mother in the work she performed, but like both a working-class woman and man in the wages she received, the very figure who theoretically should have defended the naturalness of separate spheres threatened to collapse the difference between them" (*Uneven Developments*, 127). As keepers of middle-class children and thus keepers of the future, governesses exercised important influence and power on the middle class, and Poovey explains that middle-class parents desired to employ only middle-class women as guardians of their children because they feared working-class women would usurp their positions through marriage and disrupt middle-class stability. Unsurprisingly, several women from the fiction of the time, including Jane Eyre, Becky Sharp, Mary Lawrie, and Lucy Graham (Lady Audley), who enter or consider entering January–May marriages, find themselves among the middle class because of their positions as governesses. The age disparities in these relationships emphasize the economic structures hidden beneath sexual desire, since the large differences in age seem to justify a correspondingly large leap in wealth and position.

The valuation of the woman's youth originates from motivations both pleasurable and practical. Since the younger woman's age tests social taboos like incest, child molestation, and homosexuality, she provides a normalized point of access to otherwise deviant behaviors. Secondly, the younger wife's theoretically higher potential for reproduction gives her husband a greater likelihood of producing a male heir. In Austen's *Persuasion* (1818), for example, Anne Elliot is concerned about her father's relationship with her sister's young companion, the widow Mrs. Clay, because if they marry, a male heir could alter the sisters' inheritance. In Eliot's *Middlemarch*, Casaubon marries Dorothea to "leave behind him that copy of himself which seemed so urgently required of a man" (175). Thus, as both "babies" and "baby-makers," young wives were valuable commodities to older husbands.[14] The commercial reciprocity inherent in these relationships appears obvious, and, in one sense, age thereby rationalizes the overturning of class identities. Yet because class barriers also serve to demarcate notions of gender through women's work, the transgression of those boundaries, for desires or for legacies, is unsettling. Charlotte Brontë's *Jane Eyre* illustrates the efforts of women to maintain the guises of morality and respectability in a blatantly sexual economy. Characters accept youth and class as marketable wares in both of Rochester's romantic interests. Jane's initial rival for Rochester's affection, Blanche Ingram, is much younger than he, and the housekeeper Mrs. Fairfax explains her understanding that the age difference between Rochester and Blanche is clearly too great: "Oh! yes. But you see there is a considerable difference in age: Mr. Rochester is near forty; she is but twenty-five" (163). What compensates for the age disparity is Blanche's financial disadvantage. Blanche Ingram and Rochester belong to the same social class, but "neither she nor her sister have very large fortunes. Old Lord Ingram's estates were chiefly entailed, and the eldest son came in for everything almost" (163). When Rochester reveals his desire to make Jane his "girl-bride" instead of Blanche, Mrs. Fairfax is even more surprised by the greater disparity in age and position. Initially she tries to convince herself that she only dreamt Rochester told her he was to marry Jane, and she asks that Jane not laugh at her ludicrous query: "Now, can you tell me whether it is actually true that Mr. Rochester has asked you to marry him? Don't laugh at me. But I really thought he came in here five minutes ago, and said, that in a month you would be his wife" (262). In the following exchange, she expresses her incredulity, musing "he . . . has always been called careful" (262). Convinced of the offer at last, she discouragingly says, "there are twenty years of difference in your ages. He might almost be your father" (263). While Mrs. Fairfax seems naïve regarding the exchange of youth for wealth, she confirms Poovey's explanation that a governess "could not be trusted to regulate her own sexuality" when she knowingly warns Jane to "keep Mr. Rochester at a distance" (262) and voices her uneasiness at having found Jane and Rochester both missing the night before. For Mrs. Fairfax, Jane and Rochester's engagement seems the flaunting of a doubly violated social taboo in which class and age boundaries, and their accompanying gender norms, will be subverted through sexuality and legitimized through marriage.

The hitch in the marriage plot temporarily forestalls their wedding, though it reminds the reader of the economic implications of the match. Immediately after Jane learns of the existence of Rochester's first wife and Rochester proposes keeping Jane as his mistress, Jane decides to flee Thornfield because her knowledge ruptures the delicate boundary between legitimate and illegitimate sexual exchanges. What was already a socially precarious leap for Jane from her lower position as governess to a higher position as wife is now impossible. Rochester's attempted bigamy forces her recognition of their overt sexual exchange and taints both positions of governess and wife by equating them with common prostitution. Even Rochester places her departure in economic terms, suggesting that he can no longer pay enough for the "kisses" and "caresses" that are now "forbidden" (295). Hoping their relationship to be immune to base economics, he scathingly derides the terms he fears have led to their broken contract: "It was only my station, and the rank of my wife, that you valued? Now that you think me disqualified to become your husband, you recoil from my touch as if I were some toad or ape" (299). Without the social and legal legitimacy marriage gives, Jane knows that she risks collapsing the thin barriers between serving Rochester as his governess, serving him as his wife, and serving him as his personal prostitute. Because she desires to stay, she wrestles with her wishes and the uncertain future that a position as an unmarried woman would provide, and confirms her resolution to leave only after she hears Rochester's deprecating remarks about his former mistresses: Céline, Giacinta, and Clara. Rochester bought his way out of relationships with each of these foreign women. Of Clara, described as "singularly handsome" and "honest and quiet," he explains that "I was glad to give her a sufficient sum to set her up in a good line of business, and so get decently rid of her," and unashamed, he admits, "I now hate the recollection of the time I passed with [them]" (359). Jane can therefore envision no financial or emotional security as his prostitute, projecting that she will "become the successor of those poor girls" and that "he would one day regard me with the same feeling which now in his mind desecrated their memory" (308–9).

Convinced that her position would be precarious, Jane fortifies her resolution to leave by enlisting the social "laws and principles" that prohibit the exchange of money for sex. She declares she will "keep the law given by God; sanctioned by Man" (312), and she uses this dual system of morality and expediency to brace her will to leave and to clarify that she is not a mistress or a prostitute. Knowing that she will need money to remove herself from the area, she nonetheless leaves behind "the beads of a pearl necklace Mr. Rochester had forced me to accept a few days ago" (315). Though Jane nearly faces starvation on her journey because she has no money, the importance of reinforcing the boundaries between governess, prostitute, and wife dictates her actions. The risk Jane runs regarding her health and life might appear irrational, but it makes perfect sense to Jane, and Brontë intends readers to applaud Jane's decision to place herself in physical jeopardy rather than to blend willfully categories of women's work. It is not until Jane inherits her own fortune, and Rochester has lost much of his, that she can return to him and resume their relationship. The transgression of class boundaries resolves when Jane becomes his financial equal, and, like Emma Woodhouse and Dorothea Brooke, Jane can now afford to marry for love. Indeed, *Jane Eyre*'s success as a love story stems from Jane's return to Rochester despite the lack of financial necessity, and Jane's move from following reason to acting on emotion facilitates the sentimental ending that made the novel popular with nineteenth-century audiences but remains problematic to feminist readers today.

A look at one of the Victorian period's most infamous fictional governesses, Lucy Graham, exposes how the construction of femininity caves under the social pressures of distinguishing between governess, prostitute, and wife, as the age difference of the January–May marriage underscores the permeable boundaries between the three. On multiple levels, Mary Elizabeth Braddon's sensational thriller *Lady Audley's Secret* attacks Victorian assumptions about gendered identities, and while it conforms to the moral precept that murder will out, the novel strips away the illogic and hypocrisy disguising the sexual economies of marriage. In contrast to the helpless and vapid model of the angel in the house (like *The Woman in White*'s Laura Fairlie), Lucy Graham defies the expectations formed by her delicate, fair-haired, fair-skinned body to protect her position and revenge her desertion. *Lady Audley's Secret* shocks audiences with its unpleasant revelations about masculinity and femininity and its unflinching reflection of nineteenth-century sexual economies.

*Lady Audley's Secret* relates the rise and fall of Lucy Graham, a beautiful twenty-one-year-old governess for the Dawson family. In their employment, she comes into the society of Sir Michael Audley, a fifty-five-year-old baronet. He proposes to Lucy, and she rises considerably in her social position by becoming Lady Audley. Her "secret" is that she has already been married, though she has not heard from her husband in over three years. When her roaming first husband returns, the chain of violence begins, as she struggles to preserve her new position and separate herself from her past. The overwhelming influence of material wealth on the plot is unmistakable, but Braddon calls attention to the marriage market: "The truth was that Lady Audley had, in becoming the wife of Sir Michael, made one of those apparently advantageous matches which are apt to draw upon a woman the envy and hatred of her sex" (11). Because of Sir Michael's age (from his first marriage, he has a daughter, Alicia, only three years younger than Lucy), the marital bargain appears cut and dried; he will gain the sexual pleasure of a young wife, and she will gain the advantages of a higher station.

Braddon challenges reductive readings of the terms of this exchange, pointing out that it was only an "apparently" advantageous match. Instead of placing all of the blame on Lucy, as Millais attempts to do to the young wife in *Married for Rank*, Braddon holds Sir Michael responsible for his willing participation in the sexual exchange.[15]

Braddon succinctly establishes that sexual desire resides at the base of Sir Michael's "love" for Lucy. Her beauty, after all, is persuasive, and its powers are not limited to middle-aged men: "For you see, Miss Lucy Graham was blessed with that magic power of fascination by which a woman can charm with a word or intoxicate with a smile. Every one loved, admired, and praised her" (11–12). Although Lucy, quite disturbed, objects to the possibility that she could ever have knowingly encouraged Sir Michael's affections, he falls victim to her charms, and "He could no more resist the tender fascination of those soft and melting blue eyes; the graceful beauty of that slender throat and drooping head, with its wealth of showering flaxen curls; the low music of that gentle voice; the perfect harmony which pervaded every charm, and made all doubly charming in this woman; than he could resist his destiny" (12). Noting that his first marriage, which ended in his wife's death seventeen years ago, had not involved love "but a poor, pitiful, smouldering spark, too dull to be extinguished, too feeble to burn," Sir Michael finds that his pent-up desire is ready to burst for Lucy, for whom he feels "this fever, this longing, this restless, uncertain, miserable hesitation" (12).

Sir Michael realizes that his desires may not be fulfilled, and the "hesitation" that he acknowledges festers from his awareness of the difference between their ages and his loss of conventional masculinity. Though he guesses that "she looked little more than twenty" (13), he is painfully certain of his own years. In a turbulent panic, Sir Michael faces the contradictory forces of reason and desire. Before he can propose to her, he recognizes "that his age was an insurmountable barrier to his happiness" (12) because he no longer conveys a youthful masculinity. He admits to "this sick hatred of his white beard; this frenzied wish to be young again" and longs for "glistening raven hair, and a slim waist, such as he had had twenty years before" (12). Despite his station and wealth, Sir Michael realizes that he might not be sexually desirable, and while he accepts his superior financial position, he bewails how age has devalued his marketability as a husband. He finds that the power he has enjoyed as a biological male is not stable and that other physical markers challenge his claim to a masculinity that remains problematically centered on his body. Weighing the strength of his sexual desire and his lack of physical masculinity, Sir Michael steels himself to make a bargain for sex.

Sir Michael's proposal is alternately poignant and ludicrous as he attempts to release himself from the economic implications of the marriage and his participation in a transaction close to legitimized prostitution. He circles around his proposition, "knowing that he could hardly expect to be the choice of a beautiful young girl, and praying rather that she would reject him, even though she broke his heart by doing so, than that she would accept his offer if she did not love him" (15). Sir Michael hopes that in rejecting him Lucy will save him from himself and his willingness to trade money for sex. He consequently opens his proposal of marriage with the following admonition to Lucy:

> I scarcely think there is a greater sin, Lucy . . . than that of the woman who marries a man she does not love. You are so precious to me, my beloved, that deeply as my heart is set on this, and bitter as the mere thought of disappointment is to me, I would not have you commit such a sin for any happiness of mine. If my happiness could be achieved by such an act, which it could not—which it never could, . . . nothing but misery can result from a marriage dictated by any motive but truth and love. (15)

Lucy responds passionately that his conditions are "noble" and "generous," but she speaks truthfully and simply when she replies to his request for love: "you ask too much of me. You ask too much of *me*!" (16). Lucy describes her childhood and the conditions that drove her to seek employment as a governess, and despite the other lies she constructs throughout the story, her story here matches the one she tells Sir Michael in confession at the end of the novel: "From my very babyhood I have never seen anything but poverty. My father was a gentleman; clever, accomplished, generous, handsome—but poor. My mother—But do not let me speak of her. Poverty, poverty, trials, vexations, humiliations, deprivations! *You* cannot tell; you, who are amongst those for whom life is so smooth and easy; you can never guess what is endured by such as we. Do not ask too much of me, then. I *cannot* be disinterested; I cannot be blind to the advantages of such an alliance. I cannot, I cannot!" (16). Whatever one feels for Lucy later in the novel (when she pushes her first husband to the bottom of a well and abandons him to die) should be tempered by her initial honesty and by her accurate description of the economic frustrations of a woman in the nineteenth century.[16]

By the end of the scene, Lucy's honest revelation of her necessary materialistic concerns deserves more respect than Sir Michael's "noble and generous" disclaimer to his proposal. Contradicting his aforementioned requirement of reciprocated love from his wife, he begins to hedge away from his ideal. Though he had hoped to be relieved of an awareness of his willing exchange of money for sex, he artfully rescinds his stipulation as he continues to barter for her hand:

"Lucy, Lucy, speak plainly. Do you dislike me?"
"Dislike you! No, no!"
"But is there any one else whom you love?"
She laughed aloud at his question. "I do not love any one in the world," she answered. (16–17)

Sir Michael is "silent for some moments" before he replies, "Well, Lucy, I will not ask too much of you. I dare say I am a romantic old fool; but if you do not dislike me, and if you do not love any one else, I see no reason why we should not make a very happy couple. Is it a bargain, Lucy?" (17). Sir Michael's rapid backsliding from viewing women marrying men for their money as a "sin" to a "bargain" forces the reader to reconsider his ability to stand by his principles. And as a new fiancé, he is not without a degree of self-disgust. Although he idealistically hopes he retains enough of his masculinity to attract a bride, he finds that "he must be contented, like other men of his age, to be married for his fortune and his position" (17).

Sir Michael's knowledge that he has lost his grasp on conventional masculinity causes a "strong emotion at work in his heart—neither joy, nor triumph, but something almost akin to disappointment" (17). Braddon further describes that disappointment as "some stifled and unsatisfied longing which lay heavy and dull at his heart, as if he had carried a corpse in his bosom" (17). The abjection that Sir Michael feels grows not only from the consciousness of his personal loss of masculinity, but also from the instability arising from the loss of a larger faith in a construction of masculinity. Both of these losses center on the body, although one stems from an increased appreciation of male embodiment, and the other from an overall devaluation of the physical body. Sir Michael finds first that his access to a masculine identity and authority has changed as his body has aged, and then that money and class contribute more to power than the masculine body. Neither privileging nor transcending the body offers Sir Michael much optimism, and "he carried the corpse of that hope which had died at the sound of Lucy's words" (17). He apprehends that linking power to the masculine body leads to the dissolution of power through aging or death. But linking masculinity to wealth and position also means that masculinity is a commodity that can redistributed to serve other ends, like sexual desire. Sir Michael takes this disturbing dual realization from Lucy's qualified acceptance of his proposal.

The age difference between Sir Michael and Lucy initiates the novel's challenges to broader male power, and Braddon frames the January–May theme with the hard economic realities facing the women of the day, refusing to temper even same-age male-female relationships with idealized features. Moreover, she portrays working middle-class women as active, albeit limited, agents in a commercial economy. Though Lucy self-critically remonstrates that she has been "selfish from my babyhood," the narrative clarifies that her selfishness has grown from necessity. Because of the insufficiencies of both father and husband, Lucy has fended for herself in a society ill at ease with the idea of women working. At the novel's conclusion, Lucy articulates what is often left unsaid regarding women and marriage: "I had learnt that which in some indefinite manner or other every schoolgirl learns sooner or later—I learned that my ultimate fate in life depended on my marriage" (345). Lucy reasons that in such a culture, it is difficult to marry for love. Even her first husband, the young, dashing George Talboys, can be deemed her rescuing "prince" only with bitter sarcasm. Despite George's embodiment of the physical traits of conventional masculinity—"a dark face, bronzed by exposure to the sun," "handsome brown eyes," height and a powerful build—his worth fades under economic hardship. Too realistic to be romantic about love, Lucy explains, "I loved him very well, quite well enough to be happy with him as long as his money lasted" (347). And George feels acutely the threat that poverty poses to his manhood. When Lucy criticizes him for misleading her into an unfortunate marriage, he abandons her and their infant son, leaving them penniless, with only a note explaining he has gone in search of his fortune and will not return until he is a rich man. At eighteen, Lucy has no financial security from her marriage, and no legal recourse to seek a divorce. Three and a half years pass with no word from George, and yet he believes as he returns on the ship from South Africa that she will welcome him back in spite of his desertion. He muses, "Poor little girl, how pleased she'll be! . . . how pleased and how surprised!" (18). The surprise, of course, is for George when he finds that he is still without masculine power, which has been overthrown by the dynamics of the January–May marriage. Lucy's mercenary tactics and willing admission of the motivations behind her marriage(s) are too much for the men in the novel, as well as for most readers. To her stepdaughter, she is "a practised and consummate flirt" (106). To her nephew Robert Audley, she is a "poor unhappy little golden-haired sinner" (250). The painting of Lucy that exposes her identity to George conveys her as the men would have her—not as legitimate wife but as brazen prostitute. Lucy's portrait depicts "a lurid lightness to the blonde complexion, and a strange, sinister light to the deep blue eyes" (72). The "pre-Raphaelite" painting has also given Lucy's "pretty pouting mouth [a] hard and almost wicked look" and, "as if you had burned strange-coloured fires before my lady's face," turned her into a "beautiful fiend" (72). Creating her as they secretly want her to be, the artist and those who interpret Lucy's portrait imagine her sexually on fire: "Her crimson dress, exaggerated like all the rest in this strange picture, hung about her in folds that looked like flames, her fair head peeping out of the lurid mass of colour, as if out of a raging furnace. Indeed, the crimson dress, the sunshine on the face, the red gold gleaming in the yellow hair, the ripe scarlet of the pouting lips, the glowing colours of each accessory of the minutely-painted background, all combined to render the first effect of the painting by no means an agreeable one" (72). Metaphorically aflame from the desire of those around her and the fusion of the roles of governess, wife, and prostitute, Lucy is a fearful sight, and the text shows that the men in the novel would like the wages of Lucy's sin to be everlasting death, burning in hell for her unfeminine privileging of economic well-being over love.

Without love, sexual exchange becomes a pecuniary matter even in marriage, and throughout the century, the age differences in January–May marriages underlined the blurry division between wife and prostitute. In his *An Essay on the Principle of Population* (1798), Malthus notes with disapproval marriages that were made to raise the wife's economic position, claiming that unions of young women and older men are "little better than legal prostitutions" (184). Other factors troubled boundaries between wives and prostitutes. Linton, by no means a feminist advocate, notes in "Womanly Dependence" the inequalities of the gendered economy: "As it is, men have the right to demand from their wives absolute attention to their wishes, because they are their property, their dependents, creatures whom they feed and clothe in return for certain services" (226–27). Reports of "wife sales" like the one that opens Thomas Hardy's *The Mayor of Casterbridge* brought marriage and prostitution logically closer in the public mind (Perkin, 117). Near the end of the century, the same analogy operates in texts like Bernard Shaw's *Mrs Warren's Profession*, which draws explicit connections between January–May marriages and prostitution and was banned by the Lord Chamberlain because of its radical treatment of the sex market.

Much of the concern about the play arose not from its depiction of conventional prostitution, but through the proposed January–May marriage of Sir George Crofts to Mrs. Warren's daughter Vivie, which equates marriage with prostitution. Crofts negotiates the marriage with Mrs. Warren, who, as a former prostitute and current madam, is accustomed to the exchange of money for sexual gratification. He reasons that "I'm not fifty yet; and my property is as good as ever it was. . . . And a baronet isn't to be picked up every day. . . . Why shouldn't she marry me?" (115). Hoping to shelter her daughter from life's sexual economies, Mrs. Warren refuses to entertain his proposal, but Crofts continues: "I'd die before her and leave her a bouncing widow with plenty of money. Why not?" (115).[17] When Mrs. Warren remains firm, Crofts "suddenly becom[es] anxious and urgent as he sees no sign of sympathy in her" and begs, "Look here, Kitty: you're a sensible woman: you needn't put on any moral airs. I'll ask no more questions; and you need answer none. I'll settle the whole property on her; and if you want a cheque for yourself on the wedding day, you can name any figure you like—in reason" (115). Here, marriage fails to conceal the explicit exchange of money for sex. Both Vivie and her mother/madam stand to profit from the arrangement, and marriage emerges as nothing less than socially endorsed prostitution.

As a late-nineteenth-century "new woman," Vivie rejects Crofts's offer of marriage so she can forge her career in the male-dominated business world of Chancery Lane, but the play's implicit link between mercenary marriage and prostitution remains powerful, keeping the play from print until 1898 and off the public stage until 1926. In the play's preface, Shaw explains that his intent was "to draw attention to the truth that prostitution is caused, not by female depravity and male licentiousness, but simply by underpaying, undervaluing, and overworking women so shamefully that the poorest of them are forced to resort to prostitution to keep body and soul together. Indeed all attractive unpropertied women lose money by being infallibly virtuous or contracting marriages that are not more or less venal. If on the large social scale we get what we call vice instead of what we call virtue it is simply because we are paying more for it" (3). The January–May proposal of Crofts to Vivie illustrates Shaw's point, but the age difference only emphasizes the corruption that threatens all marriages when women have unequal access to power. Malthus's designation of marriage as "little better than legal prostitutions" and Shaw's tethering of marriage to prostitution frame the century, and legal efforts such as the Contagious Disease Acts of the 1860s, which endorsed the detention and examination of prostitutes under the pretext of medical precautions, can be read as part of a larger social effort to distinguish between prostitution and culturally sanctioned sexual exchanges.

In most of these marriage proposals, the young women are active agents in a larger sexual economy. However, some works emphasize young wives as innocent victims in a system of exchange that gives them neither choice nor agency; authors adhere closely to Rubin's theories about the traffic in women when the young wives are betrothed to their husbands by their fathers or families, and not by their own choice. Though less subversive in respect to male agency than some of the other January–May marriages, these unions nonetheless protest against the traditional system of male economic superiority, even as they indulge in reinstating male systems of power by assigning the "saving" of the younger wife (or would-be wife) to her younger male lover. Presenting the male-dominated sexual economy as corrupt, Dickens's *Nicholas Nickleby* attempts to correct the problem of the passive female victim by way of the story of Madeline Bray and Arthur Gride, who are prevented from taking their January–May marriage vows by Nicholas's timely intervention. Here, the failure of the January–May engagement is vital to the novel's happy ending and to readers' expectations, since the novel construes the relationship between Madeline, who is eighteen, and Gride, who is "seventy or seventy-five years of age" (703), as sexual perversion not to be bought at any price. The January–May marriage plot provides Dickens with the material to execute a number of objectives: he criticizes old men and their corrupt economy, he preserves wifely submission and a feminine ideal, and he attempts to restore a noble masculinity through the figure of the rightful young lover. [18]

On the surface, the marriage between Madeline and Gride follows the economic pattern of the other January–May marriages examined in this chapter. Madeline's father owes Gride and his friend Ralph Nickleby a substantial amount of money, and they promise to forgive his debt if he arranges a marriage between his daughter and Gride. Addressing Gride, Ralph Nickleby explains that he considers the exchange "fair and easy" because "you have money, and Miss Madeline has beauty and worth. She has youth, you have money. She has not money, you have not youth. Tit for tat—quits—a match of Heaven's own making" (714). The incentives for the marriage draw on the broader associations between wives and prostitutes, and the intent of the father to sell his daughter for his own financial gain allows Dickens to criticize failing patriarchal and economic systems simultaneously. His mission, however, is not to overturn or disrupt the gender binary that exists, but to replace the flawed patriarch with a younger, less problematic masculine figure. Thus, Dickens paints the sexual dimension of the exchange with grotesque detail, hoping to disgust the reader so much that his idealized young masculinity will be accepted with open arms.

Dickens portrays Gride as almost dead, a "shriveled and yellow" corpse whose "jaws had fallen inwards from loss of teeth" (703). "[L]acking the power" (802) of his gender, Gride shows no "manly feeling" (803) and embodies neither masculinity nor humanity: "The whole air and attitude of the form, was one of stealthy cat-like obsequiousness; the whole expression of the face was concentrated in a wrinkled leer, compounded of cunning, lecherousness, slyness, and avarice" (703–4). In contrast, Madeline is not "some old hag," as Ralph Nickleby predicts, but "a young and beautiful girl; fresh, lovely, bewitching, and not nineteen" (707). She appears as a consumable and tactile commodity when Gride catalogs her physical attributes with continual nods to their sexual delectability: "Dark eyes—long eyelashes—ripe and ruddy lips that to look at is to long to kiss—beautiful clustering hair that one's fingers itch to play with—such a waist as might make a man clasp the air involuntarily, thinking of twining his arm about it—little feet that tread so lightly they hardly seem to walk upon the ground—to marry all this, sir,—this—hey, hey!" (707). Food imagery abounds in Gride's descriptions of his desire for Madeline. For him she is a "delicate morsel" (710), and Gride, as a capitalistic and metaphorical cannibal, is willing to part with seventeen hundred pounds to eat her up. As Gride fantasizes about the marriage, the singsong meter of his banter lends an especially eerie dreadfulness to readers' expectations of the sexual union to come. He repulsively queries, "pretty Mrs Arthur Gride—a tit-bit—a dainty chick—shouldn't I have her Mrs Arthur Gride in a week, a month, a day—any time I chose to name?" (710).

Despite the horror Gride's proposal inspires, Madeline remains steadfast in her role as dutiful daughter and prepares herself for the sacrifice of her body so that her father can prosper. Dickens needs to keep Madeline untainted by the problematic associations of the sexual economy, so he stresses that she marries for the financial gain of her father, not for herself.[19] She explains to Nicholas, "I do *not* love this gentleman; the difference between our ages, tastes, and habits, forbids it. This he knows, and knowing, still offers me his hand. By accepting it, and by that step alone, I can release my father who is dying in this place, prolong his life, perhaps, for many years, restore him to comfort" (797).

Madeline's refusal to go against her father's wishes initiates Nicholas's intervention in her engagement. Though he fashions himself as Madeline's savior, Nicholas enters the commercial exchange in women and thus participates in Madeline's prostitution. His language emphasizes her marriage as a financial transaction: he refers to "this sale of Madeline," "this business," "fraud," "price," "coin," and "account," and asks Gride how much money he would accept to break his engagement. Although Nicholas has little financial capital himself, he relies on the good will of the Cheeryble brothers and his own threatening physicality to urge Gride, "Bate some expected gain, for the risk you save, and say what is your price. . . . Miss Bray has wealthy friends who would coin their hearts to save her. . . . Name your price, defer these nuptials for but a few days, and see whether those I speak of shrink from the payment" (803). He reasons that he descends to financial bargaining because he is left with no other choice: "I take the only ground that can be taken with men like you, and ask what money will buy you off" (803), but he bargains nevertheless and, in doing so, advances his own desires to make Madeline his. Dickens unintentionally reveals that in a male-dominated economy even same-age marriages make prostitutes of women by awarding them to the highest bidders.

Dickens intends the failure of the January–May marriage plot to stabilize masculine and feminine constructions. Madeline's father's timely death acts as the *deus ex machina* that allows Nicholas to carry Madeline off (literally) to the household that he heads. The older men, Gride and Ralph, find their circumstances altered for the worse. Madeline is no longer bound by duty to marry Gride, and both Gride and Ralph suffer immediate financial disasters. With aging masculinity overthrown—Nicholas tells Gride and Ralph, "Your day is past, and night is coming on" (818)—and conventional domestic femininity preserved, Dickens clears Nicholas's path to fulfill the psychological and mythic fantasy of fathering a new and more just masculinity for society. In a Dickensian sense, he succeeds, becoming "a rich and prosperous merchant," purchasing back the home his father's financial mismanagement had lost, and fathering numerous children with Madeline, who sweetly places flowers on the grave of Smike, the unfortunate offspring of the most powerful representative of older masculinity, Ralph. It is a picturesque fairytale ending of domestic relations restored, of normative sexuality reaffirmed, and of gender identities clarified, yet the thinness of the picture remains apparent, as Madeline's close encounter with legitimized prostitution and Nicholas's desire to participate in her exchange reveal. Dickens intends to resolve nineteenth-century anxieties about gender by adapting the January–May plot, but he instead reminds readers of the instability of gender identities and their inevitable associations with economic realities.

Are women often exploited in nineteenth-century January–May marriages? Certainly. But to focus solely on this exploitation directs attention away from the challenges to masculine power that the sexual economy fosters. These texts haggle over the value of older husbands in a market that prizes youth and beauty, and they disclose a traffic in men as much as a traffic in women. Even when drawings like *Married for Rank* and texts like *Nicholas Nickleby* attempt to reinforce gender identities by criticizing men and women who exploit the sexual economy, those stabilizing moves fail. And works that include mercenary marriages demonstrate that power need not be tied to the physical body. When aging, effeminate husbands with financial advantages marry strong young women, they prove that masculinity is not essential to power. Moreover, when they transfer wealth to young women, they trump patriarchal authority with genderless, capitalist clout. And looking at these marriages in the light of a male-dominated economy also creates problems for marriage as a stable social institution. January–May marriages collapse class and gender distinctions as young wives work as governesses, as wives, and, by implication, as prostitutes in the sexual marketplace.

CHAPTER 6

JANUARY–MAY LOVE AND THE
SACRIFICIAL IDEAL

As Christopher Herbert relates in "Filthy Lucre: Victorian Ideas of Money," by mid-century, many individuals felt deeply ambivalent about money, and its acquisition formed a Victorian social taboo—revered as a key to power, yet viewed as polluting, dirty, and at odds with a Christian lifestyle. Herbert writes, "Christianity idealizes poverty and anathematizes money; it teaches Christians to recoil from the contaminating uncleanness of worldly riches" (190). Herbert theorizes that a love of money and adherence to Christianity led to a cultural schizophrenia, with individuals torn between money worship and a nonmaterialistic religion. Many nineteenth-century texts consequently uphold New Testament ideals of selflessness and love, and January–May marriages that successfully secure both money *and* love convey the social ideal. The marriages of Emma Woodhouse, Jane Eyre, and Marianne Dashwood, for example, instruct readers away from marriages solely for money, while Lucy Graham's marriage warns of disaster due to the inability to love (although Braddon suggests this is not entirely Lucy's fault). In the most successful January–May relationships, love develops amid more practical elements, complicating readings of these marriages and their implications regarding gender and power.

Love between fictional husbands and wives is difficult to approach intellectually; despite the numerous theories of love that have circulated since Plato's *Symposium*, it is difficult to reflect on love in the same way as gender, class, or power.[1] Near the end of *Child-Loving*, James Kincaid explains, "Love as a center has a nice ring to it but it is no less a dragon than power, should we let it take up permanent residence. We really have no notion of what it would be like to center love, I think, since the forms of love we have now all seem perverse and battering" (389). This critical dilemma about "center[ing] love"—that is, giving it primary importance—is especially true regarding January–May marriages, which have been so long subjected to pragmatic or cynical interpretations involving sex and money that it has become hard to believe they could be founded on compassionate feelings, selfless emotions, or reciprocated desire. As developed in the Western imagination, romantic love often encourages a narrative logic that defies reason and therefore proves difficult to reason about. Whereas an individual jockeying for economic superiority over another person, class, race, or gender captures the quintessential struggle for the preservation of self-interest, love often directs the focus away from the self and, counter to evolutionary logic, emphasizes instead the preservation of something outside of self.[2] Despite other motives, love persists in January–May literature, and to ignore love and its relationship to power would be to render an incomplete summary of the theme's dynamics. Love of a wife for a husband, or a husband for a wife, and love that is mutually shared surface in numerous nineteenth-century January–May plots, and love forms an interesting revision of the motives initiated by monetary concerns, a counterpoint that is no less integral than incest, aesthetics, or horror to the formation of gender identities within these triangles.

January–May marriages appear in several of Trollope's novels, most notably the much-sentimentalized marriage of Eleanor Bold to Francis Arabin in *Barchester Towers* (1867); the novel also includes in its humorous portrayal of Mr. Thorne's fascination with Madeline Neroni the following commentary on January–May love, which is so revealing of the theme's ability to idealize intergenerational romance that it must be quoted at length:

> It is, we believe, common with young men of five-and-twenty to look on their seniors—on men, say, double their own age—as so many stocks and stones—stocks and stones, that is, in regard to feminine beauty. There was never a greater mistake. . . . Men of fifty don't dance mazurkas, being generally too fat and wheezy; nor do they sit for the hour together on river banks at their mistresses' feet, being somewhat afraid of rheumatism. But for real true love—love at first sight, love to

devotion, love that robs a man of his sleep, love that will 'gaze an eagle blind', love that 'will hear the lowest sound when the suspicious thread of theft is stopped', love that is 'like a Hercules, still climbing trees in the Hesperides'—we believe that the best age is from forty-five to seventy; up to that men are generally given to mere flirting. (358–59)

January figures in Trollope are in many ways parodies of middle-age and middle-class masculinity, but, as in the passage above where he moves assumptions about older men's motivations from lust to love, they also challenge the tradition in remarkable ways.[3]

In this chapter, I discuss Trollope's *An Old Man's Love* after two January–May novels by Dickens not covered in Chapter 2: *David Copperfield* and *Bleak House*. These novels convey what I term the sacrificial ideal. Rather than suggesting that a submissive nature is vital to true love, such novels support an economy of love far removed from the self-centered practices of the older husbands in *Middlemarch* or *Lady Audley's Secret*. These examples offset nineteenth-century associations of individuality with masculinity and sacrifice with femininity, demonstrating another means for the theme's blurring of gender identities, and the sacrificial acts of these husbands encourage sympathy for them and for the deviancies of the January–May marriage. Whether the sacrifice releases the young woman from her wedding vows or removes the possibility of the January–May marriage altogether, the end is the same: the sacrifice makes desire for intergenerational love proliferate.

## SACRIFICING FATHERS IN *DAVID COPPERFIELD* AND *BLEAK HOUSE*

Sydney Carton's sacrifice for Lucie Manette in *A Tale of Two Cities* (1859) serves as a fitting preface for a return to Dickens's use of the January–May theme and for a query into the importance of love within the motif of the sacrificial ideal. Carton is only about fifteen years older than Lucie, though his flamboyant lifestyle, including "orgies late into the night" (90), makes him appear more aged than he really is. Upholding normative same-age sexuality in place of his own unrequited January–May desires, Carton saves Lucy's younger husband by taking his place at the guillotine, and while Carton famously proclaims, "It is a far, far better thing that I do, than I have ever done" (390), he signals how the reader should read his sacrifice, but ironically, through his death, ensures the mythologizing of January–May love. Following the example set by John the Carrier in *The Cricket on the Hearth*,

Carton and some of Dickens's most sympathetic older lovers and husbands are prepared to relinquish their January–May relationships in favor of the normative tendencies of their younger May counterparts. Incestuous dynamics remain, as I explore more fully in Chapter 2, but Dickens offers endearing renderings of these father figures by exploring the idea of the unwanted older husband or fiancé who is ready to make a personal sacrifice.

Sympathy first emerges when the older male appears to be (or is) rejected because the younger woman prefers a younger man. As these are "good" men—kind, fair, and otherwise benevolent individuals who appear undeserving of the sexual retribution of cuckoldry—the novels take advantage of the reader's competing expectations of what "should" happen. Even if the reader understands or advocates the younger woman's "natural" inclinations to normative, same-age sexuality, compassion for the good older man solicits sympathy for him in his slighted position, and this consideration for the husband's plight increases when he acknowledges his weakened status by withdrawing his claim to sexual fidelity from his younger wife. Sacrificing his desire for hers, the older husband reinforces his position as a favorable character, and though many feminists have cringed at John Jarndyce's gifting of his young fiancée Esther to her same-aged admirer, the outlandishly homosocial exchange of a woman between these men encourages renewed consideration of women's power within intergenerational marriages.

This sacrificial element might appear to promote heteronormativity over deviancy, but the disruptive effects of such sacrifice should not be overlooked. On the surface, sympathy for the older husband inspires a restored faith in benevolent masculinity and a return to traditional male-female power relations, but because the older husband remains connected to aberrant desires like incest, sympathy for him correlates to endorsement—on some level—of the domestication of deviant sexualities. The willingness of an older man to sacrifice himself for a younger woman initiates a complex process of reverse psychology, and whether or not the plot demands the sacrifice, readers must negotiate their mixed feelings about the older man's loss. Reading these texts with attention to the sympathetic portrayal of the aging husband and his frustrated love offers new possibilities for understanding the January–May marriage theme.

The January–May marriage in *David Copperfield* may not appear subversive, and some critics have emphasized the conservative implications of the novel's relegation of women to positions of childishness and subservience. Kelly Hager objects to what she sees as Dickens's idealization of the child wife: "Those happy, successful marriages, or at least those marriages which Dickens would have us see as such, are ones in which the wife has been disciplined or subdued to her husband's liking. Annie sits for long hours and listens to her husband read from his everlasting Dictionary" (1014).[4] Annie Strong, the much-younger wife of David's teacher, Doctor Strong, does sit subordinately and listen admiringly to her husband, whom she addresses passionately as "my husband and father" (606), thus she simultaneously fulfills readers' expectations of wifely and daughterly duty as their ages seem to place them even more firmly within a traditional age and gender hierarchy.

The marriage is inundated with standard tropes of older man and younger woman marriages. Doctor Strong knew Annie's father and saw Annie "from a baby six months old," and the novel explains that he had saved her from a life of poverty, because "she had not a sixpence, and had a world of poor relations" (226). In education, economics, and experience, Annie is the weaker of the two. While Hager rightly argues that it is important to be mindful of implicit systems of gender and generational power, the dynamics at play here can be read too simply if read too quickly. The Strong marriage challenges several gender assumptions about the balance of power, and Annie wields surprising sexual and emotional authority in her marriage. Doctor Strong emerges as a man to be pitied as much as admired, and the novel lauds his capacity for self-sacrifice rather than his traditional masculinity. The Strong marriage placates anxieties about gender identities by fulfilling expectations of feminine sexual virtue, but it undermines the stabilizing effects of marriage by idealizing nonnormative familial and sexual bonds.

Although Annie is forty-three years younger than her husband (she is twenty while he is sixty-three), their marriage is, appropriately, one of Dickens's "strong" January–May marriages, and its disruption is not the novel's happy-ever-after conclusion, but rather a ploy to intensify readers' longing for marital restoration. The narrative of the Strong marriage adheres to a classical comedic formula with action falling into a crisis of potential infidelity, followed by a happy affirmation of the marriage vows. Yet for much of the novel, the marriage seems doomed to failure as a result of "so much disparity in point of years" (568), and as narrator, David teases the reader with the possibility of Annie's affair with her cousin Jack Maldon, drawing out the reader's uneasiness (and conveniently giving the reader ample opportunity for imagining Annie's unfaithfulness) for almost half the novel.

Dickens introduces Doctor Strong and Annie through the eyes of young David, and his unreliable narration deliberately encourages an initial misreading of their relationship. David's description stresses their differences in age and appearance, and their arrangement appears a curious oddity even to a boy.[5] David explains that "Doctor Strong looked almost as rusty, to my thinking, as the tall iron rails and gates outside the house. . . . [H]is clothes [were] not particularly well brushed, and his hair not particularly well combed. . . . [He] reminded me of a long-forgotten blind old horse" (215). In contrast, David describes "a very pretty young lady—whom he called Annie, and who was his daughter, I supposed" (215–16). David then adds that "I was much surprised to hear Mr Wickfield, in bidding her good morning, address her as 'Mrs Strong,' and I was wondering could she be Doctor Strong's son's wife, or could she be Mrs Doctor Strong" (216). This logical progression from daughter to daughter-in-law to wife is quick, and although David and the reader soon learn the apt designation for their connection, the text continues to mix familial adjectives playfully: "It was very pleasant to see the Doctor with his pretty young wife. He had a fatherly, benignant way of showing his fondness for her, which seemed in itself to express a good man" (227). Annie's mother likewise directs, "Annie, Doctor Strong will not only be your husband, but he will represent your late father: he will represent the head of our family, he will represent the wisdom and the station, and I may say the means, of our family" (229). As in his other January–May texts, Dickens emphasizes incestuous elements amid the humor of the mother-in-law's mercenary motives, but the message is clear that, as Annie puts it, Doctor Strong is her "husband and father" (606). When a few sentences later her mother criticizes her for being "a little unnatural towards your own family" (230), a double meaning seems implicit. The Strong marriage is decidedly strange but idealized nonetheless.[6]

When Uriah Heep forces suspicions about Annie's infidelity on Doctor Strong (while all other characters encourage his ignorance and, consequently, the prolongation of the sexually deviant triangle), Doctor Strong chooses not to perform irate masculinity or even disappointed paternity. Neither jealous nor scolding, he feels understandably dejected, but assumes a decidedly submissive and sacrificial stance toward the charges against his wife. Blaming himself, he begs forgiveness: "If I did her wrong; as I fear I did, in taking advantage (but I never meant it) of her gratitude and her affection; I ask pardon of that lady, in my heart!" (570). Strong legitimizes his wife's sexual yearnings, rationalizing that it is "natural" that she should have "some regretful feelings" (571) toward her cousin. Strong confirms that he wishes Annie to be financially and sexually independent, and he redrafts his will to emphasize that on his death he "gives her all unconditionally" (605). He prepares "to bear the knowledge of the unhappiness I have occasioned, as submissively as I can" and looks forward to his death, which will "release her from constraint" (571). Dickens intends his audience to respect Strong's recognition that their age difference troubles the marriage, but because Dickens develops the audience's compassion for Strong as a "good man" and not for Jack, he indicates that what is normative, expected, or even "natural" is not what the audience should want.

Annie may throw herself at her husband's feet when confronting the charges of her adultery, but she does so only to rise—conveniently supported by Mr. Dick—with a surprisingly masculine tone of authority. When her mother and Strong attempt parentally to silence her sensational semipublic confession, she defies them both, and "looking down upon her husband" (608) from her new vantage, affirms that her sexual and emotional needs are not what everyone supposes. In front of the audience of her mother, Mr. Dick, Betsey Trotwood, and David, whom the display "thrilled," Annie details her motivations for marriage, repeatedly demanding more opportunity to speak: "Do not speak to me yet!," "A little more!," and "Another word!" (611, 612). Contrary to what her mother and Wickfield have suggested, Annie announces that she married not for money, but for love. She admits that she once had feelings for her cousin, but declares, in retrospect, that their normative, same-age marriage would have "been most wretched" (610). She stresses that she *prefers* her marriage to her husband and eagerly displays her physical affection for him. Falling again to the floor, she embraces him, and the audience rejoices in their marital bliss. The final image of the couple displays them intertwined: "She had her arms around the Doctor's neck, and he bent his head down over her, mingling his grey hair with her dark brown tresses" (612). Defying gender norms and social taboos, this portrait of intergenerational love disputes more than it restores.

The witnesses to Annie's confession are delighted that Strong's sacrifice is not wanted, but his promise of self-sacrifice has already succeeded in winning sympathy for the aging husband and the January–May marriage. In this novel filled with unhappy same-age relationships (David's mother and Mr. Murdstone, Betsey Trotwood and her husband, Mr. and Mrs. Micawber, David and Dora, Steerforth and Emily), January–May marriages and the affectionate cohabitations of these "fathers" and "daughters" provide a happy alternative to their more conventional counterparts. Seldom mentioned is that David's mother Clara and his biological father were themselves a May and January, which helps to explain his mother's early widowhood. Clara, who was in a lower class position than David's father, was "a very Baby" and "not yet twenty" (14) upon marriage, while David's father was "double [his] mother's age" (13). Nevertheless, Clara declares, "We were very happy. . . . Mr Copperfield was only too good to me" (17), and she is in an empowered position as a young widow when the novel begins. Her degradation and death come only after she enters into a same-age relationship with Murdstone.[7] Other intergenerational couples cohabitate happily. Alcoholism seems the real danger in the Wickfield home—not the "diseased" love between Agnes and her father—and Emily, who traverses many social and sexual boundaries in the novel, starts life anew with her uncle and father figure, albeit seemingly platonically, in Australia.[8] Intergenerational and familial cohabitation reads favorably in comparison to the normative counterpart, and here the January–May marriage appears as its literary, social, and sexual culmination.

\* \* \* \* \*

The sacrificial decision of John Jarndyce to "give" Esther Summerson to her young lover Allan Woodcourt confused contemporary readers of *Bleak House*. A writer in *Bentley's Miscellany* explains that

> Of Mr Jarndyce and Esther Summerson we hardly know what to say. We should like to have substantial faith in the existence of such loveable, self-merging natures, whether belonging to elderly gentlemen or young maidens. But we cannot say that we have. Indeed, the final disposal of Esther, after all that has gone before, is something that so far transcends the limits of our credulity, that we are compelled to pronounce it eminently unreal. We do not know whether most to marvel at him who transfers, or her who is transferred from one to another, like a bale of goods. (74)

While this critic objects to the novel's open portrayal of economies that traffic in women, the main doubt lies with the questionable selflessness of the January–May couple and the forfeit of personal interest within the frame of sexual loss and gain. Unlike the January husbands of *The Cricket on the Hearth* and *David Copperfield*, who offer to release their wives without having to follow through with their promises, Jarndyce does sacrifice himself, informing Esther that he is relinquishing "the old dream I sometimes dreamed when you were very young, of making you my wife one day" and that he was wrong to have his happiness "too much in view" (751–52). The novel supports Jarndyce's sacrifice, however "unreal," by a similar selflessness displayed by another January figure, Sir Leicester Dedlock, the husband of Esther's mother.[9] Though Sir Leicester, who is already married, is in no position to make a "gift" of his wife to her same-aged lover Captain Hawdon, who is dead, he allows his reputation to suffer by ignoring public demands for a divorce and gives his wife his unyielding approval and, as much as he can, her good name. "Self-merging natures" dissolve the age and gender differences of these "elderly gentlemen [and] young maidens" and undermine conventional power structures.

The novel indicates that both Esther's and her mother's attraction to same-aged men is natural and to be expected. Esther informs us at the end of her narrative that she has been married to Woodcourt for "full seven happy years" (767), and Honoria Dedlock dies pining outside the graveyard of her same-aged lover. However "natural" Honoria's desire for same-age love appears, the novel concludes that it is destructive for her, for her husband, and for her lover.[10] And because the novel presents the reader with "deviant" intergenerational love only to leave that desire unfulfilled, it encourages a longing for what will never be.

As with Dickens's other novels, some of the deviancy stems from the relationship's incestuous overtones. Esther's illegitimacy allows for a tangle of kinship structures that are crucial to the novel's plot, and in this novel of lost mothers and fathers, it is fitting that her relationship with John Jarndyce be multifunctional. Jarndyce is not her biological father, but Dickens does not disclose that fact for much of the novel. From her childhood Jarndyce is her surrogate father and her seducer; he offers to take charge of her when she is twelve and assumes responsibility for her when she is fourteen, saving her from an uncertain future by sending her to a "first rate establishment" for her education and proper grooming to be his "Dame Durden" (23). Riding with her in the coach to her new school, he paternally wipes the tears from her eyes and plies her with sweets: "the best plum-cake that can be got for money—sugar on the outside an inch thick, like fat on mutton chops" (25). When Esther is summoned from school to live in Jarndyce's house as companion to Ada, she gives thanks for "that Father who had not forgotten me" (27), and although the capitalization of Father denotes its author's religious intent, her words carry a double meaning, as her earthly, as well as heavenly, father has remembered her.[11] As Esther is twenty and Jarndyce "nearer to sixty than fifty" when she comes to live in his home, his paternal role to Esther and to his other wards is well established. No one raises an eyebrow when he puts his arms around the waists of Ada and Esther and kisses them "in a fatherly way" (60).

In the beginning, Esther's position as eldest child to her fatherly guardian appears appropriate. She addresses Jarndyce as "my guardian" rather than calling him by name, and, for a short time, their kinship remains clear. However, as she assumes duties more commonly associated with a wife than a daughter, their relationship becomes more problematic.[12] Esther serves as a big sister and a little mother to her wayward companions Ada and Richard, and soon after her arrival, she receives the keys to the house, affirming her symbolic position as mistress of Bleak House long before her engagement to Jarndyce. As Esther fulfills cross-generational duties within this nonnuclear family, her familial connection to Jarndyce grows more suspect, and by the time of her convalescence from smallpox, the reader no longer knows how to interpret their interactions. When Jarndyce lovingly embraces Esther, calling her alternately "My dear, dear girl," "My little woman," and "my love, my love" (434–35) over the course of a few short moments, the muddled state of their relationship surfaces. Although Esther continues to call Jarndyce "my guardian," her feelings for him are uncertain, and when she expresses her relief that he doesn't mind her appearance, the layered meanings of her words reveal that she begins to reciprocate his unconditional love: "He has seen me, and he loves me better than he did; he has seen me, and is even fonder of me than he was before; and what have I to mourn for!" (434).

Indeed, Esther's pockmarked appearance encourages the disintegration of the boundary between their familial and romantic feelings for one another, and with the loss of Esther's youthful face, Jarndyce's progress from guardian and father to lover and husband comes easily. For Jarndyce, Esther's marred beauty seems to erase some of the years that separate them, and though he does not say as much in his letter to Esther that proposes marriage, she "well" knows that "when I had been better-looking, he had had this same proceeding in his thoughts, and had refrained from it" (538). Exactly how their relationship could change becomes an important issue. Preparing Esther for his proposal before he gives her the letter, Jarndyce makes her promise repeatedly that "nothing can change me as you know me" (536), and Esther does so. In truth, they had long collapsed the roles of father and lover and of daughter and wife, and even though Jarndyce is "past the prime of life; on his having attained a ripe age, while [Esther] was a child," Esther readily admits that she "had expected the contents" of the letter that makes her "happy in the undeserved love of the best of men" (537–38). After their engagement is settled, Esther continues to refer to Jarndyce as her "guardian" instead of calling him her fiancé, and when she says that their new family structure "made no difference" (540) in their lives, she attests to the comfortable amalgamation of kinship roles they had already formed.[13]

But their engagement does make a difference. Esther now puts her arms around Jarndyce's neck and kisses him with the feeling of a wife, not a daughter. She takes a new position by the side of her "guardian's" chair, and, with two hundred pounds, which Jarndyce provides for her trousseau in his dual role as father and suitor, she begins "to make such preparations as [she] thought were necessary" (748) to her wardrobe so that it will be suitable for a new bride. Esther frets over what and when to tell Ada of her altered status in the home, and Ada, trying to negotiate her own family romance with her cousin Richard, laments the confusion of Bleak House's kinship structure: "O when I think of all these years, and of his fatherly care and kindness, and of the old relations among us, and of you, what shall I do, what shall I do!" (606). Ada's question is rhetorical because there is no easy way to reconcile the joy of Esther's and Jarndyce's anticipated happiness with the deviances initiated by their generational gap.

The awkwardness of the age difference is understood by all. While Mrs. Woodcourt had earlier predicted that Esther would marry "some one, very rich and very worthy, much older—five-and-twenty years, perhaps—than yourself" (367), her marriage to Jarndyce, who is almost forty years her senior and already established as her father figure, remains an uncomfortable subject. To control criticism and gossip, Esther and Jarndyce plan for their wedding to be carried out in "the most private and simple manner" (748). Because of their ages and history, they treat the wedding as a dirty secret—embarrassing, abnormal, and uncomfortable; however, because of their love, it is a secret that the reader wants to share.

For the novel's bittersweet ending to be successful, Dickens had to make sure that on some level every reader would mourn the arrested development of Esther's and Jarndyce's relationship. Jarndyce is not a bad man. Allowing him a dark side when the wind is in the East, Dickens nevertheless makes certain that Jarndyce is a likeable, noble, and openhanded character. Esther confirms on numerous occasions that she is truly fond of her guardian. She memorizes the words of his proposal letter, she affectionately touches him, and she delights in his company, worrying about his health when they are not together. Esther likes Jarndyce, and so does the reader. Perhaps this is the reason Dickens spares him from outright rejection. When Woodcourt returns from abroad to extend his offer of normative, same-age, exogamic love, Esther is already committed to Jarndyce, and she refuses Woodcourt, explaining that "in the future, which is clear and bright before me, I am most happy, most fortunate, [and] have nothing to regret or to desire" (732–33). Despite her feelings for Jarndyce, she loves Woodcourt too, and it is left to Jarndyce to act on his awareness of the mutual desire of the young lovers.[14]

The plot demands that not everyone in this triangle will end happily, but in having Jarndyce step aside, Dickens only appears to condone Esther's move to Woodcourt as Jarndyce's sacrifice redefines traditional notions of what it means to be the better man. Showing Esther his creation of her own "bleak house" to share with Woodcourt, Jarndyce clarifies his decision to release her from their engagement: "When it was that I began to doubt whether what I had done would really make you happy, is no matter. Woodcourt came home, and I soon had no doubt at all" (752). Not wishing his "love," his "ward," and his "child" to "sacrifice her love to a sense of duty and affection," Jarndyce sacrifices his own interests instead. Esther trembles "violently" and, weeping, puts her head on Jarndyce's chest and her arms around his neck when she learns of his resolution. Jarndyce restores their relationship, assuming it needed restoration, to expected father-child dynamics. Pressing Esther to his chest, he instructs her to "Lie lightly, confidently, here, my child. . . . I am your guardian and your father now" (752). Jarndyce's sacrifice exponentially increases the sympathy he has already enjoyed as an embodiment of "good" masculinity, and because he can be pitied for his loss, his recent associations with incest and pedophilia can be overlooked. Jarndyce lifts Esther's head to kiss her "in his old fatherly way again and again" (753), and she clings to him in a renewal of their respective positions as father and daughter.

The idea that this renaming of their familial positions stabilizes heteronormative sexuality is unavoidably problematic, if not, in the words of the critic in *Bentley's Miscellany*, "eminently unreal" (74). When Jarndyce urges Woodcourt to "take from me, a willing gift, *the best wife that ever a man had*" (753, emphasis added), his use of the past tense calls attention to the spousal relationship that he had already enjoyed with his ward.[15] Esther has never chosen to change her designation of her "guardian" to "John" or anything denoting a deliberate forgetting of their parent-child relations, and thus the suggestion that

Jarndyce is her father and guardian "now" but not "then" is a narrative sleight of hand that Dickens performs, perhaps intentionally, not so well. The disconnect that should separate Esther and Jarndyce from their romantic relationship is faulty, and thus when Jarndyce sanctions Esther's marriage to Woodcourt, giving his "knowledge and consent" as both father and lover, the gifting of Esther that transfers her "like a bale of goods" from one man to another undermines rather than supports a system of male privilege because it connects same-age sexuality with an intergenerational, incestuous love. Esther's love of Jarndyce as more than guardian is not forgotten, nor is his love of her as more than his dependent ward. The scene of this transferal is ridden with pathos for Jarndyce, and it is decidedly romantic. Esther describes their farewell as lovers as they take on their normative positions: "He kissed me once again; and now the tears were in his eyes, as he said more softly: 'Esther, my dearest, after so many years, there is a kind of parting in this too. I know that my mistake has caused you some distress. Forgive your old guardian, in restoring him to his old place in your affections; and blot it out of your memory'" (753). The ambiguous "it" is their mingling of the roles of parent, child, and lover, and the call to forget "it" proves all but impossible.

Jarndyce's sacrifice ensures that he is more loved by Esther and by the reader than ever before, and Dickens encourages the perpetuation of intergenerational desire through his idealization of what will not be fulfilled. Looking back on her relationship with Jarndyce as she closes her story, Esther reflects, "I try to write all of this lightly, because my heart is full in drawing to an end; but when I write of him, my tears will have their way" (769). Esther cries for what is lost. Jarndyce and the loving January figure that he represents take on an almost mythic grandeur, not only as a "good man" but also as "the fondest father," "my husband's best and dearest friend," "our children's darling," "the object of our deepest love and veneration," and, indeed, "a superior being" (769). Dickens suggests that the ideal relationship blurs kinship roles and emotional ties, and instead of becoming nothing to Esther, Jarndyce becomes everything.

Jarndyce's sacrifice of himself becomes the very agent of the January–May theme's continuation within the domestic sphere of the middle-class home. In a strangely modern arrangement, Esther and Woodcourt build a separate "growlery" for Jarndyce in their new Bleak House to accommodate him during his visits, and Esther admits that although she is married to Woodcourt, her relationship with Jarndyce remains sufficiently confused. In the midst of detailing his superlative appellations, she provocatively queries, "to me, he is what he has ever been, and what name can I give to that?" (769). She explains, "I am so familiar with him, and so easy with him, that I almost wonder at myself" and verifies that, despite her being another man's wife, very little has changed regarding the romantic tension that has characterized her relationship with Jarndyce: "I have never lost my old names, nor has he lost his; nor do I ever, when he is with us, sit in any other place than in my old chair at his side. Dame Trot, Dame Durden, Little Woman!—all just the same as ever; and I answer, Yes, dear guardian! just the same" (769). Notably, this place by Jarndyce is not the one she occupied as his "child"; Esther earlier identifies the position by his side as one that clearly denotes her changed status in the home: "I was sitting in my usual place, which was now beside my guardian's chair. That had not been my usual place before the letter, but it was now" (606). Slipping in and out of daughter and wife roles as she meaningfully relocates herself in the room, Esther expresses her continued desire for Jarndyce—the sacrificial ideal.

## *An Old Man's Love* and the Sacrificial Ideal

At age twenty-five, Mary Lawrie is "altogether alone in the world" (2), and her dead father's best friend William Whittlestaff invites her into his comfortable bachelor home. Mary's only other plan is to become a governess, though Whittlestaff concludes "that plan he was quite sure would not answer" (3). To Whittlestaff, the twenty-five-year age difference between them would prohibit any sense of impropriety, and like Dickens's fatherly lovers, he reasons, "I can do just what I please with her . . . as though she were my own girl" (4). Trollope emphasizes Whittlestaff's nonsexual intentions: "By this he meant to imply that he would not be expected to fall in love with her, and that it was quite out of the question that she should fall in love with him" (4), but, as readers are already aware from the title of the novel, Whittlestaff protests too much about the romantic impossibilities of his actions from their very inception. When he announces his plan to bring Mary into the home "as though she were my own daughter" to his housekeeper Mrs. Baggett, she expresses her doubts about the platonic arrangement he envisions and warns Whittlestaff about his naivety: "You ain't a young man—nor you ain't an old un; and she ain't no relation to you. That's the worst part of it. As sure as my name is Dorothy Baggett, you'll be falling in love with her" (5–6). Mrs. Baggett, of course, is right.

The platonic, familial nature of their relationship lasts for over a year, but the novel makes it clear that it is Mary's resistance rather than Whittlestaff's that prevents things from developing. Trollope explains that "An old gentleman will seldom fall in love without some encouragement; or at any rate, will not tell his love. Mary Lawrie was as cold to him as though he had been seventy-five instead of fifty. And she was also as dutiful,—by which she showed Mrs. Baggett more strongly even than by her coldness, that any idea of marriage was on her part out of the question" (7–8). Nonetheless, if Whittlestaff had really hoped that his age would protect him from the complications of a romantic attachment, he finds that, at fifty years, he occupies a position between an elderly sexual ambiguity and a youthful virility. Though the novel's title, his name "Whittlestaff," and repeated descriptions throughout the work characterize him as old if not sexually impotent, the text also indicates that perceptions of age, like perceptions of gender, are subjective. While Whittlestaff's hair is beginning to turn gray, he is nonetheless an "impressive" man; the novel attests that he was "a much better looking man than he had been at thirty" (21). He is also healthy, "as fit, bodily and mentally, for hard work as ever he had been" (12). Whittlestaff equivocates about how he should interpret his own age, not because he wants to deceive himself or Mary, but because the implications of his age on his sexuality are truly confusing: "He was not a young man, because he was fifty; but he was not quite an old man, because he was only fifty" (16).[16] He comes to understand that the pliability of his age offers him two very different approaches to Mary: he could exaggerate his age and take on the role of a seventy-five-year-old (although this incorrectly presumes that seventy-five-year-old men are not sexual, which Arthur Gride's character would refute) or he could accentuate his youthfulness to court his ward. Speaking of their present guardian-ward arrangement, he muses, "She might come to accept it all and not think much of it, if he would take before himself the guise of an old man. But were he to appear before her as a suitor for her hand, would she refuse him?" (16). As time passes and he debates over which role to assume with Mary, he finds himself increasingly desirous of replacing his role as guardian with that of husband.

The pecuniary aspects of their relationship prove just as unsettling to Whittlestaff as his age. He, like Sir Michael Audley, initially rejects the idea of purchasing a wife with the financial security that he offers. He reasons to himself, "as the girl did receive from his hands all that she had—her bread and meat, her bed, her very clothes—would it not be better for her that he should stand to her in the place of a father rather than a lover?" (16). Whittlestaff wants to marry for love and to find that love reciprocated. He distances himself and his potential wife from what he envisions as a working-class perspective that accepts mercenary motivations for marriage: "Mrs. Baggett looks on [the marriage] only as a question of butchers and bakers. There are, no doubt, circumstances in which butchers and bakers do come uppermost. But here the butchers and bakers are provided." He continues, "I wouldn't have her marry me for that sake. Love, I fear, is out of the question. But for gratitude I would not have her do it" (19). Whittlestaff clearly values love over money, but like other characters in January–May relationships, Whittlestaff discovers that it is difficult to rise above economics.

Despite his observations, the "bread and meat" and "butchers and bakers" affect all of the characters' outlooks on Mary's obligations to Whittlestaff, and they couch their perceptions of her dependence in the same economic metaphor of "bread and meat" as Whittlestaff. For her own complex reasons, Mrs. Baggett is the one who initially encourages Mary to "sit close up" (31) to Whittlestaff as a sign of her willingness to accept his affections. Correctly reading Whittlestaff's hereto unexpressed longings for Mary, Mrs. Baggett tells her that she should let him "have his own way" because she is a young woman "who has had so much done for her" (31). After all, "Mary had eaten his bread, as bestowed upon her from sheer charity" (57). After Mrs. Baggett's urging, Mary reflects on the possibility of becoming Whittlestaff's wife. She inwardly muses,

> Did she not eat his bread; did she not wear his clothes; were not the very boots on her feet his property? And she was there in his house, without the slightest tie of blood or family connection. He had taken her from sheer charity, and had saved her from the terrible dependency of becoming a friendless governess. Looking out to the life which she had avoided, it seemed to her to be full of abject misery. And he had brought her to his own house, and had made her the mistress of everything. She knew that she had been undemonstrative in her manner, and that such was her nature. But her heart welled over with gratitude as she thought of the sweetness of the life which he had prepared for her. (32–33)

Despite the repetition of food imagery, Whittlestaff, unlike Arthur Gride, does not seem to want to consume Mary as a delicate morsel, and neither does the erotically suggestive fact that he owns her clothes give him moral license to make her take them off. Yet it is difficult even for Whittlestaff to keep to his honorable intentions. When he does eventually propose, he reminds her of her "ambition" and clearly outlines the social and material advantages he can offer her: "As my wife, you will fill a position more honourable, and more suitable to your gifts, than could belong to you as a governess or a companion" (54). The financial benefits that their marriage would afford never fade into the background of the novel, which lingers over practical concerns about money.

Yet the pervasiveness of financial matters does not prevent love from shaping the plot, even though Mary struggles with the question of her love for Whittlestaff. Following the conventions of the triangular January–May plot, her reluctance to commit herself to Whittlestaff originates from her affections for a younger man named John Gordon, whom she had known at home but who had gone away to seek his fortune. John had often visited her, and Mary considered him to be "the personification of manliness" (44). But John had not given her a promise of his love or any reason to expect his return. John's memory nonetheless keeps her from fully committing to Whittlestaff; she tells herself that "she could in truth have loved him,—had it not been for John Gordon" (54).

The tangled interrelationship between sexual desire and love also disturbs Mary as she contemplates their legal and physical union as man and wife. On the one hand, she reads her body as a part of the economic exchange—a material object that is subjected to a binding legal contract. She affirms to herself that she would not be sexually unfaithful if she were to marry him: "She was sure that she would be true to him, as far as truth to his material interests were concerned" (43), but, on the other hand, she assumes she will have to feign interest in their sexual relations. Directly alluding to the age difference, she pledges to herself that "she would be as tender to him as the circumstances would admit. She would not begrudge him kisses if he cared for them. They were his by all the right of contract" (43). Mary's allusion to sexual intimacy reminds readers that a husband had a legal right to more than kisses, and though she prepares herself mentally for this aspect of married life, she physically recoils from Whittlestaff when he asks her to kiss him "as a wife kisses her husband" (51).[17] Mary's reluctance to consummate their relationship suggests that she cannot love this man who is not, for her, the "personification of manliness," yet she wavers back and forth over the question of her love.

To be forthright, she tells Whittlestaff of her love for John Gordon before she accepts his proposal. Although she verbally agrees with Whittlestaff's suggestion that her feelings for John were "just a fancy," she later assumes that her confession of love for John releases her from any expectations of loving Whittlestaff. When she later halfheartedly attempts to break the engagement and he urges her "not to accept any man that you cannot love," she silently protests, "Had she not told him that she did not love him;—even that she loved another?" (55). But Mary has not told Whittlestaff that she did not or cannot love him, and her frustrated and confused memory relies too much on a monogamous ideal of love. She has even told herself that she loves him: "And it is not that I hate him. I do love him. He is all good" (45). Mary's befuddled "love" fluctuates as she compares him against her sexualized masculine ideal.

At first, Mary's ability to love Whittlestaff is inseparable from his age and its associations with conventional masculinity, even though, as he himself does, she finds his fifty years to be an ambiguous marker of gendered power. Immediately after she accepts his proposal, she finds that he looks "older than she had ever remarked him to be before" (43), but later, when she reveals that she is considering breaking the engagement and he sternly objects, she thinks "he did not now appear so old" (54). Associating masculinity and youth with power, she envisions Whittlestaff as older and more feminine when he submits, as when he accepts her confession of love for John, and younger and more manly when he acts aggressively. When Whittlestaff appears younger, Mary becomes aware that "There was a power of speech about the man, and a dignity" (54), and she admits after he forcefully kisses her on the lips that "he had displayed more of power than she had ever guessed at his possessing. A woman always loves this display of power in a man" (56). Mary's appreciation of Whittlestaff's power changes, however, when John Gordon returns just hours after Mary has engaged herself to Whittlestaff.

When John arrives and officially declares his love for Mary, he embodies a youthful and sexual masculinity, and, for the rest of the novel, serves as a foil to the aging Whittlestaff. During the three years he has been gone, he has mined diamonds in South Africa and returned rich, having "carried his purpose through with a manly resolution" (69). Mary also reflects on his masculine appearance and "How like a man he had looked" (88). Though Mary's use of the simile "like a man" nods to the unstable and transitory nature of John's phallic masculinity, which will also be challenged with time, others recognize the value of John's youthful masculinity and deem Mary's choice between her older and younger suitors an easy one. Speaking to his own fiancée, the Reverend Montagu Blake declares, "A lady always prefers a young gentleman to an old one. Only think what you'd feel if you were married to Mr. Whittlestaff" (143). Although John's return makes Mary regret her decision to marry Whittlestaff, she resolves to keep her promise, and Whittlestaff, meanwhile, wrestles with the question of whether he should release Mary from her commitment.[18] The question of whether to break off the engagement becomes an issue of sacrifice and emerges as a gendered issue: Should Mary suppress her love for John or should Whittlestaff suppress his love for Mary? For many, dutiful sacrifice was an accepted component of being a woman, as Sarah Stickney Ellis advised British women that their "highest duty" was "to suffer, and be still" (94) in her book *The Daughters of England* (1842). Expecting conventional feminine submissiveness, Mrs. Baggett believes that "Mary was bound to deliver herself body and soul to Mr. Whittlestaff, were 'soul sacrifice' demanded from her" (57). Mrs. Baggett makes it clear that society expects sacrifice from women, not from men, and she reveals that self-sacrifice can be an effeminizing characteristic as she rallies Whittlestaff to hold Mary to her engagement: "When you've said that you'll do a thing, you ought not to go back for any other man, let him be who it may,—especially not in respect of a female. It's weak, and nobody wouldn't think a straw of you for doing it. It's some idea of being generous that you have got into your head. . . . I say it ain't manly, and that's what a man ought to be" (212). Whittlestaff likewise recognizes that letting Mary go would compromise his manhood: "as it came to be known that he himself had given up the girl whom he loved, he could read the ridicule which would be conveyed by the smiles of his neighbors" (218). Mary, on the one hand, fulfills the feminine role expected of her, and she acknowledges that she is willing to lie to Whittlestaff and perform wifely affection to keep him from any regret about their marriage. Yet Whittlestaff, on the other hand, finds masculine selfishness difficult to accept. Aware that "it behoved him to learn to become stern and cruel," he discovers that he cannot hold Mary to her promise (123). Despite Mary's objections, Whittlestaff assumes a feminized position and willingly makes the sacrifice.[19]

Although Whittlestaff wants to make Mary his wife, he comes to realize "He could not alter his own self. He could not turn round upon himself, and bid himself be other than he was" (117). He cannot perform the sternness and cruelty required of him, and he is guided to his rejection of masculine norms, regardless of public opinion, by his love for Mary. Unlike Mary, he commits to the sacrifice not from a sense of obligation from eating someone's bread, but from a less material concern for her happiness more in line with the ideal of romantic sacrifice. Trollope writes, "He could not conceive it possible that he should be required by duty to make such a sacrifice; but he knew of himself that if her happiness, her true and permanent happiness, would require it, then the sacrifice should be made" (168). Thus, January–May love allows Whittlestaff to move beyond the framework of material logic or advantage and to maintain the ideology of gender and age while producing the terms of its revision. When Whittlestaff tells John that he is willing to release Mary from the engagement, he makes it clear that the acquiescence is painful for him: "If I know what love is, I loved her. If I know what love is, I do love her still. She is all the world to me" (231). Relying again on the ambiguities of his age, Whittlestaff determines to be a father if not a lover to Mary and continues to welcome Mary in his home until her wedding to John can be arranged. He promises to be her friend if she needs him in the future, and treating her as if she were his daughter, he even takes care of the "money matters" necessary to prepare for her wedding to his young rival (258). While it is difficult, Whittlestaff fully assumes a sacrificial position and relinquishes the legal and social power he held as her fiancé, and when Mary refers to him as an "angel," she correctly appropriates the metaphor commonly associated with Victorian women.[20]

Whittlestaff joins numerous January figures in nineteenth-century literature who prove true the adage that a young wife is often "a young man's slave and an old man's darling" (232). In addition to undermining gendered notions of sacrifice and duty, these submissions by January "husbands" to their May "wives" endorse feminine sexuality as a powerful and genuine social force, since they habitually include the older man's acceptance of the young woman's sexual life with another. While these sacrifices often result in the breaking of January–May engagements, their contributions are critical to the broader implications of the theme's disruption of gender identities. On one level they directly contradict the machinations of a sexual economy that I explored in Chapter 5, and, in acknowledging the validity of intergenerational love, reject stereotypical readings of these relationships that have perpetuated since the time of Chaucer. While mercenary marriages privilege the pragmatic over the romantic, both marrying for money and marrying for love challenge gender roles and power distributions.

Love's destabilizing effects are not limited to the actions of the older men in January–May relationships; love works less predictably than money, and in works that capture the passionate love of younger wives for their older husbands, the erratic irrationality of love also troubles gendered norms. In *David Copperfield*, Annie Strong's love for her much-older husband defies everyone's logic, and, however disturbing feminine infidelity might be, even innocent young David seems to believe it quite natural that she would rather have sex with Jack Maldon than be in a monogamous relationship with her elderly husband. Depictions of the January–May marriage like that of Annie and Doctor Strong test understandings of aesthetics and sexual desire, playing with perversity while simultaneously mitigating that play by crediting it to the theoretically transcendent nature of love. For example, in George Eliot's *Middlemarch* Dorothea Brooke is free to marry whom she wants, since she has been left financially well off after the deaths of her parents. She astounds her family and neighbors in accepting the proposal of the aging scholar Casaubon over the young and handsome Sir James Chettam. Despite Chettam's masculine virtues, Dorothea bluntly explains, "If he thinks of marrying me, he has made a great mistake" (26). She prefers Casaubon, regardless of his stooping shoulders, sunken eyes, and hairy moles. Perplexed, Mr. Brooke scrambles to reappraise youthful masculinity: "One never knows. I should have thought Chettam was just the sort of man a woman would like, now" (26).

The possibility of Dorothea's love for Casaubon has been largely dismissed. Dorothea's actions are considered a "perversity" (43) contrary to nature by Sir James and "the most horrible of virgin-sacrifices" (225) by Will Ladislaw. Literary critics have been only slightly less unkind. Bert Hornback reads the marriage between Dorothea and Casaubon as a great mistake that derives from Dorothea's misconception of her husband and herself. Hornback deems the marriage "not a relationship at all" and asserts that "because her marriage has taught her what love is not, she is ready—almost—to learn what love is" (125). Though the marriage fails to bring Dorothea any sexual, emotional, or intellectual satisfaction, it does not follow that Dorothea does not love her husband. *Middlemarch* makes a point of the irrationality of love, which can be seen through various other matches, such as Mary Garth's preference of Fred Vincy over Farebrother or Lydgate's illogical attachment to Rosamond—all relationships that don't make "sense" but are driven by inexplicable motives. Having fallen in love, Dorothea is "childlike" and "stupid" in spite of "all her reputed cleverness," and the Middlemarch community derides her for "throwing herself, metaphorically speaking, at Mr Casaubon's feet, and kissing his unfashionable shoe-ties as if he were a Protestant Pope" (33).

Nevertheless, "from the wealth of her own love" she would have liked "to have kissed Mr Casaubon's coat-sleeve, or to have caressed his shoe-latchet" (127). Even the sexual disappointments that begin during her honeymoon do not prevent Dorothea from attempting to instigate physical intimacy with her husband on numerous occasions, and Eliot often describes Dorothea's hands as seeking contact with Casaubon's body, although her efforts usually meet with little or no response from her husband. In Book IV, "Three Love Problems," Dorothea softly wraps her arm around Casaubon's "rigid" arm after he has spoken with Lydgate about his failing health, and later that night, she waits for Casaubon to come upstairs so that she can "put her hand into her husband's" (266) to accompany him to bed. Eliot provides several other illustrations of Dorothea's love for Casaubon. She is slow to understand the nature of Casaubon's jealousy toward Ladislaw; if she finds Ladislaw attractive, she never contemplates the possibility of Ladislaw's youthful masculinity overturning her affections for her husband. Like the sacrificial older husbands, Dorothea is prepared to give up her happiness for the happiness of another, and she resolves to bind herself to Casaubon's selfish request that she follow his instructions after his death regarding the chaotic mess that is his *Key to all Mythologies*. And I believe she truly laments his death, as her shocked response on finding his lifeless body expressively reveals: "Wake, dear, wake! Listen to me. I am come to answer" (299).

I am not suggesting that Dorothea *should* feel or behave this way, or that Casaubon is deserving of Dorothea's love. Love defies intellectual "shoulds" and rational readings. Because of love, Dorothea's dutiful allegiance to her wifely role is more subversive than not. Though it superficially fulfills conventions of womanly obedience, selflessness, and submission, it undermines conventional masculinity by demonstrating how love can value what "rationally," via the mind, or "naturally," via the body, should not be valued. Wives who fall in love with older husbands illustrate this seemingly illogical rejection of masculine power. Jane Eyre refuses St. John Rivers, who projects a youthful masculinity, to wed Rochester, who is emasculated by his blindness and injuries as well as his age. It is no surprise that Eleanor Bold prefers the older Mr. Arabin to his younger rival, Mr. Slope, even though the latter offers to help her father. Just as the January–May marriage illustrates how money shifts power away from masculine control, so January–May love demonstrates how masculinity does not lead to predictable outcomes within heterosexual romance narratives.

In the unique social and economic climate of the nineteenth century, money and love provide distinct but complementary methods of accessing and evaluating the worth of masculinity and femininity to the middle class. The January–May marriage works from within the existing economy, and, in following a heterosexual marriage plot, plays its game with gender identities by the rules. Much of the theme's subversive potential comes from its superficial acceptance of established nineteenth-century constructions like class-aligned gender differences, a male-dominated economic world, and the overwhelming power of love. Yet by grafting age onto these already overburdened concepts, the January–May marriage theme reveals their underlying fragility and encourages readers to reconsider the distribution of power across the lines of gender, class, and generation.

# Conclusion

The peculiar combinations of age and gender in January–May marriages manipulate incest, aesthetics, horror, economics, and love in ways that appealed to nineteenth-century authors and readers—in ways that continue to appeal to readers today. Because these marriages fulfill such diverse patterns and because these patterns address different objectives, older man and younger woman romances are a perfect medium for exploring anxieties about gender and power. The pliability of the theme allows for different arguments in different situations and even permits contradictory arguments in similar situations. The ambiguity of how these relationships can be interpreted is a key to their popularity. The January–May marriage theme eludes reductive readings about its objectives, and its patterns demonstrate that there is much more to intergenerational relationships than the oppression of women in a masculine hierarchy. Age alters gender in intricate ways. Viewing these marriages as evidence of masculine privilege is only one way of understanding the theme, and women often assume more powerful positions in nineteenth-century January–May marriages than they would in same-age alternatives.

Apart from the use of parodic excess and the exploration of a triangular romance—the two prevailing elements of January–May marriages that I discuss in my introduction and in my case study of *Don Juan* in Chapter 1—that bind these intergenerational relationships together, this book's topic-driven structure highlights that January–May marriages might have little in common or a great deal in common; thus, more important than providing organizing strategies for contemplating January–May marriages, the patterns that I have identified within the broader theme demonstrate the need to read these marriages in their unique contexts. Some January–May texts incorporate a number of these patterns within their retelling of the theme. Some might incorporate only a few.[1] I recognize the challenges and limitations of the classifications that I have formed, and at the end of this project I see that there is still much more to be said about the January–May marriage in literature.

The nineteenth-century fascination with these marriages intersects with a number of social concerns I have not been able to address at any length. For example, W. T. Stead's *The Maiden Tribute to Modern Babylon* (1885) corresponds directly to the nexus of age, gender, and power encapsulated by the January–May marriage. Stead, in a crusade to fight child prostitution, participated in the purchase and manipulation of thirteen-year-old Eliza Armstrong, which included chloroforming her to silence her protests and a vaginal exam to have her virginity verified. His sensational description of her treatment and her terror was shocking—and titillating—but not as much so as the revelation of his involvement. Even though Stead's journalism and the ensuing public outcry led to the passing of the Criminal Law Amendment Bill and the raising of the age of consent for girls from thirteen to sixteen years, he was sentenced to three months of imprisonment for the abduction and indecent assault of Eliza. This scandal was one of many attempts to save young women and girls from abuse that inevitably sexualized and infantilized those they tried to protect.

Victorian interest in child marriages in colonial India increased around the same time as the W. T. Stead affair. Girls in India were often wed at eight or nine years old to adult men before criticism, both in India and England, led to limited reform in the 1880s and early 1890s that, like Stead's campaign, raised the age of consent. As Antoinette Burton describes, "It looked at first as if the whole question of procuring underage girls—the very issue that had fueled 'the Maiden Tribute' controversy—was going to be revisited in the Indian context" (1134). Public statements by Rukhmabai Bhikaji, a young bride who refused to live with her husband, increased popular criticism of "infant marriages" and "infant widowhood" and highlighted the idea that age discrepancies in marriage often led to a gender-based double standard. Rukhmabai asked her readers to consider the injustice of "the edifying spectacle of a green old man of sixty, who is visited with the great misfortune of losing his second or third wife, preparing to play the young bridegroom, and sending his creatures out to seek a girl of ten or eleven to bless the remaining days of his natural life" (Burton, 1139). Toward the end of the reform movement, an eleven- or twelve-year-old named Phulmonee Mati hemorrhaged and bled to death after her husband forced her to have sex with him, solidifying sentiment against child marriage.[2] While the Stead case and child-marriage debate allowed for the displacement of unease about intergenerational unions onto criminal outcasts or foreign cultures, social causes like these brought prostitution, pedophilia, and marriage uncomfortably close in the public eye, and more work should be done to elucidate the relationships between them and the January–May marriage theme in British literature.

Because this study is focused on literature rather than biography, I have not attempted to offer any cohesive coverage of real-life examples of January–May marriages and romances of the period. As I explain in the introduction, incomplete public records regarding the ages of partners at marriage make it difficult to formulate theories about older husbands and younger wives as a complex social reality.[3] Several famous January–May romances involving writers, however, repeatedly creep into conversations whenever I share my work in academic circles, and it seems fitting to mention briefly some of the most interesting here. In 1858, John Ruskin, aged thirty-nine, met Rose La Touche, aged nine. Ruskin waited nine more years before he proposed to Rose, and though they never married, their January–May romance—best characterized by both pedophilia and frustration—has been an important touchstone in my study of the literature of the period.[4] Robert Polhemus ties Dickens's scandalous relationship with the eighteen-year-old Ellen Ternan to the author's "Lot complex," and biography is certainly one way of making sense of Dickens's investment in the January–May marriage theme. In *Men in Wonderland*, Catherine Robson details several examples of child loving among nineteenth-century writers, including Thomas DeQuincey's string of lost girl-loves and Lewis Carroll's infatuation with Alice Liddell. The pornographic exploits of "Walter" in the anonymous account *My Secret Life: An Erotic Diary of Victorian London* also extend some insight into a middle-aged man's sexual infatuation with young women and girls.

I am also intrigued by relationships that manifest January–May tendencies in nonconventional ways. For example, fifteen years separate the late-Victorian lesbian partners Katherine Bradley and Edith Cooper, who are best known by their united pseudonym "Michael Field," and I am interested in how their age difference affects their efforts to negotiate gender and power outside a heterosexual frame. Since Bradley is also Cooper's aunt, who moved into Cooper's home when she was very young, taking on many of the responsibilities of raising Cooper because her mother was ill, their relationship also offers new ways of reading incest narratives within the January–May theme. Similarly, the fifteen-year gap between Oscar Wilde and Lord Alfred "Bosie" Douglas presents another real-life revision of the heterosexual rubric. Queer theorists point out that older partners have traditionally introduced those who are younger into homosexual encounters, but I believe that queer readings of age, gender, and power in such relationships would benefit from considering similarities to and departures from the larger January–May tradition.[5]

Many other nineteenth-century January–May texts influenced my thinking for this project, but, due to the constraints of time and space, I was not able to discuss them at any length. In his pastoral poem "Michael" (1800), Wordsworth's sympathetic older husband adopts traditionally feminine domestic duties in caring for his much-loved son. Twenty years older than his wife Isabel, Michael dotingly performs "female service" (154) through "acts of tenderness" (157) and "with a woman's gentle hand" (158). Austen's juvenilia abound with marriages between older men and younger women; Austen, it appears, found the topic quite amusing as an adolescent, though her tone changes in both *Sense and Sensibility* and *Emma*, the latter of which remains one of my favorite examples of the struggle for age- and gender-based power in marriage.[6] Robert Browning's *Pippa Passes* (1841) contains the January–May marriage of Luca and Ottima and is significant for being, as far as I know, the only Victorian work from a canonical British author that allows for the consummation of the extramarital affair with the younger lover, in addition to being the only nineteenth-century text with a murder of the older husband by the younger man and woman. Many of Browning's poems, including "My Last Duchess" (1842) and "Andrea del Sarto" (1853) merit more attention than I could give in this study, and *The Ring and the Book*'s (1869) retelling of the violent end of an intergenerational marriage deserves much scrutiny. Thackeray's *The Memoirs of Barry Lyndon, Esq.* (1844) includes the intriguing marriage of an older Sir Charles and a younger Lady Lyndon, where power appears to rest in Lady Lyndon's hands. Sir Charles reports: "Look at me. I am dying, a worn-out cripple at the age of fifty. Marriage has added forty years to my life. When I took off Lady Lyndon, there was no man of my years who looked so young as myself. Fool that I was!" (183). After Sir Charles's death, Lady Lyndon's power continues, to an extent—Barry takes the Lyndon surname when they marry. Charlotte Brontë's *Villette* (1853) and *The Professor* (1857) participate in the tradition to varying degrees. Both novels emphasize the husband as teacher, and *Villette* teases the reader with "a marriage between a poor and unselfish man of forty, and his wealthy ward of eighteen" (566) just as it teases the reader with the potential marriage between the same man and Lucy Snow, little more than five years older than his ward. Elizabeth Gaskell's *North and South* (1855) illuminates life after a January–May marriage; Mrs. Shaw, Margaret Hale's aunt, is a widow of a much-older husband, and though she asserts that "disparity of age is a drawback" (6) in marriage, she presents a positive image of Victorian widowhood that stresses women's freedom.

Trollope's *Orley Farm* (1862) employs the marriage of Joseph and Lady Mason as the starting place for an investigation of primogeniture, gendered economies, and secret lives and offers a second January–May engagement between Lady Mason and Sir Peregrine Orme for contemplation. As in *An Old Man's Love* and *Barchester Towers*, Trollope treats his older lovers sympathetically, explaining: "But that old man's heart is as soft as thine, if thou couldst but read it. The body dries up and withers away, and the bones grow old; the brain, too, becomes decrepit, as do the sight, the hearing, and the soul. But the heart that is tender once remains tender to the last" (265). *Orley Farm* also explores the idea of an older man raising his wife from childhood like Rousseau's *Julie, or the New Heloise* (1761) through the characters of Felix Graham and Mary Snow. Trollope does not depict this "moulding" of a wife favorably: "Such a frame of mind comes upon a bachelor, perhaps about his thirty-fifth year, and then he goes to work with a girl of fourteen. The operation takes some ten years, at the end of which the moulded bride regards her lord as an old man" (329). In *He Knew He Was Right* (1869), Trollope twists the typical January–May scenario, making the same-aged husband of Emily Trevelyan the jealous spouse, while Colonel Osborne, "nearly sixty" (180), figures as the extramarital third. Much of the gender fun in the novel comes from mixed social stereotypes about aging masculinity and the propriety of "innocent" friendships between younger women and older men. Colonel Osborne has known Emily her entire life; he is both a friend of her father and "old enough to be the lady's father" (347), which is the argument used to diffuse Louis Trevelyan's jealous actions throughout the plot. However, Trollope's revelation that Osborne's intentions are not entirely void of romance rejects myths of male sexual decline and affirms nontraditional portrayals of later life. Emily is not romantically interested in Osborne, but through this alteration of the January–May triangle, Louis Trevelyan is shown to be entirely in the wrong, even though "he knew he was right." Other texts employ the January–May theme to manipulate their audiences' responses against older husbands. Because of widespread fears of aging and nonstandard sexual relationships, the January–May marriage was prone to assumptions about wicked aging men who abuse and destroy beautiful and young heroines, and recalling such abuses of power by way of the January–May marriage funneled readers' sympathy toward same-age, however problematically adulterous, desire. Wilkie Collins's *The Woman in White* (1860) tells the story of Laura Fairlie, aged twenty, who marries Sir Percival Glyde, aged forty-five. Glyde physically and emotionally abuses Laura while he robs her of her private fortune until finally, needing even more funds, he stages her death and has her locked into an insane asylum. In case this was not enough to prejudice readers against Glyde, the age difference drives the point home. Walter Hartright, the young lover of Laura, neatly summarizes the intended effect: "even the mention of his age, when I contrasted it with hers, added to my blind hatred and disgust of him" (78). George du Maurier's wildly famous *Trilby* (1894) also capitalizes on tacit aged-based alliances to guide readers' sympathies, using anti-Semitic hostility in addition to prevalent enmities surrounding the January husband. By the end of the novel, the menacing and decidedly Jewish Svengali is "nearly fifty" (223) while Trilby is only twenty-three, and interracial and intergenerational tensions heighten the problems associated with Svengali's use of hypnotism to control Trilby's mind and body. Swept up in both age and race discrimination, Svengali becomes one of the most infamous January husbands in English literature, and a word in the English language: "one who exercises a controlling or mesmeric influence on another, frequently, for some sinister purpose." *The Wyvern Mystery* (1869) by Joseph Sheridan Le Fanu boasts not one, but two frightening January figures. Twenty-year-old Alice Maybell escapes the amorous advances of her aging guardian "the old squire," whose "Come, lass, do ye like me?" is prefaced by this description: "She saw no object in the room but the tall figure of the old man, flushed with punch, and leering with horrid jollity, straight before her like a vivid magic-lantern figure in the dark" (21). Alice eventually elopes with the old squire's son, but as the novel makes clear, at age forty-three, "young Mr Fairfield [the son] is old enough, I think, to be your father" (1). "Young" Fairfield's age and their January–May marriage introduces Alice to terrible plot developments, including bigamy, attempted murder, and child abduction. To an extent, Glyde, Svengali, and the

Fairfields fit the framework I established regarding Gothic horror, but these villains are more one-dimensional than Philottson, Varney, or Dracula, and they do not elicit much sympathy through their roles as older husbands.

As a "New Woman" novel, Sarah Grand's *The Heavenly Twins* (1893) directly connects the January–May marriage to issues of power and gender. Angelica is the stronger of the "heavenly twins," but she finds that her brother Diavolo will enjoy countless gender-based privileges as they mature. As a child she rejects the notion that "she should marry a rickety king" and reverses the gender roles of Rousseau's *Heloise*: "I think the wisest plan for me would be to buy a nice clean little boy, and bring him up to suit my own ideas. I needn't marry him, you know, if he doesn't turn out well" (250). Ironically, this plan is explained to Mr. Kilroy, the friend of Angelica's parents who will later become her husband. Grand recognizes Angelica's power in the marriage; "stamping her foot at him," Angelica proposes to Kilroy, though the proposal is more a demand than a request: "Marry me! ... Marry me, *and let me do as I like*" (321). But Grand reminds the reader that Angelica's options in life are limited by her gender. Angelica dons a wig and men's clothing to impersonate her brother and forms a relationship with a beautiful young tenor, but her gender bending, both outside and within her marriage, is largely ineffectual. Shocked by the disclosure of her real gender (and marital status), the tenor dies after an accident involving Angelica, and she returns apologetically to her husband. Clinging to Kilroy, she entreats, "Don't let me go again, Daddy, keep me close. I am— I am grateful for the blessing of a good man's love" (551).[7]

Beyond the nineteenth-century British examples I have not been able to cover in depth, large fields regarding age and marriage demand further study. Chapter 1 provides a general overview of the January–May marriage theme's early tradition in British literature, but it is also helpful to view nineteenth-century January–May marriages in comparison with other literary and cultural frameworks. Set in seventeenth-century America, *The Scarlet Letter* (1850) by Nathaniel Hawthorne has much in common with the dreadful portrayals of older husbands in nineteenth-century British novels like *The Woman in White* and *Trilby*. *The Scarlet Letter* adheres to formulaic conventions of the January–May triangle, pitting the young reverend Arthur Dimmesdale against the aging and manipulative Roger Chillingworth for Hester Prynne's loyalty, but the text raises questions of the power of youthful masculinity through Dimmesdale's profound emotional and spiritual crises of responsibility. Henry James's *Watch and Ward*, published serially in *The Atlantic Monthly* in 1871, is another important American contribution to the theme in literature, closely linked to Dickens's *Bleak House* and Trollope's *An Old Man's Love* in its assessment of the permeable borders between guardian/husband and ward/wife identities. Unlike its British counterparts, however, *Watch and Ward* concludes with an endorsement of the January–May marriage between the older guardian, Roger Lawrence, and his young ward, Nora Lambert. These American examples are interesting complements to British fascination with the theme, but January–May marriages were not as integral to nineteenth-century literary negotiations of gender in America, perhaps because America had unique opportunities for investigating gender by way of the literature of the expanding frontier, the Civil War, and slavery.[8]

Early twentieth-century British and American writers continue the January–May tradition by adapting the theme to modern sensibilities with more explicit tales of sex and violence. *Summer* (1917) by Edith Wharton openly addresses aberrant sexualities surrounding the marriage of Lawyer Royall to his ward Charity Royall, who need not change her surname upon marriage. Lawyer's desire for Charity is close to both pedophilia and incest, but their marriage saves Charity from the consequences of other sexual improprieties: her sexual relations with young Lucius Harney and a subsequent pregnancy. As in *Summer*, other twentieth-century versions of the theme seem more likely than their nineteenth-century counterparts to promote intergenerational relationships as promising alternatives to same-age marriages. Though these texts present their own deviancies within the January–May connections, they privilege these alliances over same-age relationships, reversing the implicit sympathies toward youth that prevail in texts like *Nicholas Nickleby*. For example, Daphne du Maurier's *Rebecca* (1938) reveals the marriage of Maxim and Rebecca de Winter to be fraught with lies and deceit.[9] Rebecca fosters an image of herself as the perfect upper-class wife, though her performance as "angel in the house" masks a nontraditional femininity that is marked by an unapologetic individualism, violence, cunning, and sexual promiscuity. As Maxim explains, "she was not even normal" (255). Meanwhile, Maxim plays the role of dutiful husband, but the truth is that he murders Rebecca and finds love with the much-younger narrator of the story.

Modern works capitalize on dissatisfaction with same-age relationships. Many, but not all, of these versions of the older man and younger woman motif clearly depict male fantasies of middle-age revitalization. *Lolita* (1955), Vladimir Nabokov's controversial narrative of Humbert Humbert's sexual infatuation with his twelve-year-old stepdaughter, met with criticism for its eroticizing of children and its depiction of same-age relationships. Humbert is immensely bored with Lolita's mother Charlotte, and Lolita's marriage at the end of the novel is depressingly bleak, foreshadowing her early death. Idealization of intergenerational relationships predominate as the theme moves into film. *Rebecca* was adapted to film in 1940 by Alfred Hitchcock, winning the Oscar for Best Picture that year; it is one of the most successful early cinematic treatments of the theme. In *How to Marry a Millionaire* (1953), Lauren Bacall's character Schatze Page almost marries an aging Texan, but, like John Jarndyce, he encourages her to leave him for a younger man. Woody Allen's *Manhattan* (1979) is one of the most famous scene adaptations of the January–May romance and one of a number of the director's creations that center on a middle-aged man's love of a beautiful young woman, a subject so visually successful on the big screen that countless revisions and responses have emerged.[10] Some recent films in this genre include *Addams Family Values* (1993), *Greedy* (1994), *The First Wives Club* (1997), *The Human Stain* (2003), *Lost in Translation* (2003), *Notes on a Scandal* (2006), *Elegy (2008)* and the television series *Northern Exposure* (1990–1995). While many of the patterns that characterize nineteenth-century January–May marriages continue in these examples, the theme adapts to changing legal, financial, and social strictures governing gender and marriage. Increased possibilities for divorce, from January–May marriages or same-age matches, complicate contemporary fictional accounts of intergenerational romance, eliminating some of the tensions surrounding marriage in the nineteenth century and introducing new ones. Advances in women's equality and GLBTQ activism shift the points of anxiety to which nineteenth-century January–May marriages responded.[11] Historical and cultural influences also differentiate these texts from the ones I have examined; for example, Arthur Golden's 1997 novel *Memoirs of a Geisha* extends an account of a January–May romance in 1940s Japan, and the acclaimed 2006 film *Water* relates the experience of a child bride in India whose older husband dies, leaving her a widow at age eight. These works contribute to the broader January–May tradition, but necessitate a different critical framework for analysis.

The January–May marriage theme continues to resonate within contemporary culture, and a number of scandals keep older man and younger woman relationships in the public eye. Sensational media coverage of Anna Nicole Smith's 2006 U.S. Supreme Court case over the estate of her deceased billionaire husband J. Howard

Marshall II and of the strange circumstances surrounding her 2007 death directed public attention to the January–May marriage. Smith, a former *Playboy* centerfold, married Marshall in 1994 when she was twenty-six and he was eighty-nine. Upon his death fourteen months later, Marshall's son fought Smith in a Texas state probate court for his father's estate, reported to be worth 1.6 billion dollars, and won, but a federal court later overturned this decision. While Smith's case in the Supreme Court settled legal questions of federal jurisdiction over state probate rulings, in the public imagination the debate centered on the January–May marriage's peculiar negotiation of age, sex, money, and power. In 2008, American media buzzed with accounts of various illegal January–May relationships. In April, Texas Child Protective Services took into custody over four hundred children from the Fundamentalist Church of Jesus Christ of Latter Day Saints. Amid charges of polygamy, allegations of child marriage and pregnancy drew international attention. Also in April, a sixty-one-year-old Australian man, John Deaves, and his thirty-nine-year-old daughter Jenny declared their love on international television and admitted to having two children together. But breaking news of an Austrian man who imprisoned his daughter in a basement and fathered seven children with her quickly usurped the Deaves's consensual relationship in the media. As varied as these stories are, public interest in them attests to continued attraction to and repugnance of intergenerational unions.

Scenarios that reverse the age and gender structure of January–May marriages provide a fuller context for considering their implications. Older woman and younger man relationships do occur in nineteenth-century literature, although they are much less frequent and generally feature much smaller differences in age. Byron's *Don Juan* contains a number of these sexual encounters; as I note in Chapter 1, Juan is seven years younger than Donna Julia, and his youthful inexperience alters conventionally gendered distributions of knowledge and power. Juan has same-age romances with many women, including his beloved Haidee, but also enters sexual relationships with the Sultana and Catherine the Great, both powerful older women who use their rank and authority to gain access to Juan's body.[12] Juan does not object, and the narrator interrupts the plot to explain Juan's relationship with Catherine and to praise older women:

> Besides, he had some qualities which fix
> Middle-aged ladies even more than young:
> The former know what's what; while new-fledged chicks
> Know little more of Love than what is sung

In rhymes, or dreamt (for Fancy will play tricks)
In visions of those skies from whence Love sprung.
Some reckon women by their Sun or Years,
I rather think the Moon should date the dears. (10:73–80)

Byron endorses older woman and younger man relationships and thereby ingratiates himself with many of his female readers, but these love affairs are not likely to lead to marriage. Jane Austen's *Lady Susan* (ca. 1793–94) includes a number of age-disparate relationships, including the marriage of Lady Susan's friend Alicia Johnson to a man who is "just old enough to be formal, ungovernable and to have the gout—too old to be agreable, and too young to die," but Lady Susan's gender reversal of the age discrepancy makes her a wicked woman or sexy heroine, depending on the reader's response. After losing the dashing, young Reginald De Courcy, Lady Susan settles for the young, bumbling but rich Sir James, a man she originally intended her daughter to marry.[13] Kidderminster, a member of Sleary's circus troop in Dickens's *Hard Times*, enters a gender-reversed January–May marriage. With his characteristic lisp, Sleary updates Sissy and Louisa about Kidderminster's life: "He'th married too. Married a widder. Old enough to be hith mother" (209). Sleary's description of this marriage comes only in passing, and though Sleary adds that the couple had two children together and that the wife, once a tightrope walker, is now too fat for the job, Dickens does not offer enough information for much further analysis of their marriage. Another example that deserves comment is Thackeray's *Henry Esmond* (1852). In this novel, Henry is torn between his love for his mistress Rachel, who is eight years his senior, and her daughter Beatrix, eight years his junior. Henry eventually marries Rachel, and though their age difference is not that large, their ages complicate their relationship. When Henry meets Rachel, he is twelve and she is twenty, and the maternal role she first assumes with him affects her later claims to power as an ideal wife. Kate Chopin's novella *The Awakening* is a late nineteenth-century example of older woman and younger man love in American literature, though again, the age difference is less than ten years.

In the twentieth and twenty-first centuries, relationships between older women and younger men have assumed a more prominent place in literature and culture. The films *The Graduate* (1967) and *Harold and Maude* (1971) explore sexual relationships between older women and younger men that boast significant age gaps, and the raunchy teen flick *American Pie* (1999) popularized the acronym MILF: "Mom I'd like to fuck." Though the tabloid coverage was relatively positive, actor

Demi Moore's marriage to Ashton Kutcher in 2005 received additional scrutiny because of their fifteen-year age difference. But Mary Kay Letourneau's relationship with, and eventual marriage to, Vili Fualaau is one of the most scandalous older woman and younger man romances of recent years. Mary Kay, Vili's schoolteacher, was thirty-four years old and he thirteen when they began their sexual relationship in 1996. She served over seven years in prison, having two daughters with Vili while in custody, before being released in 2004 and marrying Vili in 2005.[14] In contemporary literature, a number of recent works respond to the increased popularity of this theme. *What's Eating Gilbert Grape* (1991) by Peter Hedges includes an older woman–younger man affair between the title character and Betty Carver, wife of a local insurance agent. Antonya Nelson's *Nobody's Girl* (1998) has a number of similarities to the Letourneau-Fualaau case. In this novel, Birdy Stone, a high school English teacher in her thirties, has an affair with her seventeen-year-old student Mark. The aptly named *A Much Younger Man* (1998) by Australian author Dianne Highbridge has a strikingly familiar plot: Aly, a thirty-five-year-old English teacher, has a passionate romance with Tom, the fifteen-year-old son of her best friend. Additionally, there is a three-novel series entitled *The Cradle Robbers* (2003–04) that explores several comparable romances.[15] In contemporary literature, the narratives usually avoid the subject of marriage, focusing on sexual relationships outside of marriage in a manner that has much more in common with Byron than with most Victorian writers, and while these texts do contribute to the theme's negotiation of power through age and gender, the patterns and implications of these works are very different from those in which marriage is proposed, considered, and finalized.

My research into critical gerontology led me to consider how other cultures link the effects of time on the body to issues of gender identity. One of the most striking examples I have encountered is that of the Gabra nomads of East Africa, a tribe whose older men become *d'abella* by assuming a feminine gender. John Colman Wood, whose fascinating study *When Men Are Women* (1999) explores this subject at length, explains that

> d'abella are regarded as women (nad'eni). They do not dress like women or act like women, though they regard their dress and aspects of their behavior as feminine. D'abella are not transvestites or transgendered. They say they are women. Others refer to them with feminine pronouns. There are special rules governing their behavior, and that of others toward them, which place d'abella in the same category

## Conclusion

as women. Offenses against d'abella, for instance, are adjudicated and punished the same as those against women. D'abella tie their cloth on the left side, like women. They walk behind men, like women. When a d'abella urinates, he squats and does not hold his penis, as if, like a woman, he did not have one. (72)

Wood points out that, as women, *d'abella* oversee rituals and advance peace, placing crucial social responsibilities in the hands of "women" in an otherwise distinctly male hierarchy. As I believe my preceding chapters make clear, I do not argue that aging masculinity demands that older men become feminized. However, my readings about the Gabra *d'abella* encouraged me to consider more closely how age constructs gender and destabilizes its position as a monolithic category that is inextricably tied to the body.

Considering these other contexts for age-based gender negotiation has helped me to theorize about nineteenth-century marriages like the one between Jane Eyre and Edward Rochester beyond the assumptions of second-wave feminism. While I value efforts to call attention to the economic and legal inequalities that often contribute to age disparities in marriage, narrowing the focus to one element of the complex gender-age-power nexus blinds critical efforts to understand the forces that created and consumed this literature. My goal for this book is that it will reinvigorate scholarly discussions about January–May marriages, and, in this sense, I extend here more of an introduction than a conclusion, because there remains so much more to be said.

# NOTES

## INTRODUCTION

1. Further explanation of the January–May theme in Chaucer can be found in Chapter 1. I am aware that other combinations of months can describe these intergenerational marriages—December–May is the most common alternative—but variations of months often work to suggest smaller differences in age. For example, Thomas Hardy's *The Hand of Ethelberta* (1876) uses November–June in the following passage: "'Ho-ho-ho—Miss Hoity-toity!' said Lord Mountclere, trotting up and down. But, remembering it was her June against his November, this did not last long" (310). Since I see Chaucer as vital to the theme's presence in British literature, I have chosen his "January–May" as the most appropriate designation.
2. Sinclair investigates the etymology of the word "cuckold" (30–49). See also *Oxford English Dictionary*, 2nd ed., s.v. "Cuckold."
3. The traditional Anglican marriage ceremony includes the verse, "For this reason a man shall leave his father and mother and be joined to his wife, and the two shall become one flesh" (Mark 10:7–8).
4. Gates reverses the logic of Audre Lorde to make his point. I differ from Gates in that I see this method as one means of subversion—not the only one.

## CHAPTER 1

1. Ryder details specific examples of this type of behavior.
2. The cycles at York, Chester, and Wakefield present Joseph as being too old to procreate with his young wife, Mary. George discusses this aspect of the play at length.
3. Before age sixty, Capellanus sees little problem with age differences in sexual relationships. The first dialogue in the book responds to a woman's complaint that "I am rather young, and I shudder at the thought of receiving solaces from old men." The man replies, "Old age is certainly not a thing to disapprove of" (39), and he lists his many accomplishments as evidence of his superiority to young men.

4. Matthews, Tavormina, Hartung, and Boothman make various connections between these works.
5. Morse provides a detailed explanation of those who brought Chaucer to his nineteenth-century audience.
6. There are a number of European works of art from the late fifteenth and early sixteenth centuries depicting older men and younger women such as *Phyllis and Aristotle* by Hans Baldung-Grien at the Louvre.
7. *The Sack-full of Newes* was reprinted in 1861 by J. O. Halliwell from a copy dated 1673, printed by Andrew Clark, and sold by Thomas Passenger at the bookseller The Three Bibles on London Bridge. Halliwell believes this is the same text referred to by Robert Laneham in a letter written in 1575.
8. Perhaps due to critical attention to racial issues, there are few scholarly treatments of the play's attention to age. Nordlund briefly addresses the important of Othello's age.
9. Here again, the January–May theme proves important across national borders. Moliere's *L'École des femmes* influenced the plot of *The Country Wife*, where the middle-aged husband foolishly believes he is ensuring his wife's fidelity (and his masculinity) by marrying a young country girl.
10. The January–May marriage theme is also central to Behn's *Oroonoko* (1688) and is one way Behn connects African and British cultures. Behn describes how Oroonoko's grandfather, the king of an African tribe, marries Imoinda, his grandson's true love. Because the elderly king is impotent, Imoinda is spared sexual relations with him, but her affair with Oroonoko inspires the king's wrath and their subsequent slavery and deaths.
11. Dawn Lewcock notes that Behn never allows Sir Patient to speak directly to the audience, while Lady Fancy addresses the audience personally on numerous occasions. Lewcock concludes that "by building such relationships through direct asides or comments to the audience by some characters and not by others Behn is able to sway the audience's sympathies to or from any particular character" (77).
12. Wilputte offers a good discussion of economics in this marriage.
13. I should note, however, that *Fanny Hill* also contains another intergenerational relationship that conveys the aging lover favorably and deserves more attention than I can give it in this introduction. Toward the end of Fanny's narrative, she describes her romance with a sixty-year-old man when she is nineteen. In this case, she sees age as a social construction; her lover appears more like "five and forty" than sixty, and she finds him a wonderful sexual partner: "as age had not subdued his tenderness for our sex, neither had it robbed him of the power of pleasing, since whatever he wanted in the bewitching charms of youth, he atoned for, or supplemented, with the advantages of experience, the sweetness of his manners, and above all, his flattering address in

touching the heart, by an application to the understanding" (206). Fanny is happily devoted to her older partner, and when he dies, leaving her his immense fortune, she grieves his loss. Another unconventional example from the period is Pope's *Eloisa to Abelard* (1717), which celebrates the love of the twelfth-century tutor and his young student.

14. In this sense, perhaps *The School for Scandal* has more in common with "The Wife of Bath's Tale," in which the erring knight is given what he wants only when he acknowledges a woman's prerogative to choose for herself.

15. Likely because their age difference is not that large, many critics have ignored how age contributes to power within the novel. Several critics refer to Dorriforth as "the young Catholic priest." Though Dorriforth is hardly elderly at thirty, designating him as "young" fails to clarify his age in relation to the age of his much-younger wife. One exception is Haggerty, who finds that "by eroticizing the 'father,' Inchbald unapologetically cuts through the tenets of sensibility, which paint the father as a superior being endowed with saintly grace, and proposes a domestic scene that is neither simple nor in any conventional sense 'happy'" (657).

16. For more on the novel's play with incest, see Ford.

17. Dismissing the age difference between Miss Milner and Dorriforth, Mortensen reads Sandford as the oppressive father figure from whom Miss Milner is saved by her young lover Dorriforth, arguing that Dorriforth does not become the oppressive father figure until the second half of the novel.

18. Curran explains this trend.

19. An evolving group of intellectual women who met in each other's homes, the Bluestockings included Elisabeth Vesey, Frances Burney, Hannah More, and Elizabeth Montagu and flourished in the years between 1770 and 1785.

20. Sterling connects important historical-scientific constructions of sex to the eighteenth and nineteenth centuries and a "crisis of gender" that corresponds with social and economic forces as well as developing scientific knowledge.

21. The following argument on Tonna and Engels originally appeared as part of my article "*Jane Eyre*, from Governess to Girl Bride," reprinted with permission from *SEL: Studies in English Literature 1500–1900* 45, no. 4 (Autumn 2005).

22. Seltzer and Ward provide more background on the shift from agrarian to industrial economies.

23. Shanley details the Infant Custody Act of 1839, the 1857 Divorce Act, and the 1870 Married Women's Property Act.

24. Despite the sympathy expressed in *The Princess* for the rights of women, Tennyson's fears of gendered reversals of power are manifest throughout

his poetry, including "Lucretius," "The Lady of Shalott," "Lady Clara Vere de Vere," and "Maud."
25. Strickland continues to be a useful source of information regarding the women in Byron's life, and Crane offers a more recent study of the struggles Byron faced with women. Recent biographies by Grosskurth, Eisler, and MacCarthy detail Byron's early years.
26. In his chapter, "'One Half What I Should Say': Byron's Gay Narrator in *Don Juan*," Gross criticizes what he sees as a scholarly focus on heterosexual aspects of the plot of *Don Juan*. Citing Butler, Gross asserts that "treating homoeroticism as 'private' perpetuates the notion that only heterosexuality is culturally intelligible" (132). Though I agree with Gross's point in theory, I maintain that homoeroticism is not limited to the confines of "male" with "male" bodies. In focusing on the January–May marriage, the essay deconstructs what appears to be a socially sanctioned heterosexual union, yet the gender dynamics are much more complex.
27. *Don Juan*'s biographical connection to Byron's life (particularly Cantos I and II) has a long-established tradition in scholarship. Steffan and Marchand both give ample evidence to suggest that Byron's life largely influenced Canto I. Steffan holds that Byron's work on his *Memoirs* led to the poet's direct infusion of immediate personal matters into *Don Juan*. This biographical interest continues into current scholarship; Gross, for example, probes Byron's own homosexual experiences to support his claim regarding the sexual orientation of the poem's narrator.
28. *Beppo*, written in the autumn of 1817, and *Mazeppa*, written between April 1817 and the autumn of 1818, explore the dynamics of age, sexual power, and adultery. *Beppo* relates the tale of a *cavaliere servente*, a middle-aged married woman, and her seafaring husband. *Mazeppa* describes the relationship between a young lover and a young wife who is unhappy with her older husband: "His wife was not of his opinion— / His junior she by thirty years— / Grew daily tired of his dominion" (167–69).
29. Though Eisler follows the biographical claim that Byron "hardly noticed" Teresa in 1818, his own words describing her position in relation to other men and his inability to get close to her in 1818 suggest otherwise. *Mazeppa* describes the young lover of "Theresa" waiting for the affair to begin: "I saw, and sigh'd—in silence wept, / And still reluctant distance kept" (244–45).
30. Teresa's own interests in the power dynamics of age are well documented. Byron criticizes her for having no tact, citing as an example that she "talks of age to old ladies who want to pass for young" (*BLJ*, 6:108). MacCarthy notes that "though she seems to have told Byron she was nineteen, the register in the Battistero di San Giovanni in Fonte in Ravenna reveals that she was twenty. Already, so young, she had

falsified her age" (356). Byron's letter of April 24 to Douglas Kinnaird describes her as twenty (*BLJ*, 6:114). Teresa continued her efforts to make herself appear younger by crossing out Byron's description of her as "nineteen years of age" and replacing it with "seventeen" (6:216).

31. Byron's letters suggest that his interest in masculine decline was a very personal one, and they convey his own concern with passing through what he considered to be the masculine prime. A letter of Byron's in July 1819 laments his inability to keep off weight since he turned thirty, the growing wrinkles around his eyes, his bad teeth that "remain by way of courtesy" and his graying and balding head. Though Byron is only thirty-one, he complains that in "my time of life . . . my personal charms have by no means increased" (*BLJ*, 6:174).

32. Butler explains the "panicked," repetitive mimicking that is gender: "It is this excess which erupts within the intervals of those repeated gestures and acts that construct the apparent uniformity of heterosexual positionalities, indeed which compels the repetition itself, and which guarantees its perpetual failure" ("Imitation and Gender Subordination," 24).

33. Granddaughter of Richard Brinsley Sheridan, Caroline Norton in the mid-1830s fought a public battle with her abusive husband George over his denial of access to their children.

34. Donelan views the discovery of the shoes as the "intrusion of the Real" into the poem. My reading resists this interpretation, as the codes of fashion that correspond with male and female shoes instead represent the ultimate in arbitrariness and mutability.

35. Graham also reads the introductory materials and Canto I as a "map" readers should use to navigate the rest of the poem. The book also makes note of Juan's age in relation to Julia and the other women with whom he has sexual encounters throughout the poem, reading age as a biographical reference to Byron's sex life as well as a device that overturns the Don Juan myth.

## CHAPTER 2

1. As Freudian scholars have duly noted, Freud's theoretical formulation of the Oedipus complex can be traced to the January–May marriage of his own parents. Jakob Freud was twenty years older than his wife, Amalie, and Jakob was already a grandfather by a child from his first marriage when Freud was born. Rudnytsky concludes that "the coincidence between Freud's biographical accidents of birth and the Oedipus drama is staggering. . . . Instead of the situation that happens in a normal family, where relationships are unequivocal and generations succeed each other diachronically, the result of Oedipus' incest is that time is frozen and each of his kinship ties *must have two names*" (16). Describing Freud by way of Edward Said's comments on incest,

Rudnytsky further explains that "because of the discrepancy between the ages of his father and mother, there is indeed a 'tangling-up of the family sequence' and Freud is confronted by the 'burden of plural identities'" (16).

2. In *Undoing Gender*, Butler points out that conventional psychoanalytic explanations of incest limit the possibilities of familial and social relations to a mother/father binary and neglect to consider homosexual, single-parent, and nontraditional family structures (158). Butler asserts, "It might, then, be necessary to rethink the prohibition on incest as that which sometimes protects against a violation, and sometimes becomes the very instrument of violation" (160). Halberstam's work on queer forgetting offers yet another method for debunking the Oedipus myth. See, for example, her essay, "'Dude, Where's My Gender?' or, Is There Life on Uranus?"

3. Freud provides a description of the "female Oedipus complex" in his 1931 essay "Female Sexuality." Herman offers a useful resource on the father's desire for the daughter. Sandra Gilbert surveys the role of fatherly desire in literature and details some important theories that extend Freud's initial work.

4. Bruhm and Hurley argue that theorists need to reconsider whether intergenerational or incestuous desire is psychologically damaging to the younger partner. Proposing that many gays and lesbians begin experimenting with sex with partners who are much older than themselves, this position demands that critics figure out "how to make sense of the child's pleasure without pathologizing it or reducing it to 'trauma'" (xxix).

5. Vivie and Frank also might be half-siblings, which adds another incestuous dimension to the play.

6. Legally, the nineteenth century was relatively free of criminal punishments for incest. During the Reformation, Puritans made incest a capital crime, but the Restoration removed that penalty, and throughout the nineteenth century in England, ecclesiastical courts handled cases of incest, not the criminal courts. Incest was considered a viable charge against a husband if a woman sued for divorce but did not become part of criminal law until the 1908 *Act to Provide for the Punishment of Incest*. Nineteenth-century silence on the matter is telling, and Parliamentary debates leading up to the 1908 decision record numerous accounts of incest in the nineteenth century. Scotland made incest a criminal act in 1857.

7. Rank's contributions to the study of the incest narrative in literature remain important, though he unfortunately, like his colleague Freud, based his theories on presumptions of male supremacy and subjectivity.

8. Dever and Sadoff are two critics who take this approach.

9. Polhemus reads this complex as a personal one for Dickens, who met Ellen Ternan, twenty-seven years his younger, in 1857 when he was experiencing marital problems. Their love affair has been accepted by numerous (though not all) Dickens scholars, including Kaplan and Slater. Other scholars see evidence of Dickens's frustrated desire for Mary Hogarth or Fanny Dickens in his idealization of daughter figures like Nell Trent or Amy Dorrit. See, for example, Goldfarb's chapter, "Charles Dickens: Orphans, Incest, and Repression" (114–38). Though my main concerns reside elsewhere, I believe a pattern emerges throughout Dickens's career that suggests his attitudes toward older man and younger woman relationships become noticeably more sympathetic as he ages.
10. For discussions of *David Copperfield* and *Bleak House*, see Chapter 6.
11. As I note elsewhere, Freud's theory of castration anxiety is difficult for me to accept, and I use it here with more humor than seriousness.
12. Polhemus notes in *Lot's Daughters* that an important and often overlooked event in the Lot myth is his offering of his virgin daughters to appease the sexual desires of an angry mob. A father's ability to use and exchange his daughter's body is thus essential to Polhemus's theory of the incest narrative.
13. For Dickens's conscious participation in this tradition, see Chapter 4 of Hollington's *Dickens and the Grotesque*.
14. Describing Nell, her great-uncle explains, "If you have seen the picture-gallery of any one old family, you will remember how the same face and figure—often the fairest and slightest of them all—come upon you in different generations; and how you trace the same sweet girl through a long line of portraits—never growing old or changing—the Good Angel of the race—abiding by them in all reverses—redeeming all their sins" (525).
15. Though Nell is only aware of the proposal of Quilp, other January–May marriages appear to threaten Nell throughout the text. Nell's great-uncle, the "single gentleman," is appalled at the thought that Nell has been married to a much-older man while working for Mrs. Jarley. Misreading the situation he encounters, her great-uncle threatens legal action to Mrs. Jarley's unsuspecting bridegroom: "Mind, good people, if this fellow has been marrying a minor—tut, tut, that can't be" (358). His hasty words reveal that the sexual deviancies he stresses "can't be"—indeed, could be—not only in his imagination, but in reality. His threats to one he thinks is "marrying a minor" are legally unfounded, since the age of consent in 1840 was still twelve, and Parliament did not raise it to thirteen until 1875 or to sixteen until 1885. And the threat of yet another January–May marriage provides further motive (at least to readers) for Nell's flight. Nell's brother initiates the plan for Dick Swiveller to marry Nell.

16. Polhemus, "Comic and Erotic Faith Meet Faith in the Child: Charles Dickens's *The Old Curiosity Shop* ('The Old Cupiosity Shape')."
17. Andrews also notes this reversal (85), as does Waters (120–35).
18. If the Marchioness is thirteen, she is, curiously, the same age as Nell.
19. The masturbatory connotations of the name "Dick Swiveller" must have amused Dickens.
20. Rousseau's idea of raising one's own wife intrigued Victorians, though many novels stress problems with the arrangement. In *Bleak House*, Jarndyce educates Esther Summerson, and though he is happy with the results, he does not benefit from them as husband. Similarly, in Trollope's *Orley Farm*, Felix Graham raises Mary Snow as his ideal wife, although he too finds his plans were not well thought out.
21. Why it is acceptable for Dick Swiveller to marry the Marchioness, and not Nell, is a question worth probing. Certainly, the class differences between Swiveller and the Marchioness help to justify the disparities in their ages (though Nell may beg, Dickens makes it clear that she does not belong in the lower class).
22. Throughout *Child-Loving*, Kincaid uses the term "child-loving" to denote the both active and passive positions of the child in the exchange of sexual power.
23. Mainardi provides a fascinating overview of this voyeuristic moment in French art in her chapter "When Seeing is Believing: The Graphic Image" in *Husbands, Wives, and Lovers*.
24. Rank, Chapter 11: "The Relationship Between Father and Daughter in Myth, Folktales, Legends, Literature, Life and Neurosis," 300–37.
25. In 1843, this "release" for people of their class would not have meant divorce.
26. Gitter reads John, Tackleton and Caleb in similar "January" positions, equally deserving of criticism for their "shameful desire" of "girls who could be their daughters" (682, 681)
27. It would be a linguistic nightmare if a woman's father were also her husband. According to the rules of kinship, her own mother would thereby be her daughter, and her brother would be her child. According to Levi-Strauss, social organization "can be achieved only by treating marriage regulations and kinship systems as a kind of language, a set of processes permitting the establishment, between individuals and groups, of a certain type of communication" (61).
28. Since I read Honoria Dedlock's marriage as a happy one before the threat of scandal, I consider this to be Dickens's only portrayal of an unsuccessful January–May marriage in his major fiction. In a short work called "Nurse's Stories," Dickens writes of other intergenerational marriages with horrific consequences. "Captain Murderer" weds young women, kills them, and then eats them.
29. Dickens makes much of the way that "innocent" social gestures like handshakes and kisses can have covert sexual implications. Recall the

kiss that Quilp solicits from Little Nell and the handshake that Gride overly enjoys from Madeline Bray. Additionally, custom dictates it is more proper for children to give rather than receive kisses from their elder acquaintances.

30. Dickens offers an even more Gothic version of this type of arranged marriage in the middle of *The Lazy Tour of Two Idle Apprentices* (1857), which he wrote with Wilkie Collins. In this story, reprinted separately as "The Bride's Tale," the young woman is horrified that she must marry her much-older guardian, and her fears prove correct as her husband kills her after their marriage. Dickens describes her foreboding: "The girl was formed in the fear of him, and in the conviction, that there was no escape from him. She was taught, from the first, to regard him as her future husband—the man who must marry her—the destiny that overshadowed her—the appointed certainty that could never be evaded" (77).

31. As Baird notes in his essay, Louisa's body was considered her husband's property, and Bounderby could have sued for the restitution of conjugal rights. Baird refers to the 1838 case between Thomas Foreman Gape and his wife Fanny Louisa, in which the husband won his "rights" to his wife in ecclesiastical court after his wife left him. For a broader analysis of this issue, see Shanley, Chapter 6.

32. Philpotts notes the addition of "Little" to the early manuscript chapters, agreeing with Butt and Tillotson that Dickens came to the name "Little Dorrit" later in composition.

33. Greenfield provides a wonderful study of the rise of this theme in literature.

34. Many Victorians were fascinated with the theme of women who breastfeed adults. In "What is a Golden Deed?" Charlotte Yonge details several examples of women breastfeeding prisoners in acts of compassion. Philpotts explains Dickens's interest in the *Caritas Romana* or "Roman Charity" theme in art: "The usual depiction was of a manacled white-haired old man reclining on the lap of a young woman feeding him from her breast as gaolers watch outside the cell or executioners enter" (237). I have chosen not to elaborate on the Electra complex as an issue within January–May marriages because it is so often associated with Freud's theory of "penis envy," which I find theoretically unsound. However, because the Electra complex is sometimes generalized as the "female" Oedipus complex, I believe Ayres's reference is important here.

35. The Marshalsea, where Mr. Dorrit and Clennam are imprisoned, is inextricably connected to Dickens's own father, who was imprisoned for debt when Dickens was twelve years old.

36. As I explain elsewhere, it was a felony to have sex with a girl under the age of ten and a misdemeanor to have sex with a girl under the age of twelve (Shanley, 90).

37. Like Dick Swiveller, Clennam is so sick that he is often unconscious, and on waking he has no idea of the extent of Little Dorrit's role in his recovery.
38. Although Clennam is forty, he exaggerates his own age, telling Little Dorrit: "my child . . . I have passed, by the amount of your whole life, the time that is present to you" (404).
39. Most Dickens scholars agree that the character of Flora is based upon Maria Beadnell. For details of Dickens's disappointed reunion with his aging sweetheart, see the chapter "Maria" in Slater, 49–76.
40. Black and Jagose offer particularly insightful readings of Miss Wade.
41. The 1850s brought important new legislation concerning married women's property and divorce law before Parliament, which resulted in the defeat of the 1856 Married Women's Property Act and the establishment of a new Court of Divorce as the result of the 1857 Divorce Act. *Little Dorrit*'s unpleasant portraits of empowered women like Mrs. Clennam and Miss Wade sharply contrast that of Betsy Trotwood in *David Copperfield*, and suggest Dickens's reconsideration of the ramifications of what could be too much gender bending.

# Chapter 3

1. In most cases, the January–May marriage theme excludes the figure of the aging woman or isolates her to the working class like *Jane Eyre*'s Mrs. Fairfax and *An Old Man's Love*'s Mrs. Baggett. One notable exception that merits scholarly attention is Flora Finching in Dickens's *Little Dorrit*. Flora, the romantic interest of Arthur Clennam in her youth, is portrayed as unattractive and annoying in middle age. Now forty years old, Clennam hopes to marry Pet Meagles and then does marry Little Dorrit, both women half his age.
2. January–May art often visually confuses familial relationships, requiring that titles clarify viewers' understanding. For example, the cover of the 1994 Penguin edition of Trollope's *Barchester Towers* depicts an elderly man and young woman, and credits the art as *The Rich Cleric and His Wife* by Peter Paul Marshall. I have been unable to locate this painting, but Artnet lists it as *The Countess Czerlaski and her Brother* as sold through Christie's on October 25, 1991.
3. Part of the material in this section first appeared in my article "Feminizing Casaubon: Gender and the Aging Husband in *Middlemarch*," *Topic: The Washington and Jefferson College Review* 55 (2007): 55–66.
4. Several portraits of Locke exist, though it is most likely that the one described by Dorothea and Celia would be that by Sir Godfrey Kneller. It depicts Locke without a wig, displaying the "iron-grey hair" and "deep eye-sockets" that Dorothea associates with Casaubon.
5. Eliot, who often joked about what she perceived as her own shortcomings in appearance, had herself been compared in appearance to

John Locke, and Eliot's wit and willingness to make herself and Casaubon the targets of aesthetic attack destabilize any idealization of self or other. Ashton offers more information on Eliot's appearance and her use of humor in regard to it in her biography (275–76, 299).

6. Later, in Rome, Eliot makes the comparison even more explicit: "Mr. Casaubon was less happy than usual, and this perhaps made him look all the dimmer and more faded; else, the effect might easily have been produced by the contrast of his young cousin's appearance. The first impression on seeing Will was one of sunny brightness. . . . Mr Casaubon, on the contrary, stood rayless" (133).
7. Graver notes that Eliot read Mill's *Subjection* at about the same time that she started *Middlemarch* and views the texts as a dialogue regarding the "woman question."
8. Pamela K. Gilbert provides more insight into the diseased body and gender subversion in Victorian literature.

## CHAPTER 4

1. O'Malley finds Gothic characteristics in the novel's interests in "traditions of sexual and religious deviance" (648). O'Malley places Hardy firmly in the nineteenth century instead of "seeing in him the unambiguous harbinger of modernism," and rightly conjectures that "the Gothic had not yet given up its hold on the Victorian novelist of the 1890s, even a novelist so central to our understanding of the protomodernist canon as Hardy" (648). But whereas critics like O'Malley locate Gothic elements in the novel's interplay between Anglo-Catholicism and aberrant sexualities, I stress Hardy's participation in the Gothic tradition by emphasizing his manipulation of the January–May marriage theme as a method for tethering the realistic with the monstrous.
2. Day identifies these two emotions as central to the Gothic.
3. Thane's chapter "'An Unfailing Zest for Life': Images and Self-Images of Older People in the Nineteenth and Early Twentieth Centuries" in *Old Age and English History* shares many examples of older people who took prominent places in society (259–72).
4. See Stearns and Gratton and Haber.
5. Austen finds this character type and its younger, mercenary counterpart amusing in "A Collection of Letters" (ca. 1791): "Oh! my dear Musgrove you cannot think how impatiently I wait for the death of my Uncle and Aunt—If they will not die soon, I beleive [*sic*] I shall run mad" (158).
6. Mary Elizabeth Braddon's 1896 story "Good Lady Ducayne" relates the frightening lengths to which older people might go to avoid death. Here the title character employs young women as her companions, then has them chloroformed so she can transfuse their "young" blood

into her own. Many of these women die, but Lady Ducayne's vampiric techniques prolong her life.

7. Katz notes that as the nineteenth century progressed, medical records began to shift from attributing death to "old age" to specific diseases and illnesses (66).

8. Rosenman and Darby give detailed summaries of the subject. The spermatorrhea panic led to the widespread circumcision of British men after the 1860s because friction caused by the foreskin was thought to increase male excitement. Medical practices endorsed and exercised other forms of genital mutilation to prevent masturbation, including cauterization of the urethral canal with silver nitrate. Darby notes that John Addington Symonds was one of many who volunteered themselves for this procedure in hopes of curing themselves of the desire to masturbate.

9. Antimasturbation literature became a cultural obsession in the nineteenth century. Rosenman makes an interesting claim that this body of literature defined an area of expertise for medical "professionals" otherwise regarded as quacks. The theories supported by the French doctor Claude Francois Lallemand were practiced in England as early as the 1830s, and his *Practical Treatise on the Causes, Symptoms, and Treatment of Spermatorrhea* was translated into English in 1847. Other important works on masturbation include William Acton's *The Functions and Disorders of the Reproductive Organs in Childhood, Youth, Adult Age, and Advanced Life* (1857) and *Masturbation: The History of a Great Terror*, by Stengers and Van Neck, which includes more images from *Le Livre Sans Titre*.

10. I was surprised to find in my research that many people continue to link masturbation with premature aging in the twenty-first century. On a Web site promoting herbal medicine for sexual concerns, an article entitled "Reversing the Effects of Over Masturbation—A Painful Journey of Recovery" details one young man's story of premature aging due to "excessive" masturbation. He believes masturbation made him look older than he was and caused his hair to fall out (http://www.herballove.com). Another Web site encourages self-abusers to come to a Gnostic Center to be cured of masturbation, which the webmasters also see as responsible for premature aging, among other dramatic consequences (http://www.anael.org/english/masturbation/consequences.htm).

11. In a Victorian version of this theme with reversed gender, Laura in Christina Rossetti's "Goblin Market" also grows prematurely old as the result of her sexual deviances.

12. In Chapter 3, I cover several of Dickens's January–May marriages in which the younger wife openly desires her husband. However, some of Dickens's incestuous January–May marriages do encourage Gothic

readings of the marriages as disruptive, even masturbatory sexual acts on the part of the older husbands. Arthur Gride's sexual fantasies of Madeline Gride and Quilp's comments about Little Nell's body are the most blatant suggestions of one-sided sexual projection in Dickens, but even John Jarndyce takes regular "cold baths," one of the methods used to discourage masturbation (*Bleak House*, 63).

13. The irony that Jude introduces the woman he loves to her future husband has been discussed by several Hardy scholars, perhaps most interestingly by Dellamora, who emphasizes the homosocial/sexual bonding embedded in this triangularity. Dellamora comments on the age difference between Jude and Phillotson in relation to Jude's search for a male mentor and connects their relationship to Hardy's with Henry Moule.

14. This depiction also fulfills stereotypical physical images of the scholar, which I discuss regarding Casaubon in Chapter 4.

15. This "gifting" of women from older men to younger men is a common January–May theme that I discuss in Chapter 6.

16. That Jude identifies sex with Phillotson as "the ultimate horror" *after* the murder-suicide of Jude's children is telling.

17. It is necessary to clarify that I am primarily addressing the nineteenth-century tradition of male vampires. Several female vampires exist in the nineteenth century, most notably Coleridge's Christabel and LeFanu's Carmilla. These women are, like the male vampires, hundreds of years old, but the texts do not construct images of them as old women. On the contrary, these female vampires look young, and these texts thrive on eroticized scenes in which female vampires and their female victims act out thinly veiled lesbian lovemaking scenes. In Stoker's *Dracula*, the female vampires who threaten to seduce Harker in Dracula's castle as well as Dracula's victim Lucy also appear young and beautiful. Only Braddon's Lady Ducayne, mentioned in a previous note, is an older female "vampire." I have several theories about why ageist fears are less likely to be grafted onto the female vampire. First, I believe that Gothic fantasies of lesbian relationships and unbridled female sexuality rivaled interest in January–May marriages: lesbian narratives contained their own sexual deviancies and gender subversions, and it was therefore unnecessary to "age" the female vampire. Secondly, aging the male vampire links the "horror" of aging to male privilege. There was less need to exaggerate aging women because they wielded less economic and social power in nineteenth-century culture. Moreover, what I find especially intriguing about the connections between the January–May and vampire themes is the intrinsic homoeroticism of the love triangle. Homosocial/sexual bonds that are submerged in January–May motifs become more explicit in vampire tales, as Aubrey, Harker, and other men are penetrated by male vampires as they fight to save young women from the clutches of their older rivals.

18. Polidori traveled with Byron and the Shelleys for a short period as Byron's physician. For information about Polidori and Byron, see Eisler's *Byron*, 518–19 and Skarde.
19. Scholarly opinions differ over the authorship of *Varney*. Varma's Arno Press edition (1970) of *Varney* cites Thomas Preskett (cited elsewhere as Peckett) Prest (1810–1879) as the author, but Humphrey Liu and other Varney experts believe the author to be James Malcolm Rymer. Both Prest and Rymer were writers employed by the publisher Edward Lloyd, and they are both attributed as possible authors of *Sweeney Todd*. I follow recent scholars in attributing *Varney* to Rymer; however, since I used the Arno edition, *Varney* is cited under "Prest" in the bibliography. In discussion, I also retained the original spelling of "Vampyre" but the bibliography reflects the Arno spelling of "Vampire."
20. I can find no record of illustrators for *Varney*.
21. The groping of her breast seems to be an imaginative addition by the illustrator; the actual text describes Varney holding Flora down on the bed by her long hair, a dominating gesture used by Hans Baldung-Grien in several of his *Death and the Maiden* paintings.
22. Dracula displays a clear preference for young bodies. The weird sisters and Lucy even crave children.
23. For a good summary of this approach, see Murfin.
24. During Mina's abstinence from sexual relations with Harker because of her "unclean" state, Harker manifests the classic symptoms of premature aging described in *Le Livre*. Dr. Seward describes Harker in his diary: "Last night he was a frank, happy-looking man, with strong youthful face, full of energy, and with dark brown hair. Today he is a drawn, haggard old man, whose white hair matches well with the hollow burning eyes and grief-written lines of his face" (263). The rapid change of Harker's hair from brown to white could come from grief, but also could allude to his own masturbatory acts when deprived of his conjugal rights.
25. Queer readings of *Dracula* abound, including Schaffer's "'A Wilde Desire Took Me': The Homoerotic History of Dracula" and Halberstam's *Skin Shows*.
26. Craft reads Mina's son Quincy Harker as "the unacknowledged son of the Crew of Light's displaced homoerotic union" (130).

## Chapter 5

1. MacFarlane documents this trend (*Marriage and Love in England*, 3–19).
2. However, because of incomplete statistical evidence, to what extent the literature reflects a social desire for, rather than a social phenomenon of, age-disparate marriages remains unclear.

3. In real life, class differences between romantic partners often proportionately correspond to their age differences. Buss examines an international trend for wealthy men to pursue women much younger than themselves. In a study of German men, Buss found that men in higher income brackets wanted younger and younger women. Framing the claim in terms of economic capital, Buss writes, "Men who enjoy high status and income are apparently aware of their ability to attract women of higher value" (64). Frost cites several examples of age differences in breach-of-promise suits (59, 83, 94).
4. Later in the century, Darwin's theories regarding sexual selection support movements in favor of eugenics, which further emphasized the reproductive necessity of marriage and the need for the middle and upper classes to breed so that they might counter what appeared to be a dangerously rapid growth of the poor population. See Richardson.
5. A more thorough explanation of this connection can be found in Jann.
6. Austen experienced circumstances similar to those of the women in the Dashwood family when her father died, leaving her, her sister Cassandra, and her mother to manage on £500 a year.
7. Lamont gives an interesting reading of Austen's broader views on "old" versus "new" things.
8. Austen's works are full of women who acknowledge the necessity of marrying for money. While some, like Isabella Thorpe and Lucy Steele, appear as heartless social climbers, others make the best of the situations in which they find themselves. Austen treats Charlotte Lucas sympathetically in *Pride and Prejudice*, and it is no coincidence that Elizabeth Bennett recognizes her love for Darcy when she first witnesses the grandeur of Pemberley. Austen treats the theme of young women marrying older men for money in a number of her minor works, including *Lady Susan, The Watsons, Catherine,* "Jack and Alice," "Frederic and Elfrida," and "Lesley Castle."
9. Mary Poovey takes this stance in *The Proper Lady and the Woman Writer*, 183–94.
10. See Chambers.
11. See Jordan.
12. Shanley describes important developments affecting the system of coverture, including the famous Caroline Norton case, the 1857 Divorce Act, and the 1882 Married Women's Property Act. Different courts addressed different issues of married women's property; the courts of common law were in charge of issues concerning a husband's right to married women's property, but the courts of equity were responsible for women's separate estates. The confusion of jurisdiction was one hurdle in the movement for reform of women's property law.
13. See Hughes, 11–25.

14. Buss explains that women's limited reproductive years have encouraged a cross-cultural valuation of younger women among men who hope to produce offspring (51–52).
15. Blodgett discusses how the novel blurs contemporary standards of right and wrong.
16. Braddon had first-hand experience of the economic challenges facing women in the nineteenth century as well as the limited abilities of traditional marriage to resolve them. After her father failed to provide economic security to their home and eventually separated from her mother, Braddon turned to writing to support herself and her mother. For more information, see Wolf.
17. Objections to their marriage regarding incest are discussed more fully in Chapter 4. Young and wealthy widows from January–May marriages are not uncommon figures in nineteenth-century literature, and they can present a unique state of female financial independence. Margaret Hale's Aunt Shaw in Elizabeth Gaskell's *North and South* and Lady Mason in Anthony Trollope's *Orley Farm* are two such women. Becky Sharp even regrets missing her chance at becoming Sir Pitt Crawley's young widow in William Makepeace Thackeray's *Vanity Fair*.
18. Dickens's treatment of older men and January–May relationships changes dramatically as he ages. Eleven years after *Nicholas Nickleby*, Dickens esteems the older husband Dr. Strong and his relationship with his young wife in *David Copperfield*. *Bleak House*, *Little Dorrit*, and *A Tale of Two Cities* all include positive accounts of January–May romances, which imply that Dickens grew more sympathetic with older men and their attraction to younger women as he faced the reality of his own unhappy marriage and sought happiness with a woman twenty years younger.
19. Clarifying that a January–May marriage economically benefited the young woman's family and not just herself was a technique authors often employed to excuse "good" women from the mercenary insinuations of these unions. Charlotte Smith presents two sisters' attitudes toward an advantageous January–May marriage very differently in *The Old Manor House*. One sister, Isabella, has few scruples about marrying for money, and her siblings worry: "She knows all the pecuniary advantages that attend such a situation as the General offers her: and the question only is, whether, as she has no attachment whatever, the charms of grandeur, the chance of being a Countess . . . and being called the honourable Mrs. Tracy, are not sufficient temptations to make her forget that the husband who is to give her all these advantages is a good deal older than her father?" (286). Another sister, Selima, clarifies what a "good" woman would do: "Were father to say to me, as he has said to my sister Belle, that to see me so opulently married would make his latter days easy, and save him from those hours of anguish that now torment him about the future fate of us all, I should certainly marry

this old man, if he were ten thousand times more odious to me than he is," but she adds, "But were only myself in question: then, were I to see poverty and even servitude on one side, and General Tracy with his brother's coronet in one hand, and a settlement of ten thousand a year in the other, I do assure you that I should refuse him" (287). Her brother approves: "Generous, charming girl!" (287). Prostitution is condoned for the family but checked for the individual.

## CHAPTER 6

1. Singer offers a review of the historical development of theories of love from Plato to the modern world.
2. Some historical and anthropological studies of love suggest that the apparent paradox presented by economic and emotional reasons for marriage is less contradictory than binary characterization would imply. In *The Culture of Capitalism*, MacFarlane maintains the correlation established by theorists like Frederick Engels and Lawrence Stone between capitalism and romantic love by identifying the emergence of capitalism earlier in the Middle Ages and by crediting Christianity with the emergence of marriages for love because of the delimitation of sex to marriage.
3. Though a great deal of scholarship exists concerning Trollope's sympathy with women's concerns about marriage, little attention has been given to *An Old Man's Love* or to the use of January–May relationships in his works. In *Orley Farm*, the marriage between Sir Joseph Mason and Lady Mason has a forty-five-year age difference, and money is an important part of their marital contract as well, since she is the daughter of a bankrupt associate, and her subversion of his will after his death is crucial to the novel's plot. *He Knew He Was Right* offers an interesting twist to the January–May theme, as the same-aged husband Louis Trevelyan grows insanely jealous of his wife's friendship with the middle-aged friend of her father, Colonel Osborne.
4. Steadman tries to distinguish Annie from the more insipid young wives in the novel. She charges that "there is real *womanly* emotion in her assertion of love for Dr. Strong," but tempers her praise with the qualification: "Here we see the successful formation of a woman's character by her teacher-husband" (116).
5. Dickens employs this same strategy of misinterpretation with the (affected) deaf elderly man's reading of John and Dot's relationship in *Cricket*. Here, Dickens carefully constructs the child David as both a sexual innocent and as a knowing commentator about adult relations. Such paradoxical portrayals of children fueled Kincaid's *Child-Loving* and *Erotic Innocence* and Robson's *Men in Wonderland*. See also Mohr's "The Pedophilia of Everyday Life."

6. The Strong marriage allows a legitimized consummation of incestuous and deviant desires in much the same way that David's first marriage to Dora placates his Oedipal urge to marry his mother. The critical difference is that David's same-age marriage to Dora is disastrous while the Strong marriage is not. Had Dora not died an early death, David too clearly would have suffered from years of marriage to his child mother (until, perhaps, he had become old enough to appreciate her infantilized personality as a pedophiliac). David's same-age marriage does not realize the liberating potential of the Strong marriage because there is no age discrepancy to free the partners from the tethers of gender affiliation, and his same-age marriage lacks the same ability to link bodies to variant gender affiliations.
7. "Merde" means "shit" in French, and his name, shit stone, indicates constipation and anal retention.
8. I find it curious that Mr. Peggotty finds it necessary to mention that he hears Emily's nightly prayers only through "t'other side of the canvas screen" (798) that divides their sleeping arrangements.
9. If Jarndyce and Esther did marry and Lady Dedlock recognized her daughter, Sir Leicester would be Jarndyce's stepfather-in-law.
10. Although Honoria's flight from home could be interpreted as her rejection of her older husband, her farewell letter suggests that her departure is intended to save her husband from further disgrace: "I have no home left. I will encumber you no more. May you, in your just resentment, be able to forget the unworthy woman on whom you have wasted a most generous devotion—who avoids you, only with a deeper shame than that with which she hurries from herself—and who writes this last adieu!" (667).
11. Valenti interprets this statement as a hidden reference to Esther's biological father.
12. As I briefly mentioned in Chapter 2, Esther's illegitimacy introduces the possibility that Jarndyce could literally be her father, exponentially increasing the incestuous insinuations of their relationship.
13. Blain addresses the "sexual taint" that transfers from Honoria Dedlock to her daughter Esther. Though Blain reads this taint as the illegitimacy of sex outside of marriage, I believe the taint is inseparable from both the mother's and daughter's incestuous January–May relationships, and I contend that Esther's continued feelings for Jarndyce perpetuate nonstandard sexualities more than they "purge" them.
14. Esther's struggle between Jarndyce and Woodcourt raises questions about monogamy that Stoker's Lucy Westenra will later articulate: "Why can't they let a girl marry three men, or as many as want her, and save all this trouble?" (60).
15. I am not arguing that this relationship had been consummated, but I do call attention to Jarndyce's belief that it was indeed a romantic and marital bond.

16. Trollope was sixty-seven years old and in very poor health when he began *An Old Man's Love*. He had to dictate much of the novel to his niece Florence Nightingale Bland, who could have served as inspiration for Mary Lawrie.
17. A husband's right to his wife's body was reinforced through British law, which even guaranteed the legality of marital rape. In *The Subjection of Women*, John Stuart Mill argued that in this respect, a wife had fewer rights than a slave. See Shanley, Chapter 6: "A Husband's Right to His Wife's Body: Wife Abuse, the Restitution of Conjugal Rights, and Marital Rape."
18. Craig outlines the social and linguistic implications of promises to marry.
19. Nardin traces a chronological development in Trollope's attitude toward men and women as his later works become increasing sympathetic to women. Though Nardin does not consider *An Old Man's Love* in her critique, this last novel follows the subversive trend that Nardin identifies in more popular works like *Can You Forgive Her?* and *Orley Farm*. Wijesinha and other critics have also noted Trollope's relatively subversive stance in comparison with other Victorian novelists.
20. Coventry Patmore's *The Angel in the House* (1854) is one of the best examples of this Victorian metaphor for women.

## Conclusion

1. One motif I want to explore further depicts the older husband as a racial "Other," a trend I found in *Trilby*, *Middlemarch*, and *The Ring and the Book*.
2. Whereas the age of consent was raised from thirteen to sixteen in England, the campaign in India raised it from ten to twelve. Child marriage also related to another Indian practice that horrified the British: *sati*, or the burning of widows on their husbands' funeral pyres. See Sharma for more about the history of child marriage in India.
3. Women under twenty-one years of age would need their parents' or guardians' permission to marry.
4. I refer the reader again to Robson, who offers an interesting reading of Ruskin's relationship with Rose in the context of his *Praeterita*.
5. Bruhm and Hurley explain this argument.
6. Austen's interest could be biographical. Her aunt, Philadelphia Austen, traveled to India to make an advantageous marriage to a much-older man. Her child, Austen's cousin Eliza, was rumored to be illegitimate. Anderson includes an insightful discussion of the "little disparity in age" between Emma and John Knightley.
7. I regret that constraints of time and space prevented me from discussing these examples in more detail, but the January–May theme was so popular in nineteenth-century Britain that the list goes on and on and

makes a complete study a formidable task. Charlotte Mary Yonge wrote a number of novels that explore older man–younger woman marriages, including *Heartsease* (1854), *Hopes and Fears* (1860), *The Clever Woman of the Family* (1865), and *Magnum Bonum* (1879). Ouida's fiction throughout the 1860s and 1870s also includes a number of marriages between young women and much-older men.

8. I would be remiss if I did not mention the marriage between Frances Folsom and President Grover Cleveland in 1886. Unlike his literary counterpart in *Bleak House*, Grover Cleveland did not plan to marry his ward in "the most private and simple manner" (748). Despite an age gap of twenty-seven years, they were the first and only partners to wed in the executive mansion.

9. Daphne du Maurier is the daughter of George du Maurier, the author of *Trilby*. I find it curious that their most famous works both feature January–May marriages.

10. In *Lot's Daughters*, Polhemus dedicates an entire chapter to the Woody Allen and Mia Farrow saga, providing an important biographical context for Allen's interest in young women.

11. For example, the 1998 film *Gods and Monsters* incorporates same-sex January–May desire.

12. Of these examples, only Juan's relationship with Catherine is "January–May" by the guidelines I established in the introduction. She is forty-eight, while Juan is in his early twenties.

13. In trying to dissuade his son from pursuing Lady Susan, Reginald's father explains, "Lady Susan's age is itself a material objection, but her want of character is one so much more serious, that the difference of even twelve years becomes in comparison of small account" (58). Just as Austen found older men marrying younger women comical, she also found the gender reversal humorous from her youth. She treats older women marrying younger men humorously in "Love and Freindship" and "Jack and Alice."

14. Olsen captures this love story.

15. This series by Sadorian Publications includes *Bloom* by Linda Dominique Grosvenor, *Class Act* by T. C. Matthews, and *Misdemeanor* by Tanya Marie Lewis.

# Bibliography

Adams, James Eli. "Victorian Sexualities." In *A Companion to Victorian Literature and Culture*, edited by Herbert F. Tucker, 125–38. Malden, MA: Blackwell, 1999.
*Addams Family Values*. Directed by Barry Sonnenfeld. Hollywood, CA: Paramount, 1993.
*American Pie*. Directed by Paul Weitz. Beverly Hills, CA: Newmarket Capital Group, 1999.
Anderson, Kathleen. "Fathers and Lovers: The Gender Dynamics of Relational Influence in *Emma*." *Persuasions: The Jane Austen Journal On-Line* 21, no. 2 (2000). http://www.jasna.org/persuasions/on-line/vol21no2/anderson.html.
Andrews, Malcolm. *Dickens and the Grown-Up Child*. Iowa City: University of Iowa Press, 1994.
Armstrong, Nancy. *Desire and Domestic Fiction*. New York: Oxford University Press, 1987.
Arnold, Matthew. *Culture and Anarchy*. 1869. In *Poetry and Criticism of Matthew Arnold*. Riverside editions. Edited by A. Dwight Culler, 407–75. Boston: Houghton Mifflin, 1961.
*Art Journal*. 1 July 1884, 210.
Ashton, Rosemary. *George Eliot: A Life*. London: Hamilton, 1996.
Auerbach, Nina. *Our Vampires, Ourselves*. Chicago: University of Chicago Press, 1995.
———. and David J. Skal. Footnotes. *Dracula*. New York: Norton, 1997.
Austen, Jane. "A Collection of Letters." In *Catherine and Other Writings*, edited by Margaret Anne Doody and Douglas Murray, 151–64. New York: Oxford University Press, 1993.
———. *Emma*. 1816. Oxford: Oxford University Press, 1988.
———. *Lady Susan, The Watsons and Sanditon*. New York: Penguin, 2003.
———. *Northanger Abbey and Persuasion*. 1818. Oxford: Oxford University Press, 1988.
———. *Sense and Sensibility*. 1811. Oxford: Oxford University Press, 1988.
Ayres, Brenda. *Dissenting Women in Dickens' Novels: The Subversion of Domestic Ideology*. Westport, CT: Greenwood, 1998.
Baird, John D. "'Divorce and Matrimonial Causes': An Aspect of 'Hard Times.'" *Victorian Studies* 20 (1977): 401–12.

Banks, J. A. *Prosperity and Parenthood: A Study of Family Planning Among the Victorian Middle Classes*. London: Routledge, 1954.
Beadle, Richard, ed. *The York Plays*. London: Arnold, 1982.
Behn, Aphra. *The Lucky Chance*. 1686. In *The Rover and Other Plays*, edited by Jane Spencer, 183–270. Oxford: Oxford University Press, 1995.
———. *The Rover*. 1677. In *The Rover and Other Plays*, edited by Jane Spencer, 1–88. Oxford: Oxford University Press, 1995.
———. *Sir Patient Fancy*. 1678. In *The Works of Aphra Behn, VI: The Plays: 1678–1682*, edited by Janet Todd, 1–81. Columbus: Ohio University Press, 1992.
*Bentley's Miscellany*. Review of *Bleak House*. Reprinted in *Dickens Bleak House: A Casebook*. Casebook series, edited by A. E. Dyson, 71–75. London: Macmillan, 1969.
Black, Barbara. "A Sisterhood of Rage and Beauty: Dickens' Rosa Dartle, Miss Wade and Madame DeFarge." *Dickens Studies Annual* 26 (1998): 91–106.
Blain, Virginia. "Double Vision and the Double Standard in *Bleak House*: A Feminist Perspective." In *Bleak House*. New Casebooks, edited by Jeremy Tambling, 65–86. New York: St. Martin's Press, 1998.
Blodgett, Harriet. "The Greying of *Lady Audley's Secret*." *Papers on Language and Literature* 37, no. 2 (2001): 132–46.
Blum, Martin. "Negotiating Masculinities: Erotic Triangles in the *Miller's Tale*." In *Masculinities in Chaucer: Approaches to Maleness in the* Canterbury Tales *and* Troilus and Criseyde, edited by Peter G. Beidler, 37–52. Bury St. Edmunds, Suffolk, UK: St. Edmundsbury, 1998.
Booth, Alison. "*Middlemarch, Bleak House*, and Gender in the Nineteenth-Century Novel Course." In *Approaches to Teaching Eliot's* Middlemarch, edited by Kathleen Blake, 129–37. New York: Modern Language Association, 1990.
Boothman, Janet. "'Who Hath No Wyf, He is No Cokewold': A Study of John and January in Chaucer's Miller's and Merchant's Tales." *Thoth* 4 (1963): 3–14.
Botting, Fred. *Gothic*. New York: Routledge, 1996.
Braddon, Mary Elizabeth. "Good Lady Ducayne." In *Vampires: Two Centuries of Great Vampire Stories*, edited by Alan Ryan, 138–62. Garden City, NY: Doubleday, 1987.
———. *Lady Audley's Secret*. 1862. Edited by Jenny Bourne Taylor. London: Penguin, 1998.
Brady, Ann P. "The Metaphysics of Pornography in *The Ring and the Book*." *Browning Institute Studies* 13 (1985): 137–64.
Brontë, Anne. *Agnes Grey*. 1847. New York: Penguin, 1989.
Brontë, Charlotte. *Jane Eyre*. 1847. Boston: Bedford, 1996.
———. *The Professor*. 1857. New York: Penguin, 1989.
———. *Villette*. 1853. New York: Penguin, 1979.

Browning, Elizabeth Barrett. *Aurora Leigh*. 1856. New York: Norton, 1996.
Browning, Robert. "Andrea Del Sarto." 1855. *Poems of Robert Browning*. Riverside editions, edited by Donald Smalley, 213–19. Boston: Houghton Mifflin, 1956.
———. *Pippa Passes*. 1841. *Poems of Robert Browning*. Riverside editions, edited by Donald Smalley, 3–46. Boston: Houghton Mifflin, 1956.
———. "Rabbi Ben Ezra." 1864. *Poems of Robert Browning*. Riverside editions, edited by Donald Smalley, 281–87. Boston: Houghton Mifflin, 1956.
———. *The Ring and The Book*. 1869. Peterborough, ON: Broadview Press, 2001.
Bruhm, Steven, and Natasha Hurley. Introduction. *Curiouser: On the Queerness of Children*, edited by Steven Bruhm and Natasha Hurley, ix–xxxviii. Minneapolis: University of Minnesota Press, 2004.
Burton, Antoinette. "From Child Bride to 'Hindoo Lady': Rukhmabai and the Debate on Sexual Respectability in Imperial Britain." *The American Historical Review* 103, no. 4 (1998): 1119–46.
Buss, David. *The Evolution of Desire*. New York: Basic Books, 1994.
Butler, Judith. "Imitation and Gender Subordination." In *Inside/Out: Lesbian Theories, Gay Theories*, edited by Diana Fuss, 13–31. New York: Routledge, 1991.
———. *Undoing Gender*. New York: Routledge, 2004.
Butt, John, and Kathleen Tillotson. *Dickens at Work*. London: Methuen, 1957.
Byron, George Gordon. "Augustus Darvell." 1819. In *The Vampire and Other Tales of the Macabre*, edited by Robert Morrison and Chris Baldick, 246–51. Oxford: Oxford World Classics, 1998.
———. *Beppo*. 1818. *The Complete Poetical Works: Vol. 4*. Edited by Jerome J. McGann. Oxford: Clarendon, 1986.
———. *The Blues. The Complete Poetical Works: Vol. 6*. Edited by Jerome J. McGann and Barry Weller. Oxford: Clarendon Press, 1986.
———. *Byron's Letters and Journals*. Vol. 6. Edited by Leslie A. Marchand. Cambridge, MA: Belknap Press of Harvard University Press, 1976.
———. *Byron's Letters and Journals*. Vol. 7. Edited Leslie A. Marchand. Cambridge, MA: Belknap Press of Harvard University Press, 1977.
———. *Don Juan. The Complete Poetical Works: Vol. 5*. Edited by Jerome J. McGann. Oxford: Clarendon Press, 1986.
———. *The Giaour*. 1813. In *Byron*, edited by Jerome J. McGann, 207–47. Oxford: Oxford University Press, 1986.
———. *Mazeppa*. 1819. *The Complete Poetical Works: Vol. 4*. Edited by Jerome J. McGann, 173–200. Oxford: Clarendon Press, 1986.
———. "On This Day I Complete My Thirty-Sixth Year." 1824. In *Byron*, edited by Jerome J. McGann, 969. New York: Oxford University Press, 1991.

Caine, Barbara. *English Feminism: 1780–1980.* New York: Oxford University Press, 1997.

Capellanus, Andreas. *The Art of Courtley Love.* ca. 1184–86. Translated by John Jay Parry. New York: Ungar, 1941.

Carter, Margaret L. Preface. In *Varney the Vampire; or, The Feast of Blood*, Vol. 1, edited by Devendra P. Varma, xxxi–xlii. New York: Arno Press, 1970.

Chambers, J. D. *The Workshop of the World: British Economic History from 1820–1880.* London: Oxford University Press, 1968.

Chaucer, Geoffrey. "The Merchant's Tale." In *The Riverside Chaucer*, 3rd ed., edited by Larry D. Benson, 154–68. Boston: Houghton Mifflin, 1987.

———. "The Miller's Tale." In *The Riverside Chaucer*, 3rd ed., edited by Larry D. Benson, 68–78. Boston: Houghton, 1987.

———. "The Wife of Bath's Prologue." In *The Riverside Chaucer*, 3rd ed., edited by Larry D. Benson, 105–16. Boston: Houghton, 1987.

Cleland, John. *Fanny Hill, or Memoirs of a Woman of Pleasure.* 1748. New York: Penguin, 1998.

Cobbe, Francis Power. "What Shall We Do with Our Old Maids?" 1862. In *"Criminals, Idiots, Women, and Minors": Victorian Writing by Women on Women*, edited by Susan Hamilton, 85–107. Peterborough, ON: Broadview Press, 1995.

Collins, Wilkie. *The Woman in White.* 1860. New York: Modern Library, 2002.

Congreve, William. *Love for Love.* In *The Complete Plays of William Congreve*, edited by Herbert Davis, 205–316. Chicago: University of Chicago Press, 1967.

———. *The Old Batchelour.* In *The Complete Plays of William Congreve*, edited by Herbert Davis, 24–113. Chicago: University of Chicago Press, 1967.

Conolly, L. W. Introduction. In *Mrs Warren's Profession*, by George Bernard Shaw, 13–74. Peterborough, ON: Broadview Press, 2005.

Cowles, David L. "Having it Both Ways: Gender and Paradox in *Hard Times.*" *Dickens Quarterly* 8, no. 2 (1991): 79–84.

Craft, Christopher. "'Kiss Me with Those Red Lips': Gender and Inversion in Bram Stoker's *Dracula.*" *Representations* 8 (1984): 107–33.

Crafts, N. F. R. "Average Age at First Marriage for Women in Mid-Nineteenth-Century England and Wales: A Cross-Section Study." *Population Studies* 32, no.1 (1978): 21–25.

Craig, Randall. *Promising Language: Betrothal in Victorian Law and Fiction.* New York: State University of New York Press, 2000.

Crane, David. *The Kindness of Sisters: Annabella Milbanke and the Destruction of the Byrons.* New York: Knopf, 2002.

Crary, Jonathan. *Techniques of the Observer: On Vision and Modernity in the Nineteenth Century.* Cambridge: MIT Press, 1992.

Croft, Christopher. "'Kiss Me with Those Red Lips': Gender and Inversion in Bram Stoker's *Dracula.*" *Representations* 8 (1984): 107–33.

Crompton, Louis. *Byron and Greek Love: Homophobia in 19th Century England.* Berkeley: University of California Press, 1985.

Cruikshank, Margaret. *Learning To Be Old: Gender, Culture, and Aging.* Lanham, MD: Rowman and Littlefield, 2003.

Curran, Stuart. "Women Readers, Women Writers." In *The Cambridge Companion to British Romanticism*, edited by Stuart Curran, 177–95. Cambridge: Cambridge University Press, 1993.

Darby, Robert. "Pathologizing Male Sexuality: Lallemand, Spermatorrhea, and the Rise of Male Circumcision." *Journal of the History of Medicine and Allied Sciences* 60, no. 3 (2005): 283–319.

Davidoff, Leonore, and Catherine Hall. *Family Fortunes: Men and Women of the English Middle Class, 1780–1850.* Chicago: University of Chicago Press, 1987.

Day, William Patrick. *In the Circles of Fear and Desire: A Study of Gothic Fantasy.* Chicago: University of Chicago Press, 1985.

Dellamora, Richard. "Male Relations in Thomas Hardy's *Jude the Obscure.*" In *Jude the Obscure*, edited by Penny Boumelha, 145–65. New York: St. Martin's Press, 2000.

Deneau, Daniel P. "The Brother-Sister Relationship in *Hard Times.*" *Dickensian* 60 (1964): 173–77.

Dentith, Simon. *Parody.* New York: Routledge, 2000.

Dever, Carolyn. *Death and the Mother from Dickens to Freud.* Cambridge: Cambridge University Press, 1998.

Dickens, Charles. *Bleak House.* 1853. New York: Norton, 1977.

———. *The Cricket on the Hearth.* 1843. In *A Christmas Carol and Other Christmas Books*, 162–242. Oxford: Oxford University Press, 2006.

———. *David Copperfield.* 1850. New York: Penguin, 2000.

———. *Great Expectations.* 1861. Oxford: Clarendon Press, 1993.

———. *Hard Times.* 1854. New York: Norton, 2001.

———. *Little Dorrit.* 1857. New York: Penguin, 2003.

———. *Nicholas Nickleby.* 1839. New York: Penguin, 1978.

———. "Nurse's Stories." In *Selected Short Fiction*, edited by Deborah A. Thomas, 218–29. New York: Penguin, 1985.

———. *The Old Curiosity Shop.* 1841. New York: Penguin, 2000.

———. "A Walk in a Workhouse." 1850. In *The Portable Victorian Reader*, edited by Gordon Haight, 84–91. New York: Penguin, 1976.

Dickens, Charles, and Wilkie Collins. *The Lazy Tour of Two Idle Apprentices.* Sandy, UT: Quiet Vision, 2003.

Donelan, Charles. *Romanticism and Male Fantasy in Byron's Don Juan.* New York: St. Martin's Press, 2000.

du Maurier, Daphne. *Rebecca.* Garden City, NY: Doubleday, 1938.

du Maurier, George. *Trilby.* 1894. New York: Penguin, 1994.

Eisler, Benita. *Byron: Child of Passion, Fool of Fame.* New York: Knopf, 1999.

Eliot, George. *Middlemarch.* 1872. New York: Norton, 2000.

Ellis, R. "On The Elegies of Maximianus." *The American Journal of Philology* 5, no. 1 (1884): 1–15.
Ellis, Sarah Stickney. *The Daughters of England, Their Position in Society, Character, and Responsibilities*. London: Fisher, 1842.
Engels, Friedrich. *The Condition of the Working Class in England*. 1846. Moscow: Progress, 1973.
Fabrizio, Richard. "Wonderful No-Meaning: Language and the Psychopathology of the Family in *Hard Times*." In *David Copperfield and Hard Times*. New Casebooks, edited by John Peck, 219–54. New York: St. Martin's Press, 1995.
Fleishman, Avrom. "Master and Servant in *Little Dorrit*." *SEL: Studies in English Literature, 1500–1900* 14, no. 4 (1974): 575–86.
Ford, Susan Allen. "'A name more dear': Daughters, Fathers, and Desire in *A Simple Story*, *The False Friend*, and *Mathilda*." In *Re-visioning Romanticism*, edited by Carol Shiner Wilson and Joel Haefner, 51–71. Philadelphia: University of Pennsylvania Press, 1994.
Foucault, Michel. *Discipline and Punish: The Birth of the Prison*. Translated by Alan Sheridan. New York: Vintage, 1979.
———. *The History of Sexuality, an Introduction: Volume One*. Translated by Robert Hurley. New York: Vintage, 1990.
Franklin, Caroline. *Byron's Heroines*. Oxford: Clarendon Press, 1992.
Frost, Ginger S. *Promises Broken: Courtship, Class, and Gender in Victorian England*. Charlottesville: University Press of Virginia, 1995.
Gardiner, Judith Kegan. "Theorizing Age with Gender: Bly's Boys, Feminism, and Maturity Masculinity." *Masculinity Studies and Feminist Theory*, edited by Judith Kegan Gardiner, 90–118. New York: Columbia University Press, 2002.
Gaskell, Elizabeth. *North and South*. 1855. New York: Oxford World Classics, 1982.
Gates, Henry Louis. *Loose Canons: Notes on the Culture Wars*. New York: Oxford University Press, 1992.
George, Michael W. "Religion, Sexuality, and Representation in the York *Joseph's Troubles* Pageant." In *Intersections of Sexuality and the Divine in Medieval Culture: The Word Made Flesh*, edited by Susannah Mary Chewning, 9–18. Burlington, VT: Ashgate, 2005.
Gilbert, Pamela K. *Disease, Desire, and the Body in Victorian Women's Popular Novels*. Cambridge: Cambridge University Press, 1997.
Gilbert, Sandra. "Life's Empty Pack: Notes toward a Literary Daughteronomy." *Critical Inquiry* 11, no. 3 (1985): 355–84.
Gillooly, Eileen. *Smile of Discontent: Humor, Gender, and Nineteenth-Century British Fiction*. Chicago: University of Chicago Press, 1999.
Gitter, Elisabeth. "The Blind Daughter in Charles Dickens's *Cricket on the Hearth*." *SEL: Studies in English Literature 1500–1900* 39, no. 4 (1999): 675–89.

Godfrey, Esther. "Feminizing Casaubon: Gender and the Aging Husband in *Middlemarch*." *Topic: The Washington and Jefferson Review* 55 (2007): 55–66.

———. "*Jane Eyre*, From Governess to Girl Bride." *SEL: Studies in English Literature 1500–1900* 45, no. 4 (2005): 853–71.

Goldfarb. Russell M. *Sexual Repression and Victorian Literature*. Lewisburg, PA: Bucknell University Press, 1970.

Gottfried, Barbara. "Father and Suitors: Narratives of Desire in *Bleak House*." *Dickens Studies Annual* 19 (1990): 169–203.

Graham, Peter. *Don Juan in Regency England*. Charlottesville: University Press of Virginia, 1990.

Grand, Sarah. *The Heavenly Twins*. 1893. Ann Arbor: University of Michigan Press, 1992.

Gratton, Brian, and Carole Haber. "Rethinking Industrialization: Old Age and the Family Economy." In *Voices and Visions of Aging: Toward a Critical Gerontology*, edited by Thomas R. Cole, et al., 134–59. New York: Springer, 1993.

Graver, Suzanne. "Mill, *Middlemarch*, and Marriage." In *Portraits of Marriage in Literature*, edited by Anne C. Hargrove and Maurine Magliocco, 55–65. Macomb: Western Illinois University, 1984.

Greenfield, Susan C. *Mothering Daughters: Novels and the Politics of Family Romance*. Detroit, MI: Wayne State University Press, 2002.

Gross, Jonathan David. *Byron: The Erotic Liberal*. Lanham, MD: Rowman and Littlefield, 2001.

Grosskurth, Phyllis. *Byron: The Flawed Angel*. Boston: Houghton Mifflin, 1997.

Grosz, Elizabeth. *Space, Time, and Perversion: Essays on the Politics of Bodies*. New York: Routledge, 1995.

Hager, Kelly. "Estranging *David Copperfield*: Reading the Novel of Divorce." *ELH: English Literary History* 63, no. 6 (1996): 989–1019.

Haggerty, George E. "Female Abjection in Inchbald's *A Simple Story*." *SEL: Studies in English Literature, 1500–1900* 36, no. 3 (1996): 655–71.

Halberstam, Judith. "'Dude, Where's My Gender?' or, Is There Life on Uranus?" *GLQ: A Journal of Gay and Lesbian Studies* 10, no. 2 (2004): 308–12.

———. *Female Masculinity*. Durham, NC: Duke University Press, 1998.

———. *Skin Shows*. Durham, NC: Duke University Press, 1995.

Hallissy, Margaret. "Widow-To-Be: May in Chaucer's 'The Merchant's Tale.'" *Studies in Short Fiction* 26, no. 3 (1989): 295–304.

Hardy, Barbara. "The Miserable Marriages in *Middlemarch*, *Anna Karenina*, and *Effi Briest*." In *George Eliot and Europe*, edited by John Rignall, 64–83. Aldershot, UK: Scolar, 1997.

Hardy, Thomas. *The Hand of Ethelberta*. 1876. New York: Penguin, 1997.

———. *Jude the Obscure*. 1895. New York: Norton, 1978.

Hartung, Albert E. "The Non-Comic Merchant's Tale, Maximianus, and the Sources." *Mediaeval Studies* 29 (1967): 10–25.
Hawthorne, Nathaniel. *The Scarlet Letter*. 1850. New York: Modern Library, 2000.
Hayley, William. *A Philosophical, Historical, and Moral Essay on Old Maids*. London: Cadell, 1785.
Hays, Mary. *Appeal to the Men of Great Britain in Behalf of Women*. 1798. Garland Series: The Feminist Controversy in England 1788–1810. New York: Garland, 1974.
Hedges, Peter. *What's Eating Gilbert Grape*. New York: Poseidon, 1991.
Helme, Elizabeth. *The History of Louisa, the Lovely Orphan; or, The Cottage on the Moor*. 1787. Wilmington, DE: Adams, 1795.
Herbert, Christopher. "Filthy Lucre: Victorian Ideas of Money." *Victorian Studies* 44, no. 2 (Winter 2002): 185–213.
Herman, Judith Lewis. *Father-Daughter Incest*. Cambridge, MA: Harvard University Press, 1981.
Highbridge, Dianne. *A Much Younger Man*. New York: Soho, 1999.
Hoeveler, Diane Long. *Gothic Feminism: The Professionalism of Gender from Charlotte Smith to the Brontës*. University Park: Pennsylvania State University Press, 1998.
Hollington, Michael. *Dickens and the Grotesque*. Totowa, NJ: Barnes, 1984.
Hornback, Bert G. *Middlemarch: A Novel of Reform*. Boston: Twayne, 1988.
Hughes, Kathryn. *The Victorian Governess*. London: Hambledon, 1993.
Humphreys, Anne. "Louisa Gradgrind's Secret: Marriage and Divorce in *Hard Times*." *Dickens Studies Annual* 25 (1996): 177–95.
Hutcheon, Linda. *A Theory of Parody*. New York: Methuen, 1985.
Inchbald, Elizabeth. *A Simple Story*. 1791. New York: Oxford World Classics, 1988.
Jagose, Annamarie. "Remembering Miss Wade: Little Dorrit and the Historicizing of Perversity." *GLQ: A Journal of Gay and Lesbian Studies* 4, no. 3 (1998): 423–51.
Jalland, Pat. *Women, Marriage, and Politics, 1860–1914*. Oxford: Oxford University Press, 1986.
James, Henry. *Watch and Ward*. 1871. New York: Grove, 1960.
Jann, Rosemary. "Darwin and the Anthropologists: Sexual Selection and Its Discontents." In *Sexualities in Victorian Britain*, edited by Andrew H. Miller and James Eli Adams, 287–306. Bloomington: Indiana University Press, 1996.
Jewsbury, Geraldine Ensor. *Zoe*. 1845. New York: Garland, 1975.
Jordan, Ellen. *The Women's Movement and Women's Employment in Nineteenth Century Britain*. London: Routledge, 1999.

Joseph, Gerhard, and Herbert F. Tucker. "Passing On: Death." In *A Companion to Victorian Literature and Culture*, edited by Herbert F. Tucker, 110–24. Malden, MA: Blackwell, 1999.

Jost, Jean E. "May's Mismarriage of Youth and Elde: The Poetics of Sexual Desire in Chaucer's *Merchant's Tale*." In *Representations of the Feminine in the Middle Ages*, edited by Bonnie Wheeler, 117–37. Cambridge, MA: Academia, 1993.

Kaplan, Fred. *Dickens*. Baltimore: Johns Hopkins University Press, 1988.

Katz, Stephen. "Imagining the Life Span: From Premodern Miracles to Postmodern Fantasies." In *Images of Aging: Cultural Representations of Later Life*, edited by Mike Featherstone and Andrew Wernick, 59–76. New York: Routledge, 1995.

Keats, John. *Hyperion*. 1819. In *Selected Poetry*, edited by Elizabeth Cook, 121–43. New York: Oxford University Press, 1998.

Kelleher, Paul. "How to Do Things with Perversion: Psychoanalysis and the 'Child in Danger.'" In *Curiouser: On the Queerness of Children*, edited by Steven Bruhm and Natasha Hurley, 151–71. Minneapolis: University of Minnesota Press, 2004.

Kern, Stephen. *The Culture of Love*. Cambridge, MA: Harvard University Press, 1992.

Kestner, Joseph. *Masculinities in Victorian Painting*. Brookfield, VT: Scolar, 1995.

Killham, John. *Tennyson and* The Princess: *Reflections of an Age*. London: Athlone, 1958.

Kincaid, James R. *Child-Loving: The Erotic Child and Victorian Culture*. New York: Routledge, 1992.

———. *Erotic Innocence: The Culture of Child Molesting*. Durham, NC: Duke University Press, 1998.

Kittredge, George Lyman. "Chaucer and Maximianus." *American Journal of Philology* 9, no. 1 (1888): 84–85.

Laqueur, Thomas. *Making Sex: Body and Gender from the Greeks to Freud*. Cambridge, MA: Harvard University Press, 1990.

———. *Solitary Sex: A Cultural History of Masturbation*. New York: Zone, 2003.

Lamont, Claire. "Jane Austen and the Old." *Review of English Studies* 54 (2003): 661–74.

Le Fanu, J. Sheridan. "Carmilla." 1872. In *Three Vampire Tales*. New Riverside Editions, edited by Anne Williams, 86–146. Boston: Houghton Mifflin, 2003.

———. *The Wyvern Mystery*. 1869. Phoenix Mill, UK: Sutton, 1994.

Lennox, Charlotte. *The Female Quixote*. 1752. New York: Penguin, 2006.

Levi-Strauss, Claude. *Structural Anthropology*. Translated by Claire Jacobson and Brooke Grundfest Schoepf. New York: Basic Books, 1963.

Lewcock, Dawn. "More for Seeing than Hearing: Behn and the Use of Theatre." In *Aphra Behn Studies*, edited by Janet Todd, 66–83. New York: Cambridge University Press, 1996.

Linton, Eliza Lynn. "Nearing the Rapids." In *Prose by Victorian Women: An Anthology*, edited by Andrea Broomfield and Sally Mitchell, 377–86. New York: Garland, 1996.

———. "What Is Woman's Work?" In *The Voice of Toil: Nineteenth-Century British Writings about Work*, edited by David J. Bradshaw and Suzanne Ozment, 698–703. Athens: Ohio University Press, 2000.

———. "Womanly Dependence." In *Ourselves: A Series of Essays on Women*, 2nd ed, 226–27. London: Routledge, 1870.

MacCarthy, Fiona. *Byron: Life and Legend*. New York: Farrar, 2002.

MacFarlane, Alan. *The Culture of Capitalism*. New York: Blackwell, 1987.

———. *Marriage and Love in England: Modes of Reproduction 1300–1840*. New York: Blackwell, 1986.

Mainardi, Patricia. *Husbands, Wives, and Lovers: Marriage and Its Discontents in Nineteenth-Century France*. New Haven, CT: Yale University Press, 2003.

Malthus, T. R. *An Essay on the Principle of Population*. 1798. Edited by Philip Appleman. New York: Norton, 1976.

Mangum, Teresa. "Growing Old: Age." In *A Companion to Victorian Literature and Culture*, edited by Herbert F. Tucker, 97–109. Malden, MA: Blackwell, 1999.

Marchand, Leslie. "Lord Byron and Count Alborghetti." *PMLA* 64 (1949): 976–1007.

Masi, Michael. *Chaucer and Gender*. New York: Peter Lang, 2005.

Matthews, William. "Eustache Deschamps and Chaucer's 'Merchant's Tale.'" *Modern Language Review* 51, no. 2 (1956): 217–20.

McKeon, Michael. "Historicizing Patriarchy: The Emergence of Gender Difference in England, 1660–1760." *Eighteenth-Century Studies* 28, no. 3 (1995): 295–322.

McMaster, Juliet. "'A Microscope Directed on a Water-Drop': Chapter 19." In *Approaches to Teaching Eliot's Middlemarch*, edited by Kathleen Blake, 109–16. New York: Modern Language Association, 1990.

Medwin, Thomas. *Medwin's Conversations of Lord Byron*. 1824. Edited by Ernest J. Lovell. Princeton, NJ: Princeton University Press, 1966.

Mighall, Robert. *A Geography of Victorian Gothic Fiction: Mapping History's Nightmares*. Oxford: Oxford University Press, 1999.

Milbank, Alison. *Daughters of the House: Modes of the Gothic in Victorian Fiction*. New York: St. Martin's Press, 1992.

Mill, John Stuart. *The Subjection of Women*. 1869. In *Mill: The Spirit of the Age, On Liberty, The Subjection of Women*, edited by Alan Ryan, 133–216. New York: Norton, 1996.

Mohr, Richard D. "The Pedophilia of Everyday Life." In *Curiouser: On the Queerness of Children*, edited by Steven Bruhm and Natasha Hurley, 17–30. Minneapolis: University of Minnesota Press, 2004.

Monkhouse, Cosmo. *British Contemporary Artists*. New York: Scribner's, 1899.

Montagu, Lady Mary Wortley. "The Reasons that Induced Dr S to write a Poem call'd the Lady's Dressing room." ca. 1732–43. In *Essays and Poems and* Simplicity, a Comedy, edited by Robert Halsband and Isobel Grundy, 273–76. Oxford: Clarendon Press, 1977.

Morse, Charlotte C. "Popularizing Chaucer in the Nineteenth Century." *Chaucer Review* 38, no. 2 (2003): 99–125.

Mortensen, Peter. "Rousseau's English Daughters: Female Desire and Male Guardianship in British Romantic Fiction." *English Studies* 83, no. 4 (2002): 356–70.

Murfin, Ross. "Gender Criticism and *Dracula*." In *Dracula*, edited by John Paul Riquelme, 434–49. New York: Palgrave, 2002.

*My Secret Life: An Erotic Diary of Victorian London*. Edited by James Kincaid. New York: Signet, 1996.

Nabokov, Vladimir. *Lolita*. 1955. New York: Knopf, 1992.

Nardin, Jane. *He Knew She Was Right: The Independent Woman in the Novels of Anthony Trollope*. Carbondale: Southern Illinois University Press, 1989.

Nelson, Antonya. *Nobody's Girl*. New York: Scribner, 1999.

Newton, Judith Lowder. *Women, Power, and Subversion: Social Strategies in British Fiction, 1778–1860*. Athens: University of Georgia Press, 1981.

Nightingale, Florence. *Cassandra*. 1860. In *The Voice of Toil: Nineteenth-Century British Writings about Work*, edited by David J. Bradshaw and Suzanne Ozment, 118–38. Athens: Ohio University Press, 2000.

Nordlund, Marcus. "Theorizing Early Modern Jealousy: A Biocultural Perspective on Shakespeare's *Othello*." *Studia Neophilologica* 74 (2002): 146–60.

Olsen, Gregg. *If Loving You Is Wrong: The Shocking True Story of Mary Kay Letourneau*. New York: St. Martin's Press, 1999.

O'Malley, Patrick M. "Oxford's Ghosts: *Jude the Obscure* and the End of the Gothic." *MFS: Modern Fiction Studies* 46, no. 3 (2000): 646–71.

Origo, Iris. *The Last Attachment*. London: Cape, 1949.

Patmore, Coventry. *The Angel in the House*. 1854. London: Bell, 1892.

Perkin, Joan. *Women and Marriage in Nineteenth-Century England*. London: Routledge, 1989.

Philpotts, Trey. *The Companion to Little Dorrit*. London: Helm, 2003.

Polhemus, Robert M. "Comic and Erotic Faith Meet Faith in the Child: Charles Dickens's *The Old Curiosity Shop* ('The Old Cupiosity Shape')." In *Critical Reconstructions: The Relationship of Fiction and Life*, edited by

Robert M. Polhemus and Roger B. Henkle, 71–89. Stanford, CA: Stanford University Press, 1994.

———. "The Favorite Child: *David Copperfield* and the Scriptural Issue of Child-Wives." In *Homes and Homelessness in the Victorian Imagination*, edited by Murray Baumgarten and H. M. Daleski, 3–20. New York: AMS Press, 1998.

———. *Lot's Daughters*. Stanford, CA: Stanford University Press, 2005.

Polidori, John. *The Vampyre*. 1819. Oxford: Oxford World Classics, 1998.

Polwhele, Richard. *The Unsex'd Females*. 1798. Garland Series: The Feminist Controversy in England 1788–1810. New York: Garland, 1974.

Pool, Daniel. *What Jane Austen Ate and Charles Dickens Knew: From Fox Hunting to Whist—the Facts of Daily Life in Nineteenth-Century England*. New York: Simon, 1993.

Poovey, Mary. *The Proper Lady and the Woman Writer: Ideology as Style in the Works of Mary Wollstonecraft, Mary Shelley, and Jane Austen*. Chicago: University of Chicago Press, 1984.

———. *Uneven Developments: The Ideological Work of Gender in Mid-Victorian England*. Chicago: University of Chicago Press, 1988.

Prest, Thomas Preskett. *Varney the Vampire; or, The Feast of Blood*. 1847. Vols. 1–3. Edited by Devendra Varma. New York: Arno Press, 1970.

Radcliffe, Ann. *The Mysteries of Uldolpho*. 1794. London: Penguin, 2001.

———. *The Romance of the Forest*. 1791. Oxford: Oxford University Press, 1999.

———. *A Sicilian Romance*. 1790. Oxford: Oxford University Press, 1993.

Rank, Otto. *The Incest Theme in Literature and Legend: Fundamentals of a Psychology of Literary Creation*. Translated by Gregory C. Richter. Baltimore: Johns Hopkins University Press, 1992.

Richardson, Angelique. *Love and Eugenics in the Late Nineteenth Century: Rational Reproduction and the New Woman*. New York: Oxford University Press, 2003.

Riga, Frank P. "Dismantling Traditionalist Gender Roles: An Exotic Counter-World in Byron's *Don Juan*." In *The Foreign Woman in British Literature: Exotics, Aliens, and Outsiders*, edited by Marilyn Demarest Button and Toni Reed, 1–15. Westport, CT: Greenwood, 1999.

Roberts, Bette B. "*Varney, the Vampire*, or, Rather, *Varney*, the Victim." *Gothic* 2 (1987): 1–5.

Robson, Catherine. *Men in Wonderland: The Lost Girlhood of the Victorian Gentleman*. Princeton, NJ: Princeton University Press, 2001.

Roebuck, Janet. "When Does 'Old Age' Begin?: The Evolution of the English Definition." *Journal of Social History* 12 (1979): 416–28.

Rose, Sonya. *Limited Livelihoods: Gender and Class in Nineteenth-Century England*. Berkeley: University of California Press, 1992.

Rosenman, Ellen Bayuk. *Unauthorized Pleasures*. Ithaca, NY: Cornell University Press, 2003.

Rubin, Gayle. "The Traffic in Women." In *Literary Theory: An Anthology*, edited by Julie Rivkin and Michael Ryan, 533–60. Malden, MA: Blackwell, 1998.

Rudnytsky, Peter. *Freud and Oedipus*. New York: Columbia University Press, 1987.

Ryder, K. C. "The 'Senex Amator' in Plautus." *Greece and Rome* 31, no. 2 (1984): 181–89.

*The Sack-full of Newes*. London: Clark, 1673.

Sadoff, Dianne F. "The Dead Father: *Barnaby Rudge*, *David Copperfield*, and *Great Expectations*." *Papers on Language and Literature* 18, no. 1 (1982): 36–57.

———. *Monsters of Affection: Dickens, Eliot and Bronte on Fatherhood*. Baltimore: John Hopkins University Press, 1982.

———. "Storytelling and the Figure of the Father in *Little Dorrit*." *PMLA* 95, no. 2 (1980): 234–45.

Schaffer, Talia. "'A Wilde Desire Took Me': The Homoerotic History of Dracula." *English Literary History* 61, no. 2 (1994): 381–425.

Schor, Hilary M. *Dickens and the Daughter of the House*. Cambridge: Cambridge University Press, 1999.

Scott, Joan Wallach. "Gender: A Useful Category of Historical Analysis." *American Historical Review* 91, no. 5 (1986): 1053–75.

Sedgwick, Eve Kosofsky. *Between Men*. New York: Columbia University Press, 1985.

Seltzer, Mark. *Bodies and Machines*. New York: Routledge, 1992.

Senf, Carol. *The Vampire in Nineteenth-Century English Literature*. Bowling Green, OH: Bowling Green State University Popular Press, 1988.

Shakespeare, William. "138." In *The Complete Works of Shakespeare*, 4th ed. Edited by David Bevington, 1644. New York: HarperCollins, 1992.

———. *Othello*. In *The Complete Works of Shakespeare*, 4th ed. Edited by David Bevington, 1117–66. New York: HarperCollins, 1992.

———. *The Taming of the Shrew*. In *The Complete Works of Shakespeare*, 4th ed. Edited by David Bevington, 108–46. New York: HarperCollins, 1992.

Shanley, Mary Lyndon. *Feminism, Marriage, and the Law in Victorian England*. Princeton, NJ: Princeton University Press, 1989.

Sharma, Mani Ram. *Marriage in Ancient India*. Delhi: Agam Kala Prakashan, 1993.

Shaw, George Bernard. *Mrs Warren's Profession*. 1898. *Complete Plays with Prefaces*. Vol. 3. New York: Dodd, 1962.

Shelley, Mary Wollstonecraft. *Frankenstein*. 1818. Peterborough, ON: Broadview Press, 1994.

———. *Mathilda*. 1819. Chapel Hill: University of North Carolina Press, 1959.

Shelley, Percy. *The Cenci*. 1819. In *Shelley's Poetry and Prose*, edited by Donald H. Reiman and Sharon B. Powers, 236–301. New York: Norton, 1977.

Sheridan, Richard Brinsley. *The School for Scandal*. In *Restoration and Eighteenth-Century Comedy*, edited by Scott McMillin, 277–340. New York: Norton, 1973.

Shildrick, Margrit. *Embodying the Monster: Encounters with the Vulnerable Self*. London: Sage, 2002.

Simcox, Edith Jemima. "The Capacity of Women." In *Prose by Victorian Women: An Anthology*, edited by Andrea Broomfield and Sally Mitchell, 583–97. New York: Garland, 1996.

Sinclair, Alison. *The Deceived Husband: A Kleinian Approach to the Literature of Infidelity*. Oxford: Clarendon Press, 1993.

Singer, Irving. *The Nature of Love*. 3 vols. Chicago: University of Chicago Press, 1984–87.

Skarde, Patricia. "Vampirism and Plagiarism: Byron's Influence and Polidori's Practice." *Studies in Romanticism* 28, no. 2 (1989): 249–69.

Slater, Michael. *Dickens and Women*. Stanford, CA: Stanford University Press, 1983.

Smith, Charlotte. *The Old Manor House*. 1794. Peterborough, ON: Broadview Press, 2002.

Stead, W. T. *The Maiden Tribute to Modern Babylon: The Report of the "Pall Mall Gazette's" Secret Commission*. London: Richard Lambert, 1885.

Steadman, Jane. "Child-Wives of Dickens." *The Dickensian* 59 (1963): 112–18.

Stearns, Peter N., ed. *Old Age in Preindustrial Society*. New York: Holms, 1982.

Steffan, T. G. "Byron at Work on Canto I of *Don Juan*." *Modern Philology* 44 (1947): 141–64.

Stengers, Jean, and Anne Van Neck. *Masturbation: The History of a Great Terror*. Translated by Kathryn Hoffmann. New York: Palgrave, 2001.

Sterling, Anne Fausto. *Sexing the Body*. New York: Basic Books, 2000.

Stoker, Bram. *Dracula*. 1897. New York: Norton, 1997.

Stone, Lawrence. *The Family, Sex and Marriage in England 1500–1800*. New York: Harper & Row, 1977.

Strickland, Margot. *The Byron Women*. London: Owen, 1974.

Tavormina, M. Teresa. Notes for "The Merchant's Tale." In *The Riverside Chaucer*, edited by Larry D. Benson, 884–89. Boston: Houghton Mifflin, 1987.

Taylor, Thomas. *A Vindication of the Rights of Brutes*. 1792. Gainesville, FL: Scholars' Facsimiles and Reprints, 1966.

Tennyson, Alfred. *The Princess*. 1847. In *Poems of Tennyson*. Riverside Editions, edited by Jerome Buckley, 123–77. Boston: Houghton Mifflin, 1958.

———. "Tithonus." 1860. In *Poems of Tennyson*. Riverside Editions, edited by Jerome Buckley, 68–69. Boston: Houghton, 1958.

Thackeray, William Makepeace. *The History of Henry Esmond, Esq*. 1852. Oxford: Oxford University Press, 1991.

———. *The Memoirs of Barry Lyndon, Esq.* 1844. Oxford: Oxford University Press, 1999.

———. *Vanity Fair.* 1847. New York: Norton, 1994.

Thane, Pat. *Old Age in English History: Past Experiences, Present Issues.* Oxford: Oxford University Press, 2000.

———. "Social Histories of Old Age and Aging." *Journal of Social History* 37, no. 1 (2003): 93–111.

Tonna, Charlotte Elizabeth. *The Perils of the Nation: An Appeal to the Legislature, the Clergy, and the Higher and Middle Classes.* London: Seeley, 1843.

Tracy, Robert. "Loving You All Ways: Vamps, Vampires, Necrophiles and Necrofilles in Nineteenth-Century Fiction." In *Sex and Death in Victorian Literature*, edited by Reginia Barreca, 32–59. London: Macmillan, 1990.

Trollope, Anthony. *Barchester Towers.* 1857. New York: Penguin, 1994.

———. *He Knew He Was Right.* 1869. New York: Penguin, 1994.

———. *An Old Man's Love.* 1884. Oxford: Oxford World Classics, 1991.

———. *Orley Farm.* 1861. Oxford: Oxford University Press 2000.

Tromp, Marlene. *The Private Rod: Marital Violence, Sensation, and the Law in Victorian Britain.* Charlottesville: University Press of Virginia, 2000.

Twitchell, James. *The Living Dead: A Study of The Vampire in Romantic Literature.* Durham, NC: Duke University Press, 1980.

Valenti, Teresa. "The Forgotten Father in Charles Dickens's *Bleak House.*" *Dickens Quarterly* 17, no. 2 (2000): 88–93.

Wall, Stephen. Introduction. In *Little Dorrit*, by Charles Dickens, xi–xxvii. New York: Penguin, 2003.

Walpole, Horace. *The Castle of Otranto.* 1764. London: Penguin, 2001.

Ward, J. T. *The Factory Movement: 1830–55.* New York: Barnes, 1962.

Waters, Catherine. "Gender, Family and Domestic Ideology." In *The Cambridge Companion to Charles Dickens*, edited by John O. Jordan, 120–35. New York: Cambridge University Press, 2001.

Wijesinha, Rajiva. *The Androgynous Trollope: Attitudes to Women Amongst Early Victorian Novelists.* Washington, DC: University Press of America, 1982.

Wilde, Oscar. *The Picture of Dorian Gray.* 1890. New York: Norton, 2007.

Wilputte, Earla A. "Wife Pandering in Three Restoration Plays." *SEL: Studies in English Literature, 1500–1900* 38, no. 3 (1998): 447–64.

Witemeyer, Hugh. *George Eliot and the Visual Arts.* New Haven, CT: Yale University Press, 1979.

Wharton, Edith. *Summer.* 1917. New York: Signet Classic, 1993.

Wolf, Robert. *Sensational Victorian: The Life and Fiction of Mary Elizabeth Braddon.* New York: Garland, 1979.

Wolfson, Susan. "'Their She Condition': Cross-Dressing and the Politics of Gender in *Don Juan.*" *ELH: English Literary History* 54 (1987): 585–617.

Wollstonecraft, Mary. *Thoughts on the Education of Daughters.* 1787. Garland Series: The Feminist Controversy in England 1788–1810. New York: Garland, 1974.

———. *A Vindication of the Rights of Woman.* 1792. New York: Norton, 1975.

Wood, John Colman. *When Men Are Women: Manhood Among Gabra Nomads of East Africa.* Madison: University of Wisconsin Press, 1999.

Woolf, Virginia. *A Room of One's Own.* 1929. San Diego, CA: Harcourt Brace Jovanovich, 1989.

"A Word of Amelia Roper." *Spectator* 64 (1890): 83–84.

Wordsworth, William. "Michael." In *Selected Poems and Prefaces.* Riverside Editions, edited by Jack Stillinger, 146–56. Boston: Houghton Mifflin, 1965.

Wycherley, William. *The Country Wife.* 1675. New York: Cambridge University Press, 1996.

Yeazell, Ruth Bernard. "Do It or Dorrit." *NOVEL: A Forum on Fiction* 25, no. 1 (1991): 33–49.

Yonge, Charlotte Mary. *A Book of Golden Deeds.* London: Blackie, 1864.

# INDEX

Acton, William: *The Functions and Disorders of the Reproductive Organs in Childhood, Youth, Adult Age, and Advanced Life,* 224n9
Act to Provide for the Punishment of Incest, 218n6
*Addams Family Values,* 1n
Africa, 13, 210–11, 214n10
Allen, Woody, 232n10; *Manhattan,* 4, 207
*American Pie,* 209
Anatomy Act of 1832, 120
Anderson, Kathleen, 231n6
Andrews, Malcolm, 220n17
Armstrong, Nancy, 149
Arnold, Matthew: *Culture and Anarchy,* 157
art, 93–100, 121–23, 131–33, 136–39, 151–53, 222n2, 226n21
Auerbach, Nina, 130, 145
Austen, Jane, 223n6, 227n6, 231n6; *Catherine,* 227n8; *Emma,* 5, 54, 148, 149, 160, 164, 175, 202; "Frederic and Elfrida," 227n8; "Jack and Alice," 227n8, 232n13; *Lady Susan,* 209, 227n8; "Lesley Castle," 227n8; "Love and Friendship," 232n13; *Northanger Abbey,* 114; *Persuasion,* 161; *Pride and Prejudice,* 91, 227n8; *Sense and Sensibility,* 2, 5, 6, 11, 90, 154–56, 202; *Watsons, The,* 227n8
Ayres, Brenda, 53, 54, 83–84, 221n34

Baird, John D., 221n31
Baldung-Grien, Hans: *Death and the Maiden,* 226n21; *Phyllis and Aristotle,* 214n6
Banks, J. A., 149
Behn, Aphra, 9; *The Lucky Chance,* 23, 24–25; *Oroonoko,* 214n10; *The Rover,* 23; *Sir Patient Fancy,* 23–24, 214n11
Black, Barbara, 222n40
Blain, Virginia, 230n13
Blodgett, Harriet, 228n15
Bluestockings, 32, 39, 215n19
Boccaccio, Giovanni: *Ameto,* 16
Boothman, Janet, 214n4
Botting, Fred, 114–15
Braddon, Mary Elizabeth, 228n16; "Good Lady Ducayne," 223n6, 225n17; *Lady Audley's Secret,* 6, 11, 149, 150, 164–69, 177
Bradley, Katherine. *See* Field, Michael (Katherine Bradley and Edith Cooper)
Brontë, Anne: *Agnes Grey,* 160
Brontë, Charlotte, 2; *Jane Eyre,* 2, 3, 11, 54, 111–12, 149, 162–64, 175, 196, 211, 215n21, 222n1; *Professor, The,* 203; *Villette,* 54, 203

Browning, Elizabeth Barrett: *Aurora Leigh*, 37
Browning, Robert, 2; "Andrea Del Sarto," 119, 202; "My Last Duchess," 202; *Pippa Passes*, 202; "Rabbi Ben Ezra," 115–16; *Ring and the Book, The*, 202, 231n1
Bruhm, Steven, 218n4, 231n5
Burton, Antoinette, 200–201
Buss, David, 227n3, 228n14
Butler, Judith, 217n2, 260n26, 261n32
Butt, John, 221n32
Byron, Lord, 2, 133–35, 216–17n30; "Augustus Darvell," 133; *Beppo*, 39, 216n28; *Blues, The*, 39; *Byron's Letters and Journals*, 3, 39; *Don Juan*, 6, 9–10, 12, 37–51, 199, 208–9, 217n35, 232n12; *Don Juan*, biographical sources of, 39–41, 216n27, 217n31; *Don Juan*, feminism and, 39; *Giaour, The*, 133–34; *Mazeppa*, 39, 216n28–29; "On This Day I Complete My Thirty-Sixth Year," 118; relationships with women, 39, 47, 216n25; *Sardanapalus*, 47

*Canterbury Tales*, 16–20, 29; "The Merchant's Tale," 16–20; "The Miller's Tale," 16, 18–20, 29; "The Wife of Bath's Prologue," 16–18, 215n14
Capellanus, Andreas: *De Amore*, 16, 213n3
Carlisle, Anthony: *An Essay on the Disorders of Old Age*, 119
Carroll, Lewis, 5, 201
"Cauchemar," 132
Chambers, J. D., 227n10
Charcot, Jean-Martin: *Clinical Lectures on the Diseases of Old Age*, 119–20
Chaucer, Geoffrey, 2, 9, 20–23, 27–29, 31, 36, 147, 194, 213n1, 214n5. See also *Canterbury Tales*
Chopin, Kate: *The Awakening*, 209
Cleland, John: *Fanny Hill*, 26, 214n13
Cobbe, Francis Power: "What Shall We Do with Our Old Maids?" 2
Coleridge, Samuel Taylor, 46, 225n17
Collins, Wilkie, 2; "The Bride's Tale" 221n30; *Woman in White, The*, 12, 148, 204, 205;
Congreve, William: *Love for Love*, 25; *Old Batchelour, The*, 25
Contagious Disease Acts of 1860s, 36, 171
Cooper, Edith. *See* Field, Michael (Katherine Bradley and Edith Cooper)
Cowles, David L., 74
*Cradle Robbers, The*, 210
Craft, Christopher, 226n26
Crafts, N. F. R., 149
Craig, Randall, 231n18
Crane, David, 216n25
Crary, Jonathan, 90
Crompton, Louis, 41
Curran, Stuart, 215n18
Custody of Infants Act, 47, 215n23

Darby, Robert, 224n8
Darwin, Charles, 153, 160, 227n4
Davidoff, Lenore, 2
Day, Patrick, 223n2
Dellamora, Richard, 225n13
Dentith, Simon, 8
DeQuincey, Thomas, 201
Deschamp, Eustache, 16
Dever, Carolyn, 218n8

# INDEX

Dickens, Charles, 2, 9, 54–88, 220n29, 221n35, 222n39, 224n12; *Bleak House*, 4, 7, 12, 56, 60, 177, 182–88, 206, 220n20, 228n18, 232n8; "The Bride's Tale," 221n30; "Captain Murderer," 220n28; *Cricket on the Hearth, The*, 10, 58, 60, 66–75, 177–78, 182, 229n5; *David Copperfield*, 6, 10, 58, 60, 111, 177, 178–82, 194–95, 228n18; and Ellen Ternan, 201, 219n9; *Great Expectations*, 58, 91, 151; *Hard Times*, 3, 10, 58, 60, 75–82, 209; *Lazy Tour of Two Idle Apprentices, The*, 221n30; *Little Dorrit*, 10, 58, 60, 82–88, 222n1, 228n18; *Nicholas Nickleby*, 6, 10, 58, 59, 60–63, 130, 171–74, 206, 228n18; "Nurse's Stories," 220n28; *Old Curiosity Shop, The*, 58, 59, 62–66; *Tale of Two Cities, A*, 177, 228n18; "A Walk in a Workhouse," 117
Divorce Act of 1857, 215n23, 222n41, 227n12
Donelan, Charles, 217n34
du Maurier, Daphne, 232n9; *Rebecca*, 206
du Maurier, George, 232n9; *Trilby*, 12, 204, 205, 231n1, 232n9

Eisler, Benita, 216n25, 216n29, 226n18 Eisler, Benita, 216n25, 216n29, 226n18
*Elegy*, 12, 207
Eliot, George, 2, 222n5–6; *Middlemarch*, 4, 10, 12, 54, 101–11, 148, 161, 177, 195–96, 223n7, 231n1; *Silas Marner*, 116
Ellis, Sarah Stickney: *Daughters of England, The*, 193

Engels, Friedrich, 229n2; *Condition of the Working Class in England, The*, 35

Factory Act: of 1850, 160; of 1870s, 36
Field, Michael (Katherine Bradley and Edith Cooper), 201–2
*First Wives Club, The*, 207
Ford, Susan Allen, 215n16
Foucault, Michel, 55
Freud, Sigmund, 10, 33, 55, 58, 80, 83, 217n1, 218n3, 219n11
Frost, Ginger S., 3
Fuseli, Henry: *Nightmare, The*, 131–32

Gabra people, 13, 210–11
Gaskell, Elizabeth: *North and South*, 203, 228n17
Gates, Henry Louis, 9, 213n4
George, Michael W., 213n2
Gilbert, Pamela K., 223n8
Gilbert, Sandra, 218n3
Gillooly, Eileen, 104
Gitter, Elisabeth, 73, 220n26
Godfrey, Esther, 215n21, 222n3
*Gods and Monsters*, 232n11
Godwin, William, 33
Golden, Arthur: *Memoirs of a Geisha*, 207
gothic, 11, 113–46
governess, 147, 150, 156–57, 160–64, 166, 169, 174, 188, 190–91
*Graduate, The*, 209
Graham, Peter, 217n35
Grand, Sarah: *Heavenly Twins*, 54, 205
Gratton, Brian, 223n4
Graver, Suzanne, 223n7
*Greedy*, 207
Greenfield, Susan C., 221n33
Gross, Jonathan David, 216n26
Grosskurth, Phyllis, 216n25

252 INDEX

Grosvenor, Linda Dominique: *Bloom*, 232n15
Grosz, Elizabeth, 10

Haber, Carole, 223n4
Hager, Kelly, 179
Haggerty, George, 215n15
Halberstam, Judith, 7, 133, 218n2, 226n25
Hall, Catherine, 2
Hallissy, Margaret, 17–18
Halliwell, J. O., 214n7
Hardy, Barbara, 4–5, 170
Hardy, Thomas, 2; *Hand of Ethelberta, The*, 213n1; *Jude the Obscure*, 3, 5, 11, 54, 90, 113–14, 125–29; *Mayor of Casterbridge, The*, 56, 170
*Harold and Maude*, 209
Hartung, Albert E., 214n4
Hawthorne, Nathaniel: *Scarlet Letter, The*, 12, 205
Hayley, William: *Philosophical, Historical, and Moral Essay on Old Maids, A*, 2
Hays, Mary: *Appeal to the Men of Great Britain in Behalf of Women*, 33, 41
Health of Women Act of 1874, 160
Helme, Elizabeth: *History of Louisa, the Lovely Orphan, The*, 114
Herbert, Christopher, 175
Herman, Judith Lewis, 218n3
Highbridge, Dianne: *A Much Younger Man*, 210
Hitchcock, Alfred, 207
Hoeveler, Diane Long, 139
Hogarth, William: *Marriage á la Mode*, 93
Hollington, Michael, 219n13
homoeroticism, 38, 41, 47, 54–55, 135, 144–45, 216n26–27, 225n17, 226n25
Hoppner, Richard, 41

Hornback, Bert, 195
*How to Marry a Millionaire*, 207
Hughes, Kathryn, 227n13
*Human Stain, The*, 207
Humphreys, Anne, 79
Hurley, Natasha, 218n4, 231n5
Hutcheon, Linda, 9

Imlay, Gilbert, 33
incest, 5, 121–22, 148, 161, 176–78, 202, 215n16, 218n6, 228n17; daddy-daughter, 5, 8–10, 54, 60, 218n3, 220n27; in Dickens, 53–88, 230n6; Oedipus complex and, 10, 54–55, 58–59, 73, 81–83, 217n1, 218n2–3, 221n34, 230n6; pedophilia and, 5, 63, 66, 77–78, 81–83, 104, 121–22, 186, 201, 206; and Romanticism, 5, 57
Inchbald, Elizabeth, 9; *Simple Story, A*, 29–31, 32, 215n15
India, 12, 200–201, 207, 231n2, 231n6
Infant Custody Act of 1839, 36, 215n23

Jagose, Annamarie, 222n40
James, Henry: *Watch and Ward*, 12, 205–6
Jann, Rosemary, 227n5
Jewsbury, Geraldine Endsor, 1
Jordan, Ellen, 227n11

Katz, Stephen, 224n7
Keats, John: *Fall of Hyperion, The*, 118; *Hyperion*, 118
Kelleher, Paul, 55
Kern, Stephen, 147
Kestner, Joseph, 94, 97
Killham, John, 158
Kincaid, James, 5, 64, 176, 220n22, 229n5

Lallemand, Claude Francois: *Practical Treatise on the Causes, Symptoms, and Treatment of Spermatorrhea*, 224n9
Lamont, Claire, 227n7
Laqueur, Thomas, 33, 120–21
Le Fanu, J. Sheridan: "Carmilla," 143, 241, 225n17; *Wyvern Mystery, The*, 150, 204
Leighton, Edmund Blair: *Till Death Do Us Part*, 6, 10, 93, 97–100
*Le Livre Sans Titre*, 121–23, 133, 143, 224n9, 226n24
Lennox, Charlotte: *Female Quixote, The*, 26
Lewcock, Dawn, 214n11
Lewis, Tanya Marie: *Misdemeanor*, 232n15
Linton, Eliza Lynn: "Nearing the Rapids," 159; "What is Woman's Work?" 156–57; "Womanly Dependence," 169
Lorde, Audre, 213n4
*Lost in Translation*, 207
love, 12, 175–97

Macaulay, Catherine: *Letters on Education*, 32
MacCarthy, Fiona, 216n25, 216n30
MacFarlane, Alan, 226n1, 229n2
Mainardi, Patricia, 34, 220n23
Malthus, T. R.: *An Essay on the Principle of Population*, 118, 169, 171
Mangum, Teresa, 117–20
marriage: aesthetics, 10, 89–112; age of consent for, 3, 219n15, 231n2; breach of promise, 3, 150, 227n3; child marriage, 12, 66, 208, 231; child marriage in India, 12, 200–201, 207, 231n2; civil registration, 3; daddy-daughter (*see* incest); definition of January–May, 8–9;

Divorce Act of 1857, 215n23, 222n41, 227n12; divorce and, 34, 49, 94, 128, 168, 183, 207; financial considerations and, 147–74; gay/lesbian, 201–2, 207, 225n17; infidelity, 18, 22, 24, 27, 34, 40, 48–49, 59, 68, 73, 122, 179–80, 194; inheritance and, 24–25, 34, 118, 157, 161; love and, 12, 175–97; love triangle and, 7–10, 37–41, 46–47, 55, 83, 87, 90, 98, 129, 144, 176, 180, 186, 191, 204–5, 216n29; of older woman and younger man, 12, 16–18, 91, 208–10; parody of, 7–9, 37–38, 44–48, 55, 92, 199; polygamy and, 40–41, 208; prostitution and, 12, 78–81, 170–74, 200–201, 229n19; reproduction and, 107–8, 161–62; sexual economy, 11–12, 23, 147–74. *See also* incest
Married Women's Property Act of 1870, 93, 215n23, 222n41, 227n12
Marshall, Peter Paul: *Rich Cleric and his Wife, The*, 222n2
masturbation, 46, 120–23, 139, 220n19, 224n8–12
Matrimonial Causes Act of 1878, 93–94
Matthews, T. C.: *Class Act*, 232n15
Matthews, William, 214n4
Maximianus, 15
McKeon, Michael, 150
McMaster, Juliet, 108
Medwin, Thomas, 39
Mighall, Robert, 11, 115, 125
Milbank, Alison, 86
Mill, John Stuart, 36; *Subjection of Women, The*, 37, 107, 223n7, 231n17

Millais, John Everett: *Married for Rank*, 11, 151–53, 160, 165, 174
Mines Regulation Act of 1842, 160
Mohr, Richard D., 229n5
Moliere: *L'École des femmes*, 214n9
Monkhouse, Cosmo: *British Contemporary Artists*, 93
Montagu, Lady Mary Wortley, 26
Morse, Charlotte C., 214n5
Mortensen, Peter, 215n17
Murfin, Ross, 226n23

Nabokov, Vladimir: *Lolita*, 206–7
Nardin, Jane, 231n19
Nelson, Antonya: *Nobody's Girl*, 210
Newton, Judith Lowder, 34
Nightingale, Florence: *Cassandra*, 158
Nordlund, Marcus, 214n8
*Northern Exposure*, 12, 207
*Notes on a Scandal*, 207

Old Testament, book of Kings, 15
Olsen, Greg, 232n14
O'Malley, Patrick M., 223n1
Orchardson, William Quiller, 10, 92–97; *First Cloud, The*, 10, 93–95; *Mariage de Covenance*, 10, 93, 95–97; *Mariage de Covenance—After!*, 10, 93, 97–98

Patmore, Coventry: *Angel in the House, The*, 37, 231n20
Philpotts, Trey, 221n32
Plato: *Symposium*, 176, 229n1
Plautus, 15
Polhemus, Robert M., 10, 58, 63, 219n9, 219n12, 220n16, 232n10
Polidori, John: *Vampyre, The*, 6, 11, 129, 133–35, 226n18
Polwhele, Richard: *Unsex'd Females, The*, 33

Pool, Daniel, 3
Poor Law Amendment Act of 1834, 116
Poovey, Mary, 159, 161, 162, 227n9
Pope, Alexander: *Eloisa to Abelard*, 215n13
Prest, Thomas Preskett. *See* Rymer, James Malcolm

Radcliffe, Ann: *Mysteries of Udolpho, The*, 114; *Romance of the Forest, The*, 114; *Sicilian Romance, A*, 114 Radcliffe, Ann:
Rank, Otto, 57, 218n7, 220n24
Raymond, Michel, 132
Richardson, Angelique, 227n4
Roberts, Bette B., 141
Robson, Catherine, 5, 201, 229n5, 231n4
Roebuck, Janet, 119
Rosenman, Ellen Bayuk, 224n8
Rossetti, Christina: "Goblin Market," 224n11
Rousseau, Jean-Jacques: *Julie, or the New Heloise*, 203, 205, 220n20
Rubin, Gayle, 7, 11, 148, 171
Rudnytsky, Peter, 217n1
Ruskin, John, 201, 231n4
Ryder, K. C., 213n1
Rymer, James Malcolm: *Varney the Vampyre*, 11, 129, 135–41, 143, 205, 226n19

Sadoff, Diane, 4–5, 58, 59, 82–83, 218n8
Said, Edward, 217n1
Schaffer, Talia, 226n25
Second Reform Act of 1867, 36
Sedgwick, Eve, 7–8, 79, 133
Seltzer, Mark, 215n22
Senf, Carol, 130
Shakespeare, William: *Othello*, 21–22, 25, 104, 214n8;

Sonnet, 138, 21; *Taming of the Shrew, The*, 20–21;
Shanley, Mary Lyndon, 215n23, 221n31, 227n12, 231n17
Sharma, Mani Ram, 231n2
Shaw, George Bernard, 2; *Mrs Warren's Profession*, 56, 170–71, 218n5
Shelley, Mary Wollstonecraft: *Frankenstein*, 113–14, 133; *Mathilda*, 5, 57
Shelley, Percy: *Adonais*, 118; *Cenci, The*, 5, 57
Sheridan, Richard Brinsley, 9, 217n33; *School for Scandal, The*, 26–29, 215n14
Shildrick, Margrit, 124
Simcox, Edith: "The Capacity of Women," 158
Sinclair, Alison, 213n2
Singer, Irving, 229n1
Skal, David J., 145
Smith, Anna Nicole, 4, 147, 207–8
Smith, Charlotte: *Old Manor House*, 16, 100–101, 228–29n19
Stead, W. T.: *Maiden Tribute to Modern Babylon, The*, 12, 200
Steadman, Jane, 229n4
Stearns, Peter, 223n4
Steffan, T. G., 44
Stengers, Jean, 224n9
Sterling, Anne Fausto, 215n20
Stoker, Bram: *Dracula*, 6, 11, 115, 129, 135, 141–46, 205, 225n17, 226n22, 226n25, 230n14
Strickland, Margot, 216n25
Summary Jurisdiction Act of 1895, 93
Swift, Jonathan, 26, 102

Tavormina, M. Teresa, 214n4
Taylor, Thomas: *Vindication of the Rights of Brutes, A*, 33

Tennyson, Alfred, 215n24; "Lady Clara Vere de Vere," 216n24 ; "The Lady of Shalott," 216n24; "Lucretius," 216n24; "Maud," 216n24; *Princess, The*, 37, 215n24; "Tithonus," 118
Thackeray, William Makepeace: *Henry Esmond*, 209; *Memoirs of Barry Lyndon, Esq., The*, 202–3; *Vanity Fair*, 228n17
Thane, Pat, 2, 116
Tillotson, Kathleen, 221n32
Tissot, Samuel Auguste David: *Onanism*, 120
Tonna, Charlotte Elizabeth: *Perils of the Nation, The*, 34–36, 215n21
Trollope, Anthony, 2, 176; *Barchester Towers*, 148, 176, 196, 203, 222n2; *Can You Forgive Her?* 231n19; *He Knew He Was Right*, 37, 203, 229n3; *Old Man's Love, An*, 6, 12, 177, 188–94, 203–4, 206, 222n1, 229n3, 231n16, 231n19; *Orley Farm*, 3, 203, 220n20, 228n17, 229n3, 231n19
Twitchell, James, 130, 131–32

Valenti, Teresa, 230n11
vampires, 11, 129–46
Van Neck, Anne, 224n9
Varma, Devendra, 135, 226n19

Wall, Steven, 83
Walpole, Horace: *Castle of Otranto, The*, 114
Ward, J. T., 215n22;
*Water*, 12, 207
Waters, Catherine, 220n17
Wharton, Edith: *Summer*, 206
*What's Eating Gilbert Grape*, 211
Wilde, Oscar, 202; *Picture of Dorian Gray, A*, 89–90, 101, 111, 115

Wilputte, Earla A., 214n12
Witemeyer, Hugh, 103
Wolf, Robert, 228n16
Wolfson, Susan, 47, 48
Wollstonecraft, Mary, 33; *Thoughts on the Education of Daughters*, 32; *Vindication of the Rights of Woman, A*, 32
Wood, John, 13, 210–11
Woolf, Virginia: *Room of One's Own, A*, 158
Wordsworth, William, 5, 46, 118; "Michael," 117, 202; "Resolution and Independence," 116; "Simon Lee," 116
Wycherley, William: *Country Wife, The*, 22–23, 27, 42, 214n9

Yeazell, Ruth Bernard, 85
Yonge, Charlotte Mary, 232n7; *Clever Woman of the Family, The*, 232n7; *Heartsease*, 232n7; *Hopes and Fears*, 232n7; *Magnum Bonum*, 232n7; "What is a Golden Deed?" 221n34